A Southern Collection

Then and Now

The Junior League of Columbus, Georgia, Inc.

Additional copies of *A Southern Collection Then and Now* may be obtained at the cost of $22.95 plus $4.00 postage and handling, each book. Georgia residents add 7% sales tax, each book.

Send to:

Junior League of Columbus, Georgia, Inc.
1440 Second Avenue
Columbus, GA 31901

ISBN: 0-9606300-1-5

First Printing	15,000 copies	November, 1994
Second Printing	7,500 copies	July, 1998
Third Printing	5,000 copies	May, 2002

WIMMER
COOKBOOKS
ConsolidatedGraphics
1-800-548-2537

Table of Contents

Appetizers and Beverages 8

Soups 40

Salads and Dressings 58

Breads 78

Pasta 96

Entrées 108

Grilling 174

Vegetables.. 192

Sweets 216

Contributors 275

Index 277

 Some favorite recipes from previous Junior League of Columbus, Georgia, Inc. cookbooks are marked with a pineapple, the symbol of hospitality.

A Southern Collection Then and Now Chairmen

1993–1994 Susan Mitchell
1994–1995 Dede Upchurch
1995–1996 Pam Shuler
1996–1997 Donna Voynich
1997–1999 Linda Callier

Original Committee

Susan Mitchell, *Chairman*
Lu Ann Brandon, *Co-Chairman*
Mary Bruce, *Treasurer*
Mary Harcourt, *Recipe Chairman*
Dede Upchurch, *Marketing Chairman*
Cathy Bickerstaff, *Sustainer Chairman*

DESIGN AND LAYOUT
Angie Hart
Susan Culpepper

PRODUCTION
Courtney Farmer
Editor
Sean Norman
Proof Editor
Fonda Carter
Betsy Covington
Pam Johnson

RECIPE SECTION CHAIRMEN
Margaret Amos
Kimberly Bishop
Angela Blankenship
Lucile Flournoy
Billie Flowers
Elizabeth Graham
"J" Mize
Laura Porter
Carroll Pound
Jeanne Swift
Katie Turner

MARKETING
Allison Estes
Lisa White

RESEARCH
Ashley Holt
Patricia Hargarten

ADVISORS
T. J. Connaughty
President, 1993-94
Kathelen Spencer
President, 1994-95

Acknowledgment

The Junior League of Columbus wishes to acknowledge the efforts of William A. Becker and Jerry Christenson. These local professionals have made a tremendous contribution to the production of this publication, spending untold hours providing valuable expertise.

Bill Becker, a partner in the advertising firm of Basset & Becker, has significantly contributed to the concept, design and copywriting of this publication. The quality of the final product is indicative of Bill's talents and creativity.

Through the exquisite photography of Jerry Christenson, *A Southern Collection Then and Now* seems to come to life. Jerry's photography beautifully depicts that blending of the old and new, creating a lasting impression in our minds.

The talents of Bill Becker and Jerry Christenson are truly unmatched. With heartfelt thanks, we acknowledge their dedication and contribution to *A Southern Collection Then and Now*.

Organization

The Junior League of Columbus, Georgia, Inc. is an organization of women committed to promoting voluntarism and to improving the community through the effective action and leadership of trained volunteers. Its purpose is exclusively educational and charitable.

Proceeds realized from the sale of *A Southern Collection Then and Now* benefit programs within the Junior League of Columbus, Inc.'s focus area of Parenting and Children's Welfare.

About the Cover...

Pictured on the cover is one of the best known landmarks in Columbus – the historic house "St. Elmo." "St. Elmo" was completed in 1833 and became significant in the history of the city due to its connection with many famous individuals including two Presidents of the United States – James K. Polk and Millard Fillmore. "St. Elmo" has been a private residence since 1966, the home of Dr. and Mrs. Philip Schley, and was listed on the National Register of Historic Places in 1971.

A Southern Collection
Then and Now

In the South an invitation to dinner is like a handshake. "Having someone over" is still the best way to make friends and cement friendships. The prospect of a delightful meal, served by an attentive host and enjoyed in the company of friends and family, is something special, an event looked forward to with great anticipation.

Contrary to popular opinion, great cooking is not unique to the South. However, there is something truly unique about southern cooking. It's not just the choice of ingredients or the preparation that makes food so different. Sure, recipes are important — after all that's what this book is all about. But southern cooking, REAL southern cooking, is always served with a special ingredient you can't seem to find anywhere else. Some folks call it hospitality, but to a southern cook, no meal is complete without it.

A Southern Collection Then and Now is a compilation of some of our favorite southern recipes, assembled by The Junior League of Columbus, Georgia. Good hosts, always on the lookout for recipes and new ideas for entertaining, will welcome this book to their collection. It's filled with a pleasurable selection of recipes, old and new, that will entertain and delight. So invite a few friends over and enjoy A *Southern Collection Then and Now*. Rest assured that an ample serving of hospitality has been added to each and every page.

One of the most talked-about events of the decade was a double wedding at the Rankin House in 1905. Someone, it seems, was always getting married there. No wonder, for the house itself — with its iron-filigreed veranda, flying balcony and solid walnut double staircase — was just made for weddings. So it is today. Hardly a week goes by that vows aren't exchanged here and new beginnings forged. Radiant brides and expectant grooms exchange adoring looks and celebrate among friends with the choicest of delicacies. The house, looking on, surely smiles.

Wedding Celebration

Bridesmaid Luncheon

Mimosas
Julia's Crabmeat
Asparagus Vinaigrette
A Tomato Well Stuffed
Melt Away Muffins
Lemon Soufflé

Rehearsal Dinner

Cold Squash Soup
Beef Tenderloin
New Potatoes with Basil Cream Sauce
Broccoli Lorraine
Mother's Refrigerated Rolls
Sweet Mouthful

Walnut Crest Blanc de Blanc

Wedding Reception

Royal Chicken Crêpes
Fresh Sliced Fruit on Boston Lettuce
Crisp Tender Broccoli
Lemon Ice Cream

Estancia Sauvignon Blanc

Easter Sunday Best

Spring has always come early here in the South, at the first sign of jonquils bursting through thawed ground in vivid, yellow glory. For generations, it's been a time to don Easter bonnets and Sunday bow ties and pose in front of the just-blooming dogwood for the traditional family photographs. After Sunday service, children of all ages hunt for colored eggs. Then families sit down to lunch of the freshest of springtime fare.

Frosted Orange
Cheese Straws
Mary Mobley's Shrimp Mold
Seasoned Leg of Lamb
Spinach Soufflé
Thyme Potatoes
Miracle Rolls
Carrot Cake
Easter Bird Nests

Seghesio Zinfandel

A Cool Game of Bridge

Friends have always settled down for a game of something or other in the heat of a Southern summer afternoon. In fact, there were card and board games aplenty in most every Southern household. As the challenge heated up, the wise hostess would bring out some cool refreshment to temper the mood. Whether it's Monopoly or bridge, friends still gather in the heat of the day, in the spirit of friendly competition. The smart hostess will have something cool and refreshing handy, just to keep things light.

Chicken and Pasta Salad
Fresh Fruit
Poppy Seed Dressing
The Absolute Very Best Buttermilk Pie
Mint Tea

Estancia Chardonnay

Visitors to Sunset Terrace, the original Bradley family home, knew there was something special about the garden. Maybe it was the terraced rose garden, or the grotto and cascading waterfalls. Or maybe it was the sweeping magnificence of the swimming pool. Then, you'd expect nothing less, considering the garden's designer was Frederick Law Olmsted, the very "Father of American Landscape Architecture," designer of Central Park and Biltmore Gardens. Today's garden, which spans the distance between the Columbus Museum and the Bradley Library, is being carefully renovated, so that visitors can refresh themselves in the serene expanse and marvel, once again, in quiet, green vistas.

Garden Of Delights

Apple Blossom Punch
Sesame Asparagus Roll Ups
Sundried Tomato Cheese Spread
Ham Delights
Shrimp Curry Mold
Olive and Pecan Canapés
Whole Wheat Cheese Straws
Lemon Cheesecake Squares
Caramel Chocolate Layer Brownies
Pecan Sticks

Robert Mondavi Fumé Blanc

In the good ol' summertime …what could be finer than a picnic in the park! And what finer park than Callaway Gardens, or the many others where area families have enjoyed the great outdoors for generations. From horseshoes to hiking, picnickers work up a hefty appetite and chow down on treats galore spread out in a bountiful outdoor smorgasbord. Never mind a few ants. They come with the territory.

Picnic in the Park

Salmon Bacon Ball
Olive Surprises
Beef Shish Kabobs
Boo's Potato Salad
Cole Slaw
Sour Dough Bread
Chocolate Dish Cake

Robert Mondavi Woodbridge Cabernet Sauvignon

Patriotic Dazzle

On the 4th of July, tradition has it that barbecue grills everywhere light up for a real Southern feast. When night falls and the dishes are put away, the family often gathers for a few fireworks in private celebration of our nation's independence. Around Fort Benning, the fireworks light the night sky in dazzling tribute to those who have given their lives for our freedom. It's something folks around here always remember. Especially so on this day, when we celebrate our precious freedom.

Boursin Cheese Spread
Snappy Cheese Wafers
Rotisserie Chicken
Grilled Vegetables
Brunswick Stew
Corn on the Cob
Sour Cream Corn Bread
Peach Ice Cream
Watermelon

Ferrari Carano Chardonnay

In the Team Spirit

Nothing says fall like the traditional tailgate party. Woe be unto the losing team! There's a nip in the air. Fans sport bright and gaudy team colors, hurl friendly taunts at one another in the gathering crowds and dig into the tasty curbside feast, brimming with dishes as hearty as the spirit of the day. It's a Southern custom rich with family tradition.

Bay Point Bloody Mary
Layered Shrimp Spread
Marinated Green Beans and Artichokes
Herbed Pork Tenderloin
Curried Rice Salad
Toasted Thyme Sticks
Apple Pecan Cake

Staton Hill Pinot Noir

The front porch has been just another room in many Southern homes. It offers respite from the heat, a place for cooling your heels in the shade and sipping on a glass of lemonade, or just rocking a little and stirring up a breeze. Many a family supper has been shared on the front porch and many a sunset shared, too. It's just that way in the South. It's a pretty good way to be.

Lazy Summer Supper

Vidalia Onion Dip
Summer Tomato and Basil Salad
Low Country Boil
Dilly Cheese Bread
Fresh Fruit Tart

Robert Mondavi White Zinfandel

We never forget the richness of the land around here, for our roots run deep in the agricultural tradition. There's an abundance to be shared at harvest time, whether from the field or the family garden. It's a time of giving thanks for the bounty of the land, and sharing the wealth with family and friends with a broad menu straight from the field. There's no better way to bring the harvest home.

Harvest Home

Baked Ham
Sweet Potato Casserole
Fresh Broccoli Salad
Spicy Black-Eyed Peas · Baked Squash Casserole
Sliced Tomatoes
Cricket Tea Room Cornbread
Blueberry Cobbler

Barton Guestier Merlot

Tricks and Treats

Halloween — the night is ageless. Young and old alike get into the "spirit" of things. Tiny ghosts and goblins, pirates and fairy princesses scour the neighborhood looking for treats, while inside, grown-up spooks gather around the table for their own Halloween goodies, with a few tricks thrown in just for fun. It's festive, and wickedly delicious!

Fiesta Slush
Surprise Dip
Green Chile Tortillas
Deviled Pecans
Soul Satisfying Chili
Tangy Romaine Toss
Baked Oranges
Mexican Corn Bread
Snickerdoodles

Robert Mondavi Woodbridge Red Zinfandel

After the Hunt

It's opening day and the hunt is on. Nowhere in the country, perhaps, is wild game more abundant than in the South, where opening day has been a traditional event passed from father to son. Hunters-turned-cooks carefully prepare each brace of birds following their own "secret" concoctions. Notes of the day are compared over each tasty morsel. It's the highest expression of culinary art, Southern style.

Southern Quail
Baked Grits
Grapefruit and Avocado on Bibb Lettuce
Dressing for Fruit and Vegetables
Sautéed Green Beans
Cheddar Drop Biscuits
Crème Caramel

Walnut Crest Sauvignon Blanc

Photo compliments of Callaway Gardens

There's a universal language at the holidays, one that transcends time and place. Families the world over celebrate the holiday spirit with their own brands of tradition. But the joy and wonder, the anticipation, all remain the same — just like home. Here, families pull out the finery and feast at decorative tables amidst the glow of twinkling holiday lights. It's been done that way for ages, and probably always will be. It's our own special brand of tradition.

Holiday Memories

Holiday Dinner

Baked Pecan Brie
Oyster Spinach Soup
Elegant Beef Tenderloin
Congealed Cranberry Salad
Gourmet Potatoes · Glazed Carrots
Worth the Wait Rolls
Charlotte Russe

Errazvriz Cabernet Sauvignon

Christmas Caroling Party

Crock Pot Cider
Carnonnades Flamandes (Beef Stew)
Caribbean Salad
Sour Dough Bread
Chocolate Praline Cake

Mirassou White Zinfandel

Generations of theater buffs have gathered for performances at the historic Springer Opera House, the official State Theater of Georgia. Afterwards, dessert gets the curtain call. From rich chocolate to the finest dainties, there's something for the most discerning palate. Coffee, of course, is a must for a truly grande finale.

Grande Finale

Peach Champagne Sorbet
Melting Moments
Fresh Strawberries with Powdered Sugar · Orange Blooms
Oatmeal Lace Cookies · Chocolate Snacks
Chocolate Carmelita Bars · Sugared Pecans · Creamy Dip for Apples
Mexican Mocha Coffee

Domaine Mumm Cuvee Napa

Dinner Duet

The candles are lit, the table is set. The room wraps its warm, cozy fingers all about, shutting out the chilly night air. It's a romantic retreat that begins with dinner for two. It's a night for savoring the finest of delicacies with a special companion, a Southern tradition as old as time itself. *C'est l'amour.*

French Onion Soup
Individual Beef Wellington
A Tomato Well Stuffed
Asparagus Caesar
Miracle Rolls
Chocolate Angel Pie

Caliterra Cabernet Sauvignon

A Winter's Eve

Winters around here have always been kind. Cold, yes. But not enough to stop the party. There's no better way to spend a Southern winter evening than with friends around the fire's glow. It'll warm your toes, and your heart.

Almond Pine Cones
Bourbon Steaks
Asparagus and Pea Casserole
Corn Pudding
Parmesan Herb Loaves
Old Fashion Gingerbread

Ferrari Carano Merlot

Appetizers & Beverages

Salmon Bacon Ball

1   1-pound can red salmon
1   8-ounce package cream cheese, room
    temperature
2   tablespoons lemon juice
3   teaspoons grated onion
1   tablespoon horseradish
½   teaspoon salt
⅛   teaspoon Worcestershire sauce
⅛   teaspoon cayenne pepper
¼   teaspoon commercial liquid smoke
½   cup chopped pecans
    Minced fresh parsley
    Crackers

- Drain salmon. Remove skin and bones and flake with fork, removing all lumps.
- Blend remaining ingredients except pecans, parsley and crackers with electric mixer. Stir in salmon and shape into ball or log.
- Combine nuts and parsley on waxed paper. Roll salmon mixture in nuts and parsley until well-coated. Chill.
- Serve with crackers.

Cheese in Pastry

1   large package crescent rolls
2   7-ounce Edam or Gouda cheeses
    Butter or margarine, melted
    Sesame seeds
    Wheat crackers

- Unroll dough into one flat sheet.
- Divide in half, making two squares.
- Peel wax from cheese and set cheese in center of each dough square.
- Fold dough over cheese, pinching edges to seal.
- Brush pastry with melted butter and sprinkle with sesame seeds.
- Cook according to package directions on crescent rolls, removing from oven when lightly browned.
- Serve with wheat crackers.

8

Baked Pecan Brie

½ cup coarsely chopped pecans
1 tablespoon butter or margarine, melted
1 1-pound wheel baby Brie cheese (4-inch)
¼ cup dark brown sugar
 Stone wheat crackers or mini-bagels

- Toast pecans in butter at 300° for 10 minutes, stirring occasionally.
- Place Brie in small pie pan and cover with brown sugar.
- Sprinkle with toasted pecans and bake in a preheated oven at 325° for 15 minutes.
- Serve with stone wheat crackers or toasted mini-bagels.

Pineapple Cheese Ball

2 8-ounce packages cream cheese
1 cup crushed pineapple, drained
2 cups chopped pecans, divided
2 tablespoons finely chopped onion
1 teaspoon salt
¼ cup finely chopped green bell pepper
 Crackers

- Beat cream cheese until smooth. Add pineapple, 1 cup pecans, onion, salt and bell pepper and refrigerate until firm.
- Shape into ball and roll in remaining pecans. Wrap in plastic wrap and chill.
- Serve with crackers.

Low Fat Cheese Spread
You would never know the fat is missing!

4 ounces light cream cheese
4 ounces low fat cottage cheese
½ teaspoon dill
½ teaspoon chives
½ teaspoon basil
½ teaspoon parsley or chervil
½ teaspoon thyme
 Salt and pepper to taste
 Crackers

- Blend all ingredients except crackers together in blender or food processor. Place in greased mold and chill overnight.
- Unmold and serve with crackers.

Almond Pinecones

1¼ cups whole almonds
1 8-ounce package cream cheese, softened
½ cup mayonnaise
5 crisply cooked bacon slices, crumbled
1 tablespoon chopped green onions
½ teaspoon dill weed
⅛ teaspoon pepper
1 cup shredded sharp Cheddar cheese
1 tablespoon diced pimento
  Pine sprigs for garnish
  Crackers

- Spread almonds in a single layer in shallow baking pan. Bake at 300° for 15 minutes, stirring often, until almonds just begin to turn color.
- Combine cream cheese and mayonnaise and mix well.
- Add bacon, onions, dill, pepper, cheese and pimento, mixing well. Cover and chill overnight.
- Form cheese mixture into shapes of two pinecones on serving platter.
- Beginning at narrow ends, press almonds at slight angle into cheese mixture, forming rows. Continue overlapping rows until all cheese is covered.
- Garnish with pine sprigs and serve with crackers.

Boursin Cheese Spread

2 tablespoons parsley
1 tablespoon dill weed
2 tablespoons chopped chives
¼ teaspoon thyme
1 small garlic clove, minced
1 8-ounce package cream cheese, softened
2-3 tablespoons butter or margarine, softened
  Salt, to taste
  Crackers

- Mix all ingredients except crackers in food processor and chill overnight.
- Serve on crackers.

Sun-Dried Tomato Cheese Spread

1 8-ounce package cream cheese,
   softened
4 ounces sharp Cheddar cheese, grated
2 tablespoons sun-dried tomato bits
¼ teaspoon garlic salt
⅛ teaspoon cayenne pepper
¼ teaspoon salt
   Crackers

- Combine all ingredients except crackers, mixing well with electric mixer. Refrigerate.
- Serve on crackers.

Herbed Dip for Vegetables

2 cups mayonnaise
1 cup sour cream
2 teaspoons dill
2 teaspoons tarragon
2 garlic cloves, mashed
2 tablespoons chopped chives
2 tablespoons chopped parsley
1 teaspoon paprika
   Salt and pepper to taste
   Raw vegetables

- Mix all ingredients except vegetables and chill.
- Serve with fresh vegetables.

Curry Dip for Raw Vegetables

2 cups mayonnaise
½ cup sour cream
⅛ teaspoon turmeric
2 tablespoons curry powder
2 garlic cloves, minced, or 1½ teaspoons garlic powder
4 teaspoons sugar
2 teaspoons salt
2 teaspoons lemon juice
¼ cup minced parsley
   Raw vegetables

- Combine and refrigerate all ingredients the day before serving so flavors can blend.
- Serve with raw vegetables.

Vidalia Onion Dip
Always rave reviews

1   cup coarsely chopped Vidalia onions
1   cup mayonnaise
1   cup grated sharp Cheddar cheese
    Paprika
    Corn chips, tortilla chips or crackers

- Combine onions, mayonnaise and cheese; pour into a 1-quart baking dish.
- Sprinkle with paprika and bake uncovered in a preheated oven at 350° for 25 minutes.
- Serve with corn chips, tortilla chips or crackers.

Spinach Vegetable Dip

1½   cups mayonnaise
½   cup sour cream
     Salt and pepper to taste
½   cup chopped parsley
½   cup chopped green onion
⅛   teaspoon Worcestershire sauce
1   10-ounce package frozen chopped spinach
     Raw vegetables

- Blend first 6 ingredients well.
- Cook spinach slightly, drain and add to mayonnaise mixture. Do not put in blender as it will change color.
- Serve with raw vegetables.

Creamy Dip for Apples

1   8-ounce package cream cheese, softened
1¼   cups light brown sugar
1   teaspoon vanilla
4-6 Granny Smith apples, unpeeled and sliced vertically

- Combine all ingredients, except apples, in a large bowl and blend with electric mixer until creamy.
- Refrigerate for at least one hour and serve with apple slices.

Artichoke and Crab Dip

1   14-ounce can artichokes, minced
1   4.25-ounce (drained weight) can
    crabmeat
1   cup mayonnaise
1   cup grated Parmesan cheese
½   medium onion, chopped
1½ teaspoons lemon juice
    Crackers

- Mix all ingredients except crackers together and place in lightly greased casserole dish.
- Bake uncovered in a preheated oven at 375° for 15-20 minutes.
- Serve warm with crackers.

  Variation: Substitute 2 large jalapeño peppers (rinsed, seeded and chopped) for the crabmeat and delete the onion and lemon juice. Serve with tortilla chips.

Hot Seafood Spread

1   4.25-ounce (drained weight) can shrimp,
    drained
1   4.25-ounce (drained weight) can lump
    crabmeat, drained
1   8-ounce package cream cheese,
    softened
1   teaspoon horseradish
2   tablespoons chopped onions
1   teaspoon milk
    Paprika
    Crackers or melba rounds

- Blend all ingredients except paprika and crackers and place in a baking dish.
- Bake uncovered in a preheated oven at 350° for 15 minutes.
- Sprinkle with paprika and serve with crackers or melba rounds.

Avocado Dip

1   avocado
1   garlic clove, minced
¼   cup fresh chopped cilantro
1   tablespoon lime juice
1   cup tomatillos
2-4 tablespoons diced green chiles
2   tablespoons minced onions
¼   teaspoon cumin
    Tortilla chips

- Purée the avocado in a food processor. Add the remaining ingredients except chips and process until smooth.
- Serve with tortilla chips.

  Yield: 2 cups

Water Chestnut Dip

8 ounces sour cream
1 cup mayonnaise
1 8-ounce can water chestnuts, drained and chopped
2 tablespoons soy sauce
½ cup chopped parsley
2-3 green onions, chopped
2 drops hot pepper sauce, or to taste
  Bagel chips

• Mix ingredients well and serve with bagel chips.

Yield: 3 cups

Surprise Dip

1 10-ounce package frozen green peas
½ cup sour cream
½ cup mayonnaise
½ cup dry roasted peanuts
½ cup cooked, finely chopped bacon
¼ cup finely chopped green onion
¼ cup finely chopped celery
  Crackers

• Combine first 7 ingredients, serve with crackers.

Yield: 4 cups

Fresh Fruit Dressing

1 cup sugar
3 tablespoons all-purpose flour
  Zest of 1 orange
  Zest of 1 lemon
2 eggs, beaten
  Pinch of salt
  Juice of 2 lemons
1 cup boiling water
1 cup heavy cream, whipped

• Combine and cook first 8 ingredients slowly in double boiler until thick. Cool completely.
• Stir in whipped cream.
• Serve over fresh fruits; wonderful over melon balls.

Keeps several days in refrigerator.

Steak Dip
A great way to use leftovers

2 cups sour cream
Leftover steak, thinly sliced, then chopped
1 4.5-ounce can chopped green chiles, to taste
4 green onions, thinly sliced
Worcestershire sauce, to taste
Triscuits

- Mix all ingredients except Triscuits and chill.
- Serve with Triscuits.

Hot Tuna Dip

1 10¾-ounce can cream of mushroom soup, undiluted
1 8-ounce package cream cheese
1 6-ounce can white tuna in spring water, drained
2 ¾-ounce packages slivered almonds
1 2-ounce can sliced mushrooms, drained
1 teaspoon Worcestershire sauce
⅛ teaspoon garlic powder
⅛ teaspoon pepper
Crackers or toast points

- Combine all ingredients except crackers in saucepan and cook over medium heat until well blended and heated through.
- Pour into serving dish, sprinkle with paprika and serve hot with crackers or toast points.

Zesty Broccoli Dip

1 10-ounce package frozen chopped broccoli
2 10¾-ounce cans cream of mushroom soup
1 cup chopped onions
1 cup chopped celery
1 8-ounce package jalapeño Monterey Jack cheese
1 4-ounce can sliced mushrooms, drained
Corn chips or crackers

- Cook broccoli according to directions on package and drain.
- In a double boiler, mix all ingredients except corn chips and cook over medium heat until cheese is melted.
- Serve in chafing dish with corn chips or crackers.

Layered Shrimp Spread

1 8-ounce package cream cheese
1 tablespoon Worcestershire sauce
½ teaspoon curry powder
¼ teaspoon garlic salt
2 hard-boiled eggs, finely chopped
1 tablespoon finely chopped onion
   Chili sauce
1 4.25-ounce (drained weight) can deveined shrimp, drained, or ½ cup fresh shrimp, boiled, deveined and chopped
   Parsley, chopped
   Crackers

- Cream first 4 ingredients together and spread into the bottom of a glass serving bowl.
- Scatter eggs and onion over the top, then add just enough chili sauce to cover.
- Top with shrimp and parsley and serve with crackers.

  Variation: White lump crabmeat can be substituted for the shrimp.

  Yield: 8-10 servings

Easy Shrimp Dip

1 pound fresh shrimp, cooked, peeled and chopped
½ cup mayonnaise
1½ tablespoons lemon juice
½ cup finely chopped onion
½ cup finely chopped celery
3 ounces cream cheese, softened
⅛ teaspoon garlic powder
   Crackers

- Combine all ingredients except crackers and mix well.
- Serve hot or cold with crackers.

Marinated Broccoli

3 bunches broccoli
1 cup cider vinegar
1 tablespoon sugar
1 tablespoon dill weed
1 tablespoon Accent
1 teaspoon salt
1 teaspoon ground pepper
1 teaspoon garlic salt
1½ cups vegetable oil

- Break off tops of broccoli and discard stems. Steam broccoli if desired.
- Combine remaining ingredients and pour over broccoli.
- Refrigerate for 24 hours and drain before serving.

  Yield: 20 servings

Salmon Mousse with Sour Cream Dill Sauce
An elegant appetizer

1 envelope unflavored gelatin	• Soften gelatin in water. Add boiling water and dissolve. Let cool.
¼ cup cold water	
½ cup boiling water	• Add next six ingredients, mix well, and chill to the consistency of unbeaten egg whites.
½ cup mayonnaise	
1 tablespoon grated onion	
½ teaspoon hot pepper sauce	• Add salmon and capers. Whip cream and fold into salmon mixture.
2 tablespoons lemon juice	
¼ teaspoon paprika	• Place into 2-quart greased fish mold.
1 teaspoon salt	
2 cups salmon, drained and finely chopped	• Add cottage cheese to fill mold, if desired. Chill until set.
1 tablespoon chopped capers	• Serve with crackers.
½ cup whipping cream	
3 cups cottage cheese, optional	
Crackers	

Sour Cream Dill Sauce:

2 teaspoons dill weed	• Mix ingredients and pour over salmon mold.
1½ cups sour cream	*Yield: 2 cups*
1 egg, beaten	
1 teaspoon salt	
4 teaspoons lemon juice	
1 teaspoon onion, grated	

Pizza Dip
The hit of the party

1 8-ounce package cream cheese, softened	• Press cream cheese into the bottom of a 9-inch greased pie plate and spread with pizza sauce.
1 14-ounce jar pizza sauce	
½ cup chopped green onions	• Layer remaining ingredients except tortilla chips in order listed and bake in a preheated oven at 350° for 20 minutes.
¼ cup chopped bell pepper	
2 cups grated mozzarella cheese	
½ cup chopped ripe olives	• Serve with tortilla chips.
1 3-ounce package sliced pepperoni, chopped	
Tortilla chips	

Tex Mex

At a party, always first to go!

3 medium avocados, peeled and seeded
2 tablespoons lemon juice
½ teaspoon salt
½ teaspoon pepper
1 cup sour cream
½ cup mayonnaise
1 package taco seasoning
2 10-ounce cans bean dip
1 large bunch green onions, chopped
3 medium tomatoes, chopped
Sliced ripe olives, optional
2 cups shredded Cheddar cheese
Tortilla chips

• Mash avocados. Add lemon juice, salt and pepper.
• In separate bowl, combine sour cream, mayonnaise and taco seasoning.
• Spread bean dip in bottom of 13x9x2-inch dish. Top with avocado mixture, then sour cream mixture.
• Sprinkle onions and tomatoes on top and add olives, if desired.
• Top with Cheddar cheese and chill.
• Serve with tortilla chips.

Homemade Salsa

7 medium fresh tomatoes, diced,
or 1 28-ounce can diced tomatoes
with juice
1 3-ounce can diced mild green chili peppers
3 green onions, diced
Salt and pepper to taste
⅓ cup chopped fresh cilantro
1½ tablespoons fresh lemon juice
2 teaspoons soy sauce
⅛ cup salad oil
2 tablespoons red wine vinegar
Jalapeño peppers to taste, optional
Corn chips

• Combine all ingredients except corn chips in a large bowl and mix well. Cover and chill overnight.
• Serve with corn chips.

This keeps well for 1 to 2 weeks in the refrigerator.

Yield: 1 quart

Southern Salsa

A bit of Mexico....Southern style!

1 16-ounce can black-eyed peas, drained
2 tomatoes, chopped
1 bunch green onions, sliced
1 tablespoon chopped fresh cilantro
3 tablespoons fresh lime juice
1 tablespoon olive oil
1-2 garlic cloves, minced
½ teaspoon ground cumin
¼ teaspoon salt
   Leaf lettuce
   Tortilla chips

• Place peas in a colander; rinse with cold water and drain.
• Combine tomatoes and next 7 ingredients in a medium bowl; stir in peas.
• Cover and refrigerate at least 4 hours.
• Place in a lettuce-lined compote or bowl; serve with tortilla chips.

Mexican Cheese Dip

2 pounds ground beef
1 pound hot bulk sausage
1 medium onion, chopped
1 pound Velveeta cheese
1 10-ounce can Rotel tomatoes
1 10¾-ounce can cream of mushroom soup
1 teaspoon garlic salt
⅛ teaspoon hot pepper sauce
   Several drops Worcestershire sauce
   Corn chips

• Brown beef, sausage and onions in a skillet and drain.
• Add cheese, tomatoes, soup, garlic salt, hot pepper sauce and Worcestershire sauce. Stir and heat until cheese is melted.
• Serve in a chafing dish with corn chips.

Spinach Cheese Squares

4 tablespoons butter or margarine, melted
3 eggs
1 cup all-purpose flour
1 cup milk
1 teaspoon salt
1 teaspoon baking powder
1 pound grated Monterey Jack cheese
2 10-ounce packages frozen chopped spinach, thawed and drained well

• Pour melted butter into a 13x9x2-inch baking dish.
• In large bowl, beat eggs. Add flour, milk, salt and baking powder, mixing well. Add cheese and spinach.
• Pour all into prepared dish and bake in a preheated oven at 350° for 35 minutes.
• Cool 45 minutes and cut into small squares.

Pickled Shrimp

2½ pounds raw shrimp
Celery tops
2 tablespoons salt
2 cups thinly sliced onion
7 bay leaves
1¼ cups salad oil
¾ cup white vinegar
2 teaspoons salt
2½ teaspoons celery seed
2½ teaspoons capers and juice
⅛ teaspoon hot sauce

- Cook shrimp for 3-5 minutes in boiling water with celery tops and salt. Peel and devein.
- Alternate cooked shrimp and sliced onions in shallow baking dish. Add bay leaves.
- Mix together remaining ingredients and pour over shrimp and onions.
- Cover and store in refrigerator.

Will keep for 2 weeks in the refrigerator.

Caviar Mousse

2 envelopes unflavored gelatin
2 tablespoons cold water
½ cup boiling water
1 cup whipping cream
2 2-ounce jars red and black caviar
¼ cup mayonnaise
1 tablespoon lemon juice
1 tablespoon Worcestershire sauce
⅛ teaspoon dry mustard
Parsley
Unsalted crackers

- Soften gelatin in cold water; let stand 3 minutes. Add boiling water and stir until gelatin dissolves.
- Stir in remaining ingredients except crackers and pour into lightly greased 3-cup mold. Chill until firm.
- Garnish with fresh parsley and serve with unsalted crackers.

Mushroom Pâté

3 tablespoons chopped green onion
4 tablespoons butter or margarine
½ pound mushrooms, minced
2 tablespoons all-purpose flour
½ teaspoon salt
⅛ teaspoon cayenne pepper
1 tablespoon minced parsley
½ teaspoon lemon juice
¾ tablespoon chopped chives
1 8-ounce package cream cheese, softened
 Bagel crisps

- Sauté onions in butter for 4 minutes.
- Add mushrooms and cook 10-15 minutes.
- Add flour and mix well, cooking 2 minutes more.
- Remove from heat and allow to cool.
- Pour mushroom mixture in a large bowl and add salt, cayenne, parsley, lemon juice and chives, mixing well.
- Blend in cream cheese and refrigerate overnight.
- Serve with bagel crisps.

Zucchini Squares

3 cups zucchini, cut into matchsticks
1 cup biscuit mix
½ cup fresh grated Parmesan cheese
½ cup Cheddar cheese, grated
4 eggs, beaten
¼ cup vegetable oil
½ cup chopped onion
1-2 garlic cloves, pressed
½ teaspoon parsley
½ teaspoon salt
½ teaspoon oregano
¼ teaspoon pepper

- Mix all ingredients together, spread into a greased 13x9x2-inch dish and bake at 350° for 40 minutes.
- Cut into small squares.

Olive Surprises

¼ cup butter or margarine, softened
1 cup grated sharp Cheddar cheese
¼ teaspoon salt
¼ teaspoon paprika
⅛ teaspoon cayenne pepper
½ cup all-purpose flour
3 dozen medium stuffed olives

• Cream butter and cheese until well blended. Add remaining ingredients except olives and mix well.
• Chill 15-20 minutes.
• Shape a small portion of dough around each olive. Place on cookie sheet and bake in a preheated oven at 400° for approximately 15 minutes.

Yield: 36

Olive and Pecan Canapés

1 8-ounce package cream cheese, softened
3 tablespoons mayonnaise
10 large pimento-stuffed olives
½ cup pecans
12 slices of thin-sliced dense whole-grain bread, crusts removed

• Blend cream cheese, mayonnaise, olives and pecans in a food processor until the olives and the nuts are chopped fine.
• Spread the bread with the mixture and cut each slice into quarters.
• Serve at room temperature or broil on a jelly roll pan under a preheated broiler about 4 inches from the heat for 1 minute or until the cream cheese mixture begins to bubble.

Variation: This can also be used as a dip for small melba rounds or similar crackers.

Yield: 48 canapés

Broiled Crab Melt-A-Ways

6 English muffins
1 6½-ounce can white lump crabmeat, drained
½ cup butter or margarine, softened
1 5-ounce jar Old English sharp Cheddar cheese
1 tablespoon mayonnaise
½ teaspoon salt
½ teaspoon garlic salt

• Split muffins and quarter each half.
• Mix remaining ingredients and spread onto muffins.
• Freeze for at least 30 minutes then bake in a preheated oven at 350° for 8-10 minutes.
• Run under broiler until bubbly and brown.

Cheese and Mushroom Toast

¼ pound mushrooms, sliced
1 small onion, chopped
2 tablespoons butter or margarine
¼ cup minced parsley
1 cup shredded Swiss cheese
⅓ cup grated Parmesan cheese, divided
2 teaspoons Dijon mustard
½ teaspoon salt
⅛ teaspoon thyme
½ cup mayonnaise
6 slices bread, buttered and toasted on both sides
6 tablespoons grated Parmesan cheese

- Sauté mushrooms and onions in butter. (If too much liquid, pour off.)
- Mix other ingredients except bread and 6 tablespoons Parmesan cheese and stir into mushrooms and onions.
- Spread equal portions on bread. Sprinkle each slice with one tablespoon Parmesan cheese.
- Cut each slice of toast into quarters.
- Broil 5 inches from heat until cheese bubbles and browns.

Yield: 24 squares

Sesame Asparagus Roll-ups

20 slices white bread, crusts removed
1 8-ounce package cream cheese, softened
3 ounces blue cheese, crumbled
1 egg, slightly beaten
1 10½-ounce can cut asparagus spears
⅓ cup butter or margarine, melted
Sesame seeds

- Flatten each slice of bread slightly with rolling pin.
- Combine cheese and egg and spread evenly on each bread slice. Place one asparagus spear on each and roll up.
- Dip each roll in melted butter and then lightly in sesame seeds. Cut each roll into three equal pieces and place on greased cookie sheet cut side down.
- Bake in a preheated oven at 400° for 15-20 minutes.

Variation: To make ahead, prepare, cover and freeze individually on cookie sheets. Transfer to airtight container. To serve, bake at 400° 25-30 minutes or thaw and bake as instructed above.

Yield: 60 snacks

Green Chile Tortillas

2   8-ounce packages cream cheese, softened
2   4-ounce cans chopped green chiles, drained
4   green onions, chopped
½   teaspoon garlic salt
12 6-inch soft flour tortillas
    Picante sauce

- Combine cream cheese, chiles, onions and garlic salt in a small bowl. Spread 2 heaping tablespoons of this mixture on each tortilla.
- Roll up jelly-roll fashion and place seam side down on baking sheet. Cover and chill 2 hours.
- Slice each tortilla roll into 4 pieces.
- Serve with picante sauce.

Yield: 48 pieces

Ham Delights
Children love these

2   7.5-ounce packages Pepperidge Farm party rolls
¾   pound sliced Swiss cheese
¾   pound sliced ham
1   cup butter or margarine, softened
3   tablespoons poppy seeds
1   teaspoon Worcestershire sauce
3   tablespoons spicy mustard
1   medium onion, chopped

- Partially freeze rolls. Make one slice through middle of entire package and remove tops.
- Layer cheese and ham on bottom of rolls. Mix together butter, poppy seeds, Worcestershire, mustard and onions and spread on top of ham.
- Put tops of rolls back on and cover completely with aluminum foil.
- Bake in a preheated oven at 400° for 20-30 minutes.
- Separate rolls to serve.

Yield: 24 sandwiches

Whole Wheat Cheese Straws

1   pound sharp Cheddar cheese, grated
¾   cup butter or margarine, softened
1   cup whole wheat flour
1   cup unbleached flour
2   teaspoons salt
¾   teaspoon cayenne pepper

- Combine all ingredients. Mix well and chill.
- Roll out dough and cut into rectangles approximately ½ inch x 3 inches.
- Place on ungreased cookie sheet and bake in a preheated oven at 350° for 15 minutes.

Yield: 5 dozen

Sausage Bacon Delights

¼ cup butter or margarine, melted
½ cup hot water
1½ cups herb seasoned stuffing
1 egg, slightly beaten
¼ pound hot or mild bulk pork sausage
1 pound bacon

- Mix well the butter, water and stuffing. Add egg and sausage and blend thoroughly. Chill for 1 hour.
- Cut each bacon slice into thirds. Wrap 1 teaspoon stuffing mixture with a piece of bacon and secure with a wooden pick. Repeat.
- Place bundles on rack in shallow pan. Bake in a preheated oven at 375° for 35 minutes or until brown and crisp, turning halfway through baking time.
- Drain on paper towels and serve hot.

Note: May be made ahead, frozen, then thawed before baking.

Snappy Cheese Wafers

1 cup butter or margarine, softened
2 cups all-purpose flour
1 8-ounce package sharp Cheddar cheese, grated
½ teaspoon cayenne pepper
½ teaspoon salt
2 cups Rice Krispies

- Mix butter and flour until the texture of corn meal.
- Add cheese, pepper and salt, mixing with your hands until smooth. Stir in Rice Krispies.
- Pinch off small pieces and roll into balls. Place on ungreased cookie sheet and press down with fork.
- Bake in a preheated oven at 350° for 15 minutes.

Yield: about 125

Cheese Straws

½ pound New York extra sharp cheese, grated
6 tablespoons butter or margarine, softened
1 teaspoon salt
1 teaspoon baking powder
1 cup all-purpose flour, sifted
⅛ teaspoon red pepper or more to taste
⅛ teaspoon Worcestershire sauce

• Combine cheese and butter, mixing thoroughly.
• Sift salt and baking powder with flour. Add to the cheese and butter along with the red pepper and Worcestershire, mixing well.
• Use a cookie press to make cheese straws.
• Bake in a preheated oven at 325° for 12-15 minutes or until golden. Be careful not to overcook.

Deviled Pecans

½ cup butter or margarine, melted
1 pound pecans
1 teaspoon Worcestershire sauce
¾ teaspoon salt
½ teaspoon hot sauce

• Spread butter into a 13x9x2-inch pan. Stir together remaining ingredients, pour into pan and bake at 300° for 20 minutes, stirring twice while cooking.

Sugared Pecans

1 cup sugar
½ teaspoon cinnamon
⅓ cup evaporated milk
½ teaspoon vanilla
2¼ cups toasted pecans

• In a saucepan, mix sugar, cinnamon and milk. Boil until the mixture forms a soft ball when dropped in cold water.
• Remove from heat and stir in vanilla and pecans. Keep stirring until it crystallizes.
• Drop pecans separately on waxed paper.

Rich Cinnamon Bits

Unusual....but oh so good!

1   8-ounce package cream cheese, softened
1   egg yolk
½   cup sugar
1   king-sized loaf white sandwich bread (24 slices), crust removed
1   cup butter or margarine, melted
1½ cups sugar
1½ teaspoons cinnamon

- Mix cream cheese, egg yolk and sugar in food processor or mixer.
- Spread mixture on each slice of bread and roll up jelly-roll fashion. Dip in butter and then in mixture of sugar and cinnamon.
- Place on cookie sheet and freeze for several hours. Cut each roll into thirds and package in foil in the freezer.
- To bake, place frozen pieces on non-stick cookie sheet and bake in a preheated oven at 400° for 12 minutes.

Yield: 6 dozen

Mary Mobley's Shrimp Mold

1   8-ounce package cream cheese, softened
½   cup butter or margarine, softened
⅛   teaspoon Worcestershire sauce
    Juice of 1½ lemons, or to taste
2   tablespoons mayonnaise
1   teaspoon salt
1   small onion, finely chopped
    Pepper to taste
1   teaspoon sugar, optional
2   4.25-ounce (drained weight) cans small shrimp, washed and drained, or 1½ cups fresh shrimp, boiled and chopped (Do not cook shrimp over 1 day ahead.)
    Melba toast or crackers

- Mix all but shrimp and melba toast with electric mixer. Add shrimp and mix well.
- Pour into greased, small mold and refrigerate.
- Serve with plain melba toast or crackers.

Make ahead at least 2 or 3 days.

Yield: 8-10 servings

Shrimp Curry Mold

1 8-ounce package cream cheese, softened
½ cup butter or margarine, softened
2 tablespoons mayonnaise, preferably homemade
3 tablespoons lemon juice
1 small onion, grated
1 teaspoon salt
  Cayenne pepper to taste
⅛ teaspoon hot pepper sauce
⅛ teaspoon Worcestershire sauce
1 teaspoon curry powder
½ cup chutney
1 cup cooked shrimp
  Crackers

- Mix all but last 3 ingredients with electric mixer.
- By hand, fold in chutney and shrimp. (If shrimp are large, they should be chopped.)
- Serve in a shell or turn out on a platter.
- Serve with crackers.

  Best if made a day or two ahead.

  Yield: 10-12 servings

Chutney Bacon Cheese Hors D'Oeuvres

Bread, crust trimmed
Sharp Cheddar cheese, sliced
Chutney
Bacon, cooked

- Cut bread into quarters.
- Top with cheese, 1 teaspoon chutney, small piece bacon.
- Heat in a preheated oven at 400° for 2-3 minutes.
- Serve warm.

Mushroom Turnovers

These are sure to impress

Pastry:

1 cup butter or margarine, softened
1 8-ounce package cream cheese, softened
½ teaspoon salt
2 cups all-purpose flour

Mushroom Filling:

½ pound fresh mushrooms, finely chopped
2 tablespoons butter or margarine
½ cup chopped onion
½ teaspoon salt
⅛ teaspoon pepper
⅛ teaspoon ground nutmeg
1 teaspoon lemon juice
2 teaspoons all-purpose flour
½ cup sour cream
1 teaspoon dill weed
1 egg yolk
2 teaspoons milk

- Mix butter, cream cheese, salt and flour to form soft dough and chill overnight.
- When ready to use, break off part of dough; keep remaining dough in refrigerator until ready to roll it out.
- Roll dough out paper thin on a floured surface and cut into 2-3-inch circles with a biscuit cutter. Fill with the following:

- Sauté mushrooms and onions in butter until limp. Stir in salt, pepper, nutmeg and lemon juice.
- Blend in flour until smooth and slightly thickened. Stir in sour cream and dill weed and allow filling to cool.
- To assemble, place about a teaspoon of filling on one side of a pastry circle. Fold over and crimp edges with a fork.
- Brush tops of pastry with a mixture of egg yolk and 2 teaspoons of milk.
- Place on ungreased cookie sheet and bake in a preheated oven at 350° for 20 minutes.

These may be frozen before baking and baked when ready to use.

Yield: About 50-60

Black Bean Torte

2 cups dried black beans
2 14½-ounce cans chicken broth
1 chicken bouillon cube
2 cups water
1½ teaspoons ground cumin
1½-2 bunches fresh cilantro leaves
2 tablespoons olive oil
1 teaspoon pressed garlic
½ cup pine nuts
1 large tomato, seeded and chopped with excess juice pressed out
½ cup finely chopped red onion
4 ounces crumbled feta cheese
½ cup sour cream
Cilantro leaves for garnish
Crackers or tortilla chips

- Rinse black beans and place in a large pan. Add chicken broth, bouillon cube, water and cumin. Bring to a boil. Cover and simmer approximately 2½ hours until beans are tender. Stir mixture occasionally. Drain liquid.
- Mash 1 cup of beans. Gently hand mix remaining whole beans with mashed beans. Let cool.
- In a food processor or blender, purée the cilantro leaves, olive oil, garlic and pine nuts to make pesto. Set aside.
- Line a 4x8-inch loaf pan with plastic wrap, with edges overlapping rim.
- Gently press ⅓ bean mixture in pan, making the layer smooth. Spread cilantro pesto over the bean mixture. Press another ⅓ of bean mixture over the pesto, making the bean layer smooth. On top of beans, make an even layer of chopped tomatoes and onions. Sprinkle with feta cheese.
- Top with remaining beans, pressing gently to make a smooth loaf.
- Cover tightly with plastic wrap and refrigerate until loaf is firm.
- To serve, invert loaf onto a platter and remove plastic wrap. Spoon sour cream down the center and garnish with cilantro leaves.
- Serve with crackers or tortilla chips or loaf may be sliced into ½-inch pieces and served as a first course.

Shrimp Rémoulade

1	pound shrimp, cooked and peeled
4	shakes hot pepper sauce
½	cup chopped parsley
1	garlic clove, minced
½	cup chopped onion
4	teaspoons prepared mustard
⅓	cup tarragon vinegar
4	teaspoons lemon juice
2	teaspoons fresh ground horseradish
½	cup olive oil or corn oil
1	teaspoon salt
2	teaspoons paprika
½	cup diced celery

• Combine all ingredients and marinate overnight in the refrigerator.

Great as an appetizer or served over lettuce as a salad.

Cherry Tomatoes Stuffed with Avocado

30	large cherry tomatoes
	Salt
	Sugar
2	ripe medium avocados
2	tablespoons sour cream
2	tablespoons minced parsley
4	teaspoons lime juice
2	teaspoons lemon juice
2	teaspoons minced chives
½	teaspoon salt
¼	teaspoon hot pepper sauce
¼	teaspoon sugar

• Cut thin slices from the tops of cherry tomatoes. With a small melon ball cutter, scoop out and discard the seeds and pulp.
• Sprinkle the insides of the shells lightly with salt and sugar and invert on paper towels to drain for at least 30 minutes.
• In a bowl, mash avocados and combine with remaining ingredients. Blend the mixture well.
• Using a small knife, fill the shells with the avocado mixture. Chill.

Yield: 6 servings

Tenderloin with Béarnaise

Listen to the raves

1 tenderloin
8 egg yolks
4 tablespoons lemon juice
½ teaspoon salt
½ teaspoon hot pepper sauce
2 cups butter or margarine, melted and hot
½ cup white wine
4 tablespoons tarragon vinegar
2 teaspoons dried tarragon
2 tablespoons chopped green onion
½ teaspoon freshly ground pepper

- Cook tenderloin to desired doneness a day ahead.
- Make a béarnaise sauce by putting yolks in blender with lemon juice, salt and hot pepper sauce. Cover container and turn on low speed. Uncover and pour in hot butter in a steady stream, still on low speed. Leave in blender.
- In a small saucepan, combine remaining ingredients. Bring to a boil and cook rapidly until liquid is reduced to about 4 tablespoons. Pour this into blender and stir.
- Cover and turn on high speed for 8 seconds. Refrigerate, preferably overnight.
- Cut tenderloin into ½- or ¾-inch cubes.
- Let béarnaise sauce come to room temperature. It will be thick, but perfect for dipping.
- Place sauce in bowl, in center of tray, with cubed meat surrounding it. Dip meat into sauce with toothpicks.

Easy Sweet and Sour Sauce

1 8-ounce jar prepared yellow mustard
1 10-ounce jar apple jelly
1 10-ounce jar pineapple preserves
1 9-ounce jar horseradish sauce

- Whisk all ingredients together in a bowl.
- Refrigerate in glass container.
Great with chicken fingers.

Crock Pot Cider

1 gallon apple cider
¼ teaspoon ground cloves
½ teaspoon allspice
6 sticks cinnamon

- Pour all ingredients in crock pot and heat for 1 hour on high.

  Crock pots vary in size. Check to see if 1 gallon will fit into yours!

Tea Punch

2 cups water
6 individual size tea bags
2 cups water
1 6-ounce can frozen lemonade concentrate
1 6-ounce can frozen limeade concentrate
1½ cups cranberry cocktail juice
1 28-ounce bottle ginger ale

- Bring 2 cups water to a boil. Add tea bags and let steep for 10 minutes.
- Strain tea into a pitcher and add 2 cups cold water and the remaining ingredients, stirring well.

  Yield: 2½ quarts

Instant Cocoa Mix

1 2-pound box Nestle's Quik
1 8-quart box instant dry milk
6 ounces non-dairy creamer
½ cup powdered sugar

- Mix all ingredients. Store in tightly covered jars.
- To serve, place ¼ cup mix in a cup. Add 1 cup boiling water and stir well.

  Yield: 25 servings

Fiesta Slush

1 6-ounce can frozen limeade concentrate
1 12-ounce can frozen orange juice concentrate
10 cups of water
½ cup sugar
1½ teaspoons almond extract
1 teaspoon vanilla extract
Vodka to taste (optional)

- Mix all ingredients together and freeze.
- Thaw to a slushy state and serve.

  Yield: 12 servings

33

Georgia Mint Iced Tea

5   tea bags
1   cup sugar
5   sprigs mint
8   cups boiling water
¼   cup lemon juice

- Put tea, sugar and mint (squeeze leaves slightly but not stems) into a 2-quart container.
- Pour boiling water over and steep, covered, for 5 minutes.
- Strain, cool and add lemon juice.

Yield: 2 quarts

Yellow Bird

½   cup ice cubes
1   ounce light rum
½   ounce triple sec
½   ounce banana liqueur
½   ounce Galliano
¾   ounce orange juice

- Blend all ingredients until thoroughly mixed and frothy.
- Pour into tall glass and garnish with orange slice.
- Variation: add vanilla ice cream to blender and sprinkle nutmeg on top.

Yield: 4 servings

Rum Slushes

A welcomed treat by the pool

2   46-ounce cans pineapple juice
1   6-ounce can frozen lemonade concentrate
1   6-ounce can frozen limeade concentrate
1   liter of rum, or to taste

- Mix all ingredients in plastic container and freeze.
- Stir after 12 hours.
- Ready to serve when it reaches a slushy consistency.

Strawberry Margarita

1   10-ounce package frozen strawberries, partially thawed
2   tablespoons tequila
1   tablespoon orange liqueur
1   tablespoon freshly squeezed lime juice
1   cup ice cubes

- In a blender, combine strawberries, tequila, orange liqueur and lime juice, mixing well.
- Add ice cubes and blend until smooth.

Homemade Kahlúa

3 cups water
4 cups sugar
1 vanilla bean
1 cup boiling water
1 2-ounce jar instant coffee (Yuban preferred)
1 fifth 100 proof vodka

- Boil water and sugar for 20 minutes.
- Split vanilla bean lengthwise and add to mixture. Let stand until cool.
- Mix 1 cup boiling water and the instant coffee and allow to cool. Add to sugar water mixture. Add the vodka.
- Store in ½ gallon jar in a cool dark place for two weeks.
- Strain into bottles.

Frozen Pink Vodka

1 6-ounce can frozen pink lemonade concentrate
1 cup vodka
1 cup frozen strawberries

- Combine lemonade, vodka and strawberries in blender and mix well.
- Add enough ice to blend to a slushy consistency.

Yield: About 5 cups.

Bay Point Milk Punch

Vanilla ice cream
6 ounces brandy
2 ounces light crème de cacao
Ice
Nutmeg

- Fill blender ¾ full with ice cream.
- Add brandy and crème de cacao and fill blender to the top with ice. Blend.
- Pour into glasses and sprinkle each with nutmeg.

Yield: 4 servings

Party Punch

½ cup sugar
1 6-ounce can frozen orange juice
1 6-ounce can frozen lemonade
3 ounces lemon juice
3 quarts 7-up
1 fifth Southern Comfort

- Combine all ingredients and serve.

Yield: 25-30 servings

Mr. John's Eggnog

6 eggs, separated
6 tablespoons bourbon
6 tablespoons sugar
2 cups whipping cream
   Nutmeg

- Beat yolks well and add bourbon, 1 tablespoon at a time. Add more to taste. Be careful to add slowly, because bourbon will cook the eggs. Beat until the consistency of mayonnaise. Set aside.
- Beat whites until frothy, then add sugar, 1 tablespoon at a time. Beat until very thick.
- Whip cream. Fold egg mixture into egg whites and then fold into whipped cream.
- Pour into pretty bowl and sprinkle with nutmeg.

This is so thick you need to serve it in cups and provide spoons with which to eat it. This recipe can easily be doubled. To thin: use half the amount of whipped cream. Make up the difference with light cream added until the consistency suits you.

Bay Point Bloody Mary

2 quarts tomato juice
24 ounces vodka
   Juice of 6 lemons
1 tablespoon salt
½ tablespoon cracked black pepper
2½ ounces Worcestershire sauce

- Combine all ingredients and let stand for at least 12 hours.
- This will keep in the refrigerator for several weeks.

Yield: 8 servings

Frosted Orange

Children love this - a good way to get them to drink milk!

1 6-ounce can frozen orange juice
   concentrate
½ cup sugar
1 cup water
1 cup milk
½ teaspoon vanilla extract

- Pour all ingredients into a blender and fill remainder of blender with ice.
- Blend until smooth.

Yield: 4-5 cups

Apple Blossom Punch

A wonderful party punch

3   quarts apple juice
3   12-ounce cans frozen orange juice
     concentrate
3   quarts ginger ale

- Combine all ingredients.
- Pour over ice in a punch bowl.

   Yield: 50 servings

Raspberry Apéritif

1   10-ounce package frozen raspberries
3   ounces orange liqueur
1   bottle champagne, chilled

- Purée raspberries and strain to remove seeds.
  Reserve juice and chill until cold.
- Add liqueur and champagne and serve in
  chilled, stemmed glasses.

   Yield: 4-6 servings.

Mexican Mocha Coffee

The perfect ending

½   cup unsweetened cocoa
1   cup brown sugar, firmly packed
4   teaspoons cinnamon
1   cup instant coffee granules
     Brandy
     Whipped cream

- In a blender or food processor, mix all ingredients until well blended.
- To serve, place 2 rounded teaspoons of
  mixture in a cup. Add boiling water and stir.
  Add a shot of brandy and top with whipped
  cream.

Georgia Watermelon-Wine Punch

½   large watermelon
½   cup sugar
½   cup water
⅓   cup frozen pink lemonade, thawed
¾   cup rosé wine
1   28-ounce bottle ginger ale, chilled

- Make 2 cups melon balls from watermelon.
  Clean out rind for use as serving bowl and
  chill along with the melon balls.
- Boil sugar and water together for 5 minutes.
  Add lemonade and wine. Chill until cold.
- Combine wine mixture, ginger ale, and melon
  balls and serve in chilled watermelon rind
  bowl.

   Yield: 2 quarts

37

Yogurt Smoothie

½ cup plain yogurt
½ cup orange juice
1 banana
5 strawberries (fresh or frozen)

- Mix all ingredients in a blender until smooth.
- Serve immediately over ice.

  Yield: 2 servings

Soups

Cold Cucumber Soup

A special treat for a summer picnic

1 large cucumber, washed well and seeded
1 cup sour cream
Milk to thin (may use buttermilk)
1 teaspoon chopped parsley
1 teaspoon dill
1 teaspoon garlic powder
Parsley or dill to garnish
Salt and pepper to taste

- Process cucumber in food processor until chopped fine.
- Add other ingredients and chill.
- Garnish with fresh parsley or dill if desired.

Yield: 2 servings

Blueberry Soup

A different way to use blueberries

1 cup blueberries
1 slice lemon, seeds removed
1 cinnamon stick (⅛ teaspoon ground cinnamon if stick not available)
2 cups water
3 tablespoons sugar
Pinch of salt
1 tablespoon cornstarch
1 teaspoon frozen orange juice concentrate, optional
Whipped cream to garnish, if desired

- Combine blueberries, lemon, cinnamon and water in a saucepan.
- Bring to a boil and simmer 10 minutes. Add sugar and salt.
- Combine cornstarch with a little water and add to mixture.
- Bring to boil, then lower heat and simmer 1 minute.
- Remove cinnamon stick.
- Purée mixture in blender until smooth.
- Taste, then add orange juice concentrate for a stronger flavor, if desired.
- Serve chilled with whipped cream.

Yield: 4-6 servings

Summer Gazpacho

Terrific for the hot, hazy days of summer!

2½ cups tomato juice
1 cup finely chopped tomato
½ cup finely chopped celery
½ cup finely chopped green bell pepper
⅓ cup finely chopped green onions
2 tablespoons wine vinegar
2 tablespoons vegetable oil
2 teaspoons chopped fresh parsley
1 small garlic clove, pressed
1 teaspoon salt
¼ teaspoon pepper
½ teaspoon Worcestershire sauce
   Sour cream to garnish, if desired
   Chopped green onion to garnish, if
   desired

- Combine all ingredients and mix well.
- Cover and refrigerate 8 hours or overnight.
- Serve in bowls garnished with a dollop of sour cream and chopped onions.

Yield: 4-6 servings

Cold Squash Soup

1 pound yellow squash, thinly sliced
1 onion, chopped
1½ cups chicken stock or broth, divided
½ cup sour cream
   Salt to taste
   White pepper to taste
   Chopped fresh dill weed

- Combine squash, onion and 1 cup chicken stock in saucepan and bring to a boil.
- Cook 30 minutes or until vegetables are tender.
- Purée squash mixture in blender and pour into mixing bowl.
- Stir in remaining ½ cup stock, sour cream, salt and white pepper to taste.
- Chill.
- Garnish with chopped dill weed.

Peach Soup
A Southern favorite

3½ cups fresh peaches, peeled and diced
½ cup Chablis
1½ cups unsweetened white grape juice
1 cup water
1 3-inch cinnamon stick
½ teaspoon ground cardamom
½ teaspoon vanilla
⅛ teaspoon almond extract
   Mint leaves for garnish, optional

- Combine first 5 ingredients and bring to a boil.
- Reduce heat and simmer for 30 minutes.
- Stir in cardamom, vanilla and almond extract.
- Pour half of mixture into a blender and process until smooth. Repeat with other half.
- Chill. Serve chilled and garnish with mint leaves, if desired.

Yield: 6 cups

Cold Potato Soup with Asparagus

4 cups chicken broth
2 cups fresh asparagus, cut into ½-inch lengths (reserve tips for garnish)
2½ cups peeled and chopped potatoes
¼ teaspoon garlic powder
2 teaspoons onion powder
4 ounces shredded Jarlsberg or Swiss cheese

- In a large saucepan, bring broth to a boil. Add asparagus and boil 2 minutes.
- Remove asparagus from broth and chill, reserving broth.
- Return broth to a boil and add potatoes. Cook 10 minutes or until soft. Add seasonings and cheese.
- Whirl soup, in batches, in food processor or blender until nearly smooth. Chill.
- To serve, mix in asparagus and garnish with tips.

Yield: 4-6 servings

 *Vichyssoise*

2 medium onions, sliced
¼ cup butter or margarine
5 medium potatoes, thinly sliced
1 quart chicken stock
1 tablespoon salt, or less
3 cups milk
2 cups heavy cream, divided
Chopped chives

- In a deep kettle, lightly brown onion in butter.
- Add potatoes, stock and salt and boil 35 minutes or until very tender.
- Crush and rub through fine sieve or purée in blender or food processor.
- Return sieved mixture to kettle.
- Add milk and 1 cup cream and bring to a boil.
- Cook and run again through a fine sieve.
- Chill, then add remaining cream.
- Chill thoroughly and serve garnished with chives.

Yield: 8 servings

Quick Clam Chowder

1 10¾-ounce can potato soup
1 10¾-ounce can celery soup
1 10¾-ounce can clam chowder
1 11-ounce can yellow corn niblets
2 cups half-and-half
1 10¾-ounce can whole baby clams
Fresh chopped chives to garnish, if desired

- Mix all ingredients together in a large saucepan.
- Heat thoroughly and serve.

Variation: For a lower-fat version, use skim milk instead of half-and-half.

43

Hot and Sour Egg Drop Soup

Superior

2   13¾-ounce cans chicken broth
1   8-ounce can bamboo shoots, undrained
1   cup frozen snow peas
1   cup shredded carrots
1   4-ounce can sliced mushrooms, undrained
¼   cup sliced green onions
⅓   cup vinegar
1   tablespoon soy sauce
¾   teaspoon pepper
¼   cup cold water
2   tablespoons cornstarch
4   eggs, beaten

- Bring all ingredients except water, cornstarch and egg to a boil in a large saucepan.
- Reduce heat and simmer 5 minutes.
- Stir together water and cornstarch in a small bowl until thoroughly blended.
- Slowly stir cornstarch mixture into hot soup.
- While stirring soup, slowly pour in eggs.
- Immediately remove from heat and serve.

  The trick to making the egg cook into "strings" is to have the soup very hot and to keep stirring constantly while adding the eggs.

  Yield: 4 servings

Potato Soup

12-15 new potatoes, cooked, jackets removed
2   14-ounce cans clear chicken broth
½   teaspoon salt
¼   teaspoon white pepper
⅛   teaspoon cayenne pepper
⅛   teaspoon dry minced garlic
1   tablespoon grated onion
3   tablespoons sour cream
6   slices cooked bacon, crumbled
½   cup grated Cheddar cheese

- Purée potatoes in a blender or food processor.
- In a saucepan, combine remaining ingredients except bacon and cheese.
- Cook over low heat until hot.
- Garnish with chopped bacon and shredded cheese.

  Variation: If in a hurry, use four 10-ounce cans whole potatoes, drained, instead of fresh potatoes.

  Can be made ahead. Freezes well.

  Yield: 6 servings

Minestrone Soup
Hearty

¼ pound bacon, diced
2 quarts hot water
1½ cups tomato juice
2 15-ounce cans kidney beans
1 11-ounce can bean and bacon soup
6 beef bouillon cubes
1 cup diced carrots
1 cup diced celery
2 cups chopped cabbage
1 10-ounce package frozen spinach
1 teaspoon basil
½ teaspoon salt
½ teaspoon pepper
¾ cup uncooked rice

- In an 8-quart saucepan, sauté bacon until crisp.
- Add all other ingredients except rice.
- Cover and simmer over low heat for 1 hour or until vegetables are tender, stirring occasionally.
- Add rice and simmer 30 more minutes.

Yield: 10 servings

Broccoli Soup

2 cups chopped fresh or frozen broccoli
2 cups chopped carrots
½ cup chopped onion
½ cup chopped celery
   Chicken broth cubes
1 cup milk
2 tablespoons all-purpose flour
½ pound Velveeta cheese + cheddar
¼ teaspoon thyme
⅛ teaspoon garlic powder

- Cook vegetables until soft in chicken broth made from bouillon cubes and enough water to cover vegetables.
- Combine milk and flour and strain into soup, stirring constantly.
- Add cheese and seasonings over low heat.
- Add salt to taste.

Freezes well.

Yield: 4 servings

Cream of Broccoli Soup

Always an elegant beginning

1 bunch fresh broccoli
3 cups chicken stock
½ onion, chopped
4 tablespoons butter or margarine
5 tablespoons all-purpose flour
1 cup half-and-half
   Salt and white pepper to taste
2 tablespoons sherry, optional
   Paprika, croutons or parsley for garnish

- Cook broccoli in stock with onion until soft.
- Remove broccoli from pot and process in a blender until chopped, not puréed.
- Combine butter and flour in a saucepan.
- Cook 3 minutes over medium heat, stirring constantly.
- Add broccoli and stock. To avoid lumps, stir constantly until thickened.
- Thin on low heat to desired consistency with half-and-half.
- Add seasonings and sherry to taste.
- Garnish with paprika, croutons or parsley, if desired.

Freezes well.

Yield: 6 servings

Easy Seafood Bisque

2 10¾-ounce cans cream of asparagus soup
2 10¾-ounce cans cream of mushroom soup
3 cups milk
2 cups light cream
2 cups crabmeat
1 cup small shrimp
½ cup sherry
   Minced chives for garnish, if desired

- Combine soups, milk and cream.
- Stir in crabmeat and shrimp. Cook over low heat until almost boiling, stirring often.
- Add sherry just before serving and sprinkle with minced chives.

Yield: 10-12 servings

My Favorite Carrot Soup

4 tablespoons butter or margarine
1 large onion, coarsely chopped
⅛ cup fresh ginger, peeled and sliced thin
3 garlic cloves, minced
7 cups chicken stock
1 cup dry white wine
1½ pounds carrots, peeled and cut into chunks
2 tablespoons fresh lemon juice
Pinch of curry
Salt and pepper
Yogurt or sour cream for garnish, optional

- Sauté onion, ginger and garlic in butter in a non-stick pan for 15 minutes.
- Simmer carrots in chicken stock and wine until tender.
- Remove carrots and purée in a food processor, reserving stock.
- Add onion mixture to carrots and purée.
- Add puréed vegetables to the reserved stock, stirring well.
- Stir in lemon juice and curry. Add salt and pepper to taste. Chill.
- Garnish with yogurt or sour cream, if desired. Can be served hot or cold.

Yield: 10 servings

Chicken and Wild Rice Soup

1 cup chopped onion
1 cup chopped celery
4 carrots, chopped
¼ cup butter or margarine
1 6-ounce box long grain and wild rice
1 seasoning packet of long grain and wild rice
10 cups chicken broth
2 bay leaves
1½ teaspoons thyme
4 cups cooked, diced chicken
Salt
Pepper

- Sauté onions, celery and carrots in butter in a large pot.
- Add rice, seasoning packet, broth, bay leaf and thyme.
- Simmer 20-30 minutes.
- Add chicken, salt and pepper and heat thoroughly.

Variation: Also good made with smoked turkey.

Yield: 8-10 servings

47

Seafood and Leek Bisque

2   leeks (about 1½ pounds)
½   cup butter or margarine
1-2 garlic cloves, minced
½   cup all-purpose flour
4   cups chicken broth
½   cup dry white wine
2   cups half-and-half
½   pound fresh crabmeat, drained and flaked
1   cup small shrimp, peeled and deveined
¼   teaspoon salt
¼   teaspoon ground white pepper
    Sliced leeks to garnish, if desired

- Remove roots, tough outer leaves and green tops from leeks. Split white portion of leeks in half. Wash and cut halves into thin slices.
- Melt butter in a Dutch oven over medium-high heat. Add leeks and garlic and cook, stirring constantly, 3 minutes or until tender.
- Add flour, stirring until smooth. Cook 1 minute, stirring constantly.
- Gradually add broth and wine. Cook over medium heat, stirring constantly, until mixture is thick, about 4 minutes.
- Stir in half-and-half and next 4 ingredients. Simmer.
- Garnish with sliced leeks, if desired.

Yield: 2 quarts

Oyster and Spinach Soup

4   tablespoons butter or margarine
¼   cup finely chopped onion
1   garlic clove, minced
1   pint oysters, chopped
4   tablespoons all-purpose flour
3   cups half-and-half
1   cup chicken broth
¾   cup spinach purée (made in blender from fresh or frozen, uncooked spinach)
1   6½-ounce jar artichoke hearts
    Salt and pepper

- Melt butter and add onion and garlic. Sauté at low heat until soft.
- Add oysters and cook until they curl.
- Push aside oysters and onions and add flour and cook until foamy.
- Add half-and-half and cook until thickened, stirring.
- Mix in chicken broth, spinach and artichoke hearts and bring to a boil. Remove from heat.
- Correct seasonings and serve.

Clam Chowder

3 small onions, diced   *RED*
1 green bell pepper, diced
2 potatoes, diced
   Slice of ham, diced
24 ounces canned clams, drained and diced
   DON'T DRAIN RESERVE LIQUID
¼ cup butter or margarine
2 teaspoons salt
½ teaspoon white pepper
½ teaspoon celery salt
   Hot pepper sauce to taste
4 tablespoons butter or margarine
5 tablespoons all-purpose flour
5 cups milk
   Chopped chives to garnish

ADD THYME
ADD MILK TO LIQUID FROM CLAMS TO MAKE 5 CUPS

- Combine first 10 ingredients and cook for 20 minutes.
- In separate pan, melt butter. Add flour and stir until flour is well cooked.
- Add flour mixture to clam mixture.
- Add milk and cook slowly, stirring occasionally until chowder is hot and potatoes are tender, approximately 15 minutes.
- Add more milk if a thinner chowder is desired.
- Garnish with chopped fresh chives.

Mulligatawny Soup

1 cup butter or margarine
1 cup all-purpose flour
1 tablespoon curry powder, or to taste
6 cups milk
3 cups chicken stock
3 cups cooked chicken breasts, cut up
   Salt to taste
   Half-and-half or milk
   Apple, chopped

- Melt butter, stir in flour and curry powder.
- Heat milk and stock. Add slowly to flour mixture, stirring constantly. Season to taste.
- Add chicken to mixture.
- Thin soup to desired consistency with half-and-half or milk.
- Just before serving, put chopped apple in soup bowls and pour the hot soup over the apple. This keeps the apple crunchy.

Soup for the Hunt

Delicious starter for any lunch in the field

1   10¾-ounce can tomato soup
1   10¾-ounce can Italian tomato soup
1   10¾-ounce can beef bouillon
2¾ cups water
⅛   teaspoon hot pepper sauce

- Heat all ingredients in a saucepan, stirring constantly.
- Put in thermos jugs.

Yield: 6 servings

Vegetable Soup
A winter favorite

3 pounds beef stew meat
1 quart hot water
2 16-ounce cans tomatoes
1 15-ounce can tomato sauce
1½ cups chopped onion
2 16-ounce packages frozen mixed
   vegetables
2 cups chicken broth
1 tablespoon salt
⅛ teaspoon pepper
   Pinch each of rosemary, marjoram,
   savory and tarragon
1 tablespoon soy sauce
2 tablespoons brown sugar

- Brown beef in a large pot.
- Add water, tomatoes, tomato sauce and onions.
- Cover and cook on low for 2 hours, until meat is tender.
- Add vegetables and chicken broth. Cook another hour.
- When nearly done, mix in seasonings, soy sauce and brown sugar.

Yield: 15-20 servings

ADD: WORCESTERSHIRE

Pea Soup

1½ pounds Polish sausage, Kielbasa
1 pound dried green peas, washed
1 celery stalk, sliced
1 medium onion, chopped
1 tablespoon chopped parsley
1 teaspoon basil
9 cups boiling water
   Salt and pepper
4 carrots, sliced
2 medium potatoes, cubed

5 Cups Water 4 cups chicken Broth

USE HALF CHICKEN BROTH

- To the first 6 ingredients add the water and simmer 1 hour. Add salt and pepper to taste.
- Add carrots and potatoes; cook for 30 minutes. Add more water if necessary. Adjust seasoning.
- Remove sausage and slice, putting a few slices in each bowl. Serve.

Brunswick Stew

A perfect accompaniment with barbecue

5 pound Boston butt pork roast
7 pounds chicken
4 ribs celery, cut up with leaves
4 medium onions, quartered
2 cups smoke-flavored barbecue sauce
1 cup mustard-based barbecue sauce
2 8-ounce cans tomato sauce
1 6-ounce can tomato paste
2 16-ounce cans tomatoes, chopped, retain juice
1 cup vinegar
3 cups chopped onions
2 11-ounce cans white shoe peg corn, drained
Salt and pepper to taste
1 medium loaf of white bread

- In a large pot of boiling water, place the pork, chicken, celery and onions and simmer until well done.
- Remove the chicken and pork and strain the broth into a large bowl.
- Reserve 4 cups of the broth and refrigerate separately from the pork and chicken overnight.
- Remove fat from broth and pour broth into a stewing pot.
- Turn heat to medium and add all the ingredients except the meat and the bread.
- Stir constantly while bringing to a boil. Simmer for about 15 minutes.
- Meanwhile, shred the pork and chicken and add to stew.
- Remove crust from bread. Make bread into fine crumbs in a food processor or blender.
- Stir bread crumbs into simmering stew and cook for approximately 15 minutes on very low heat.

Be careful to cook very slowly. Stew will stick and burn easily. Freezes well.

Yield: 8 quarts

Bean and Ham Soup

2 cups dried beans, your choice
1 pound ham or 1 ham hock
1 onion, chopped
1 garlic clove, crushed
1 10-ounce can Rotel tomatoes and green chilies, diced
1 quart water
   Salt if needed

- Wash beans. Soak overnight. Drain.
- Add all ingredients in a very large pot.
- Cook 2-3 hours over low heat.

Yield: 6-8 servings

Mushroom Soup

1 pound fresh mushrooms, chopped
1-2 onions, chopped
¼ cup butter or margarine
2 tablespoons all-purpose flour
2 10½-ounce cans bouillon or consommé
2 cans water
¾ cup half-and-half
   Salt and pepper to taste
   Worcestershire sauce to taste
½ cup sherry, optional

- Sauté mushrooms and onions in butter for a few minutes.
- Stir in flour, bouillon and water and cook 5 minutes.
- Purée mushroom mixture in blender or food processor. Add half-and-half and seasonings. Stir in sherry, if desired.
- Reheat but do not boil.

Yield: 6 servings

Black Bean Soup

1	pound black beans
1	ham bone
1½	bunches green onions, cut tops and bottoms
2	bay leaves
2	garlic cloves
2	medium onions, chopped
2	celery stalks, chopped
¼	cup butter or margarine
1½	tablespoons all-purpose flour
¼	cup chopped parsley
	Salt and pepper to taste
	Lemon slices
	Chopped onion
	Sherry

- Soak beans overnight. Rinse and drain.
- Cover with 2½ quarts of water and boil 1½ hours with ham bone, green onions, bay leaves and garlic.
- Sauté onions and celery in butter until soft.
- Stir in flour and parsley. Cook, stirring a few minutes, until well blended.
- Add to beans, cover and continue to simmer 7 hours or longer.
- Remove ham bone and bay leaves.
- Force mixture through a fine sieve. Add salt and pepper to taste.
- To serve, garnish each soup bowl with a lemon slice and pass onions and sherry.

Yield: About 2½ quarts

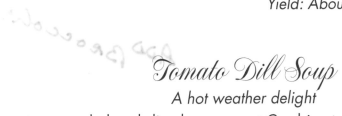

Tomato Dill Soup

A hot weather delight

3	large tomatoes, peeled and sliced
1	medium onion, sliced
1	small garlic clove
1	teaspoon salt
¼	teaspoon freshly ground pepper
2	sprigs fresh dill
1	tablespoon tomato paste
¼	cup water
½	cup cooked macaroni
1	cup chicken stock
¾	cup cream
	Fresh dill, chopped to garnish
	Chopped tomato to garnish

- Combine tomatoes, onion, garlic, salt, pepper, dill, tomato paste and water in a saucepan. Cover and simmer 15 minutes.
- Transfer to electric blender. Add macaroni and blend on high.
- Uncover and, with motor running, add the stock and cream.
- Chill. Serve garnished with fresh dill and tomato.

Gourmet Champagne Lentil Soup

1   onion, chopped
2   tablespoons butter or margarine
2   cups lentils
3   14-ounce cans chicken broth
3   tablespoons fresh lemon juice
1   teaspoon fresh grated lemon peel
2   chicken breast halves, cooked and diced
1   carrot
2   celery stalks
     Water
⅛   teaspoon basil
⅛   teaspoon tarragon
½   teaspoon salt
⅛   teaspoon pepper
½   cup dry champagne

• Sauté onion in butter, set aside.
• Place lentils in a large cooking pot.
• Add remaining ingredients except champagne.
• Bring to a boil, cover, reduce heat to simmer. Cook 2-3 hours, stirring frequently.
• Add champagne and serve.

Excellent topped with Parmesan cheese and served with French bread.

Cheese Soup ADD BROCCOLI

4   tablespoons butter or margarine
¼   cup finely chopped onion
½   cup finely chopped green pepper, optional
½   cup finely chopped carrots
5   tablespoons all-purpose flour
3   10½-ounce cans condensed chicken broth
¾   pound sharp Cheddar cheese, grated
2   cups milk
¼   teaspoon salt
⅛   teaspoon pepper
½   cup crisp croutons
     Fresh parsley, minced

• In a 3-quart pan, cook vegetables in butter for 10 minutes. Stir and remove from heat.
• Add flour to make a roux. Return to flame and cook for 1 minute, stirring constantly.
• Add broth and bring to a boil, stirring constantly. Reduce heat to medium.
• Stir in cheese by handfuls, allowing it to melt.
• Gradually add milk, then add salt and pepper.
• Bring to the boiling point, but don't let boil.
• Serve with croutons and parsley.

Freezes well.

Yield: 6-8 servings

French Onion Soup

5 large Spanish onions, sliced thinly
3 tablespoons butter or margarine
1 tablespoon oil
¼ teaspoon sugar
1 teaspoon salt
3 tablespoons all-purpose flour
2 quarts brown stock or bouillon
½ cup dry white wine
  Salt and pepper
2 tablespoons brandy
  French bread
  Parmesan cheese, grated
  Cayenne pepper
  Swiss cheese, grated

- Cook onions slowly, covered, in butter and oil in a heavy saucepan for 15 minutes. Uncover, raise the heat to moderate and add sugar and salt.
- Cook 30-40 minutes or until browned. Sprinkle in flour and cook for a couple minutes.
- Add stock, wine, salt and pepper. Simmer, partially covered, 30-40 minutes.
- Add brandy. May be made ahead to this point.
- Brush all sides of thick sliced French bread with melted butter and sprinkle with grated Parmesan and cayenne.
- Put slices of bread in bottom of bowl. Pour on soup; bread will float to top.
- Sprinkle with grated Swiss cheese and melted butter. Brown under a preheated broiler.

Tomato Consommé

1 10½-ounce can condensed consommé
1¾ cups tomato juice
  Whipped cream or thin slices of lemon
  Paprika
  Parsley sprigs

- Combine consommé and tomato juice and heat.
- Serve topped with whipped cream or thin slices of lemon.
- Garnish with paprika and a sprig of parsley.

Yield: 4 servings

Pappy Prather's Seafood Gumbo

Well worth the effort

⅔ cup plus 4 tablespoons all-purpose flour
¾ cup butter or margarine
10 garlic cloves, chopped
½ cup diced onions
¼ cup chopped green bell pepper
½ cup chopped celery
Salt to taste
Pepper to taste, if stock is not well-seasoned
½ teaspoon thyme
3 bay leaves
2 tablespoons Kitchen Bouquet
½ teaspoon chili powder
2 teaspoons hot pepper sauce
3 tablespoons Worcestershire sauce
6 pounds raw shrimp, peeled (if frozen, well thawed and drained)
1 8-ounce can tomato sauce
2 quarts fish stock
1 10-ounce package frozen sliced okra, well thawed and drained
¼ bunch parsley, chopped
1 pound lump crabmeat or Alaskan king crab
1½ pints oysters
2 tablespoons filé
Rice, cooked

- Make roux of flour and butter. Sauté garlic in roux and cook until golden brown.
- Add onion, green pepper and celery, cooking until transparent. Add next 8 ingredients.
- Add shrimp and tomato sauce, simmering for 10 minutes. Stir in fish stock and add okra, parsley and crab.
- Simmer 45 minutes-1 hour. Add oysters and filé, heating thoroughly.
- Serve in soup bowls over rice.

Yield: 20 servings (6½ quarts)

Salads & Dressings

Tomato Cheese Mold

2 envelopes unflavored gelatin
½ cup cold water
1 10¾-ounce can tomato soup
1 8-ounce package cream cheese
1 cup mayonnaise
1 cup finely chopped celery
¼ cup finely chopped green bell pepper
1 teaspoon onion juice
  Salt and pepper to taste

- Soften gelatin in cold water.
- Add tomato soup and place over low heat, stirring until gelatin dissolves and mixture is hot.
- Add cream cheese and heat until it melts. Cool mixture and stir in mayonnaise, vegetables and seasonings.
- Pour into an 8-inch square pan. Chill overnight.

Yield: 10-12 servings

 ## Tomato Aspic

1 12-ounce can tomato juice
1 10½-ounce can bouillon
1 tablespoon Worcestershire
1 teaspoon salt
¼ teaspoon hot pepper sauce
2 stalks celery with tops
1 medium onion, chopped
2 envelopes unflavored gelatin
½ cup water
  Juice of 1 lemon

- Simmer tomato juice, bouillon, Worcestershire, salt, hot sauce, celery and onions for 5 minutes. Strain mixture.
- Dissolve gelatin in water.
- Add gelatin and lemon juice to hot tomato juice and stir.
- Pour into 8 individual molds or 1 ring mold.
- Refrigerate to congeal.

Variation: chopped raw vegetables, olives, almonds, shrimp, etc., may be added.

Berries Berries Berries

"Berry" delicious!

4 cups mixed berries (blackberries, blueberries, raspberries, and boysenberries)
3 oranges, peeled and sectioned
1 cup coarsely chopped walnuts
1½ cups plain yogurt
⅓ cup cold orange juice
4 tablespoons honey

- Combine fruits and nuts and chill. Just before serving mix yogurt, orange juice and honey in a blender.
- Put fruit in chilled compotes and pour yogurt mixture over top. Serve immediately.

Yield: 8 servings

Caribbean Salad

1/4 cup vinegar
2 tablespoons water
1 package Good Seasons Italian dressing mix
3 tablespoons brown sugar
2 teaspoons Dijon mustard
3 tablespoons fresh lemon juice
2/3 cup salad oil
10 ounces fresh spinach
1/8 cup onion, sliced thin
1 avocado, cubed
1 cup fresh orange sections
Sunflower seeds

• Mix vinegar, water and dressing mix. Add brown sugar, mustard, lemon and oil.
• Tear spinach into bite size pieces and place in bowl. Layer on top of spinach the onion, avocado, oranges and seeds.
• Pour dressing over.

Yield: 6 servings

Minted Grapes in Melon Boats

2 cups red seedless grapes
2 cups green seedless grapes
1 tablespoon minced fresh mint
1 cup plain yogurt
2 tablespoons honey
1/2 teaspoon grated ginger
2 medium cantaloupes

• Toss grapes with mint and chill.
• Mix yogurt, honey and ginger in a blender.
• Combine grapes and yogurt mixture and serve in melon boats.

Curried Saffron Rice

1/4 cup chopped green onions
1/2 cup chopped green bell pepper
8-10 stuffed olives, sliced
2 6 1/2-ounce jars marinated artichoke hearts, reserve liquid
1/3 cup mayonnaise
1 teaspoon curry powder
2 1/2 cups cooked saffron rice

• Combine onions, bell pepper, olives and artichokes in a bowl.
• Mix together 1/4 cup of the reserved artichoke liquid, mayonnaise and curry powder.
• Add to vegetables and toss.
• Combine with rice and mix well.

Yield: 6 servings

Brown Rice and Almond Salad

4   cups cooked brown rice
1   cup chopped green onions
1   cup chopped red bell pepper
¾   cup coarsely chopped almonds
½   cup corn, cooked
½   cup peas, cooked
¼   cup finely chopped cilantro
4   slices bacon, cooked and crumbled
1   cup plain yogurt
½   cup mayonnaise
1½ tablespoons red wine vinegar
1   garlic clove, crushed
1½ teaspoons chili powder
½   teaspoon powdered cumin
    Salt and pepper
    Romaine lettuce

- Combine first 8 ingredients in a large bowl.
- Mix next 6 ingredients and fold into rice mixture.
- Add salt and pepper to taste.
- Serve on lettuce leaves.

  Yield: 8 servings

 # Curried Rice Salad

4   cups cooked rice
2   tomatoes, peeled and chopped
6   radishes, sliced thin
½   cup finely chopped celery
½   cup finely chopped onions
¼   cup sliced stuffed olives
    Salt and pepper
1   teaspoon curry powder
1   teaspoon Dijon mustard
2   tablespoons wine vinegar
7   tablespoons olive oil
    Lettuce leaves

- Mix together the first 6 ingredients. Add salt and pepper.
- In a separate bowl mix together curry powder, mustard, vinegar, and oil. Beat well to blend thoroughly.
- Pour over mixed vegetables. Serve in lettuce cup.

  Yield: 6 servings

Wild Rice Salad

2   4-ounce boxes wild rice
¼   cup walnuts, lightly toasted
12   sun dried tomatoes, re-hydrated
½   cup black pitted olives, preferably oil cured
1   tablespoon minced fresh parsley
½   cup olive oil
¼   cup red wine vinegar
    Salt and fresh ground pepper to taste

- Cook the rice in a big pot of boiling salted water for 35-45 minutes. Grains should double in size and still be a bit crunchy.
- Drain, rinse with cold water and drain again. Let cool.
- Combine the rice with remaining ingredients and toss gently.

Yield: 4-6 servings

Boo's Potato Salad

A must for the perfect picnic

6   medium potatoes or more
1½   cups mayonnaise
1   cup sour cream
1   teaspoon celery seed
1½   teaspoons horseradish
½   teaspoon salt
1   cup chopped fresh parsley
1   cup chopped spring onions, tops and all

- Boil potatoes in jackets. Cool, peel and cut into small pieces.
- Combine mayonnaise, sour cream, celery seed, horseradish and salt.
- Toss parsley and onions together.
- Layer potatoes, onions, parsley and dressing. Refrigerate 24 hours.
- Mix before serving.

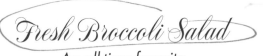
Fresh Broccoli Salad

An all-time favorite

2   bunches fresh broccoli flowerets, chopped into bite size pieces
1   cup chopped purple onion
1   cup raisins
1   cup chopped pecans
8   slices bacon, cooked and crumbled
1   cup mayonnaise
¼   cup sugar
3   tablespoons vinegar

ADD SHREDDED CHEDDAR

- Mix first 5 ingredients in a bowl and chill.
- Whisk together mayonnaise, sugar and vinegar until emulsified.
- Right before serving, pour over broccoli and toss until well coated.

Yield: 4 servings

61

New Potatoes With Dill

Superb!

5 cups new potatoes, cooked in their
   jackets until just tender, quartered
¾ cup sour cream
¼ cup mayonnaise
2 tablespoons vinegar
½ teaspoon prepared mustard
1½ tablespoons minced onion
½ cup peeled and diced cucumber
¾ teaspoon salt
¼ teaspoon pepper
¼ teaspoon celery seed (maybe a little
   more)
½ teaspoon chopped dill weed
2 hard boiled eggs, chopped
⅛ cup minced fresh parsley

- Place quartered potatoes in a bowl.
- Whisk together the sour cream, mayonnaise, vinegar, and mustard in a bowl, adding the onion, cucumber and spices. Pour over potatoes and mix lightly.
- Gently fold in eggs. Refrigerate.
- Garnish with parsley.

Yield: 8 servings

German Potato Salad

3 cups new potatoes
½ cup finely chopped celery
½ cup finely chopped fresh parsley
4 slices lean bacon, diced
½ cup finely chopped onion
⅔ cup water
1 tablespoon flour
¼ cup cider vinegar
2 tablespoons sugar
½ teaspoon salt
¼ teaspoon dry mustard
2 teaspoons poppy seeds

- Boil potatoes, whole and unpeeled; cool, peel and dice.
- In medium bowl, combine potatoes, celery and parsley.
- In non-stick skillet, cook diced bacon.
- Remove and discard fat.
- Add onions and sauté until crisp-tender, not translucent.
- In small bowl, combine water, flour, vinegar, sugar, salt, mustard and poppy seeds. Stir in onion mixture.
- Cook over medium heat until mixture thickens, 1-2 minutes.
- Pour sauce over potatoes and toss gently.
- Serve warm or at room temperature.

Yield: 6 servings

Summer Tomato and Basil Salad

5 medium tomatoes, sliced and salted
⅓ cup sliced, pitted black olives
½ cup crumbled feta cheese
½ cup olive oil
⅓ cup red wine vinegar
2 teaspoons dried whole basil or 6 teaspoons fresh
1 garlic clove, minced
⅛ teaspoon coarsely ground black pepper

- Arrange sliced tomatoes in a 13x9x2-inch dish. Top with olives and cheese.
- Combine remaining ingredients in a jar and shake vigorously.
- Pour over tomatoes and cover and chill for at least 2 hours.

Yield: 8 servings

A Tomato Well Stuffed

2 cups canned artichoke hearts
½ cup chopped celery
½ cup chopped green onions and tops
1 cup mayonnaise
6 tomatoes
2 slices bacon, cooked
Lettuce leaves

- Chop artichoke hearts and combine with celery, green onions and mayonnaise.
- Peel and scoop out 6 tomatoes and stuff with vegetable mixture. Place on lettuce leaves and sprinkle with bacon.

Holland Rusk Salad

6 Holland Rusks
6 ounces cream cheese
4 ounces Roquefort cheese
6 thick tomato slices
6-12 slices bacon, cooked and crumbled
1 head iceberg lettuce, shredded
⅓ cup ketchup
⅔ cup mayonnaise
3 hard boiled eggs, sieved
Paprika

- Place one Holland Rusk on each dinner plate.
- Mix cheeses and spread on rusk.
- Place a slice of tomato on top of cheese mixture and surround with shredded lettuce.
- Top with crumbled bacon. Whisk together ketchup and mayonnaise and spoon a generous portion of dressing on each.
- Sprinkle with egg and paprika.

Picnic Black Beans

1	pound dried black beans, soaked overnight in water
1½	cups frozen corn, thawed
1½	cups chopped and drained tomato
¾	cup thinly sliced onion
⅓	cup minced fresh cilantro
½	cup chopped red bell pepper
½	cup olive oil
½	cup fresh lemon juice
2	teaspoons salt

- Combine black beans with enough water to cover by 2 inches and simmer until beans are just tender. Drain beans and combine with corn, tomato, onion, minced cilantro and bell pepper.
- Whisk together the oil, lemon juice and salt and pour over vegetables while they are still warm.
- Let salad cool, stirring occasionally. Refrigerate.
- Serve at room temperature.

Yield: 10-12 servings

Hearts of Palm Salad

1-2	14-ounce cans of hearts of palm, drained
	Salad greens
1	4-ounce jar chopped pimientos
1	large hard-boiled egg, minced
	Vinaigrette dressing (recipe follows)

- Slice hearts of palm in half vertically. Slice in quarters if very large.
- Arrange greens on salad plates; top with hearts of palm.
- Sprinkle with pimientos, egg and Vinaigrette Dressing.
- Serve immediately.

Vinaigrette Dressing:

1	tablespoon white wine vinegar or champagne vinegar
⅛	teaspoon salt
¼	teaspoon dry mustard
6	tablespoons olive oil or combination olive oil and salad oil
	Fresh ground pepper to taste
½	tablespoon minced fresh or dried shallots or to taste, optional

- Place all ingredients in a jar with a tight fitting lid and shake until thoroughly blended; adjust seasonings.
- Dressing can be made ahead of time.

Yield: 4 servings

Spinach Mandarin Orange Salad

¼ cup chopped or slivered almonds, toasted
1 cup chopped celery
2 green onions and tops, chopped
2 small bunches spinach
1 11-ounce can mandarin orange segments, drained
1 head red leaf or Bibb lettuce
½ teaspoon salt
½ teaspoon hot pepper sauce
2 tablespoons vinegar
2 tablespoons sugar
¼ cup vegetable oil

- Combine first 6 ingredients in a large bowl and chill.
- Combine the remaining ingredients and whisk until emulsified.
- Pour over salad and toss.

Yield: 6 servings

Tangy Romaine Toss
Guaranteed to become a favorite

Romaine lettuce
1 14-ounce can artichokes hearts, drained
1 2-ounce jar pimientos, drained
1 small red onion, sliced very thin
Dressing (recipe follows)

Dressing:
⅛ cup olive oil
½ cup vegetable oil
⅓ cup red wine vinegar
½ teaspoon sugar
⅛ teaspoon black pepper
½ cup Parmesan cheese

- Wash lettuce and tear into bite size pieces.
- Combine salad ingredients in a large bowl and chill until ready to serve.
- When ready to serve, toss gently with dressing.

- Combine ingredients in a jar and refrigerate.
- Shake well before using.

Asparagus Vinaigrette

¾ cup vegetable oil
¼ cup vinegar
2 tablespoons capers, drained
1 tablespoon minced onion
1 tablespoon chopped fresh parsley
1½ teaspoons fresh tarragon (½ teaspoon dried)
1½ teaspoons chopped chives
½ teaspoon salt
⅛ teaspoon pepper
1½-2 pounds asparagus; washed, peeled, blanched and sliced diagonally into bite size pieces.

• Combine all ingredients except asparagus in a bowl and mix well.
• Add asparagus and toss. Refrigerate for several hours.

Yield: 8 servings

Curried Chicken Salad With Chutney

The perfect luncheon dish

¾ cup chutney
1¼ cups mayonnaise
1½ teaspoons curry powder
3 teaspoons grated lime peel
⅜ cup fresh lime juice
¾ teaspoon salt
6 cups cooked and diced white chicken meat
1½ cups pineapple chunks
¾ cup chopped green onions
¾ cup slivered almonds, toasted
⅛ cup currants
   Green or red leaf lettuce

• Combine first 6 ingredients mixing well.
• Combine in a bowl the chicken, pineapple, onions, almonds, and currants.
• Pour the mayonnaise mixture over the chicken and toss lightly.
• Serve on lettuce leaves.

Yield: 6-8 servings.

Sliced Chicken with Lime and Basil

6 boneless chicken breast halves
  Salt and pepper
3 tablespoons butter or margarine
1 tablespoon oil
1 teaspoon minced fresh oregano
1½ tablespoons minced fresh basil
½ teaspoon minced fresh rosemary
3 tablespoons lemon juice
  Marinade (recipe follows)
  Lettuce leaves
  Tomato wedges
  Parsley as garnish

Marinade:
1 cup fresh lime juice
4 garlic cloves
¼ cup tightly packed fresh basil, minced
½ tablespoon minced fresh tarragon
3 large shallots, chopped
1 cup Italian olive oil
⅓ cup vegetable oil
½ teaspoon sugar
  Salt and pepper to taste

- Season chicken with salt and pepper.
- Brown chicken in butter and oil with oregano, basil and rosemary.
- When both sides are nicely brown, add lemon juice and simmer until done.
- Thinly slice the cooled chicken and place in a container.
- Pour marinade over and chill for at least 12 hours.
- To serve, drain chicken and arrange on lettuce leaves with tomato wedges. Sprinkle with parsley.

- Combine all ingredients, mixing well.
  Yield: 6 servings

Chicken Salad Vinaigrette

3 cups cooked rice
¼ cup raisins
1 tablespoon minced onion
4 chicken breast halves, cooked and cut up into bite size pieces
¼ cup chopped fresh parsley
¼ cup cashews
⅔ cup chopped celery
¼ cup chutney
1 4-ounce jar sliced pimientos, drained
1 cup herb vinaigrette salad dressing
  Lettuce leaves

- Combine first 9 ingredients. Toss well with salad dressing.
- Serve on lettuce leaves.
  Yield: 6-8 servings

Sour Cream Cole Slaw

8 cups shredded cabbage or Napa lettuce
3 tablespoons chopped onion
¼ cup sugar
½ teaspoon dry mustard
⅛ teaspoon pepper
2 tablespoons chopped parsley
½ teaspoon salt
½ teaspoon celery seed
¼ cup vinegar
¼ cup oil
½ cup sour cream

- Mix cabbage and onion together in a bowl.
- Bring the next 7 ingredients to a boil.
- When mixture is cool, add oil and sour cream, blending well.
- Pour over cabbage and toss well.

Yield: 6-8 servings

Cole Slaw

1 cabbage
2 medium onions
1 green bell pepper
1 cup vinegar
¾ cup vegetable oil
½ cup sugar
1 teaspoon dry mustard
2 teaspoons celery seed
1 tablespoon salt

- Shred cabbage, onions, and bell pepper in a food processor. Remove to a bowl.
- Combine vinegar, oil, sugar, mustard, celery seed, and salt and bring to a boil.
- Pour over vegetables and toss lightly.
- Cover and let stand in refrigerator several hours before serving.

Yield: 8-10 servings

 *Shrimp Salad*

5 pounds shrimp, cooked and cleaned
1 cup mayonnaise
¼ cup Dijon mustard
¼ teaspoon salt
½ teaspoon hot pepper sauce
2 tablespoons tarragon wine vinegar
2 tablespoons chopped parsley
2 tablespoons chopped onion
2 tablespoons chopped celery
2 3-ounce bottles capers, optional

• Mix ingredients well and toss with chilled shrimp.

Yield: 8-10 servings

Shrimp Salad With Capers

1½ pounds medium shrimp, peeled and deveined
2 tablespoons oil
¼ cup minced parsley
1 medium shallot, minced
⅓ cup tomato, peeled, chopped and drained
Pinch of sugar
1-2 teaspoons chopped fresh basil
2 tablespoons capers, patted dry
½ teaspoon salt
Fresh ground black pepper to taste
1 cup mayonnaise
1 tablespoon lemon juice
1 teaspoon Dijon mustard
1 teaspoon vinegar
⅛ teaspoon cayenne pepper

• Sauté shrimp in oil over medium heat removing shrimp as they turn pink and are cooked. Drain and cool.
• Combine parsley, shallot and tomato and place in a mixing bowl. Add sugar, basil, capers, salt and pepper and toss.
• Combine mayonnaise with lemon juice, mustard, vinegar and cayenne. Add this to the vegetable mixture and blend.
• Combine with shrimp and marinate in refrigerator for at least 2 hours.

Yield: 6-8 servings.

Sea Island Salad

2   cups raw shell macaroni
½   cup mayonnaise
½   cup sour cream
2   tablespoons pimiento
1   tablespoon celery seed
1   can LeSueur peas, drained
2   tablespoons diced green bell pepper
½   teaspoon onion salt
1   cup diced mild Cheddar cheese
1   6-ounce can chunk white tuna, drained
    Pepper to taste

• Cook macaroni, according to package instructions and cool.
• Mix together mayonnaise and sour cream and toss with macaroni.
• Gently mix in other ingredients and chill.

Shrimp Aspic

1   10¾-ounce can tomato soup
3   3-ounce packages cream cheese, softened
2   envelopes unflavored gelatin
½   cup cold water
1   cup mayonnaise
¾   cup finely chopped celery
¾   cup finely chopped onions
2   cups cooked shredded shrimp

• Heat soup to boiling. Add cream cheese, stirring constantly until well mixed.
• Dissolve gelatin in water. Stir into soup. Allow to cool.
• Add mayonnaise, stirring until well blended. Add celery, onion, and shrimp to mixture.
• Pour into greased 5-cup ring mold. Refrigerate overnight or until gelatin is set and will come out of mold easily.
• Serve as a salad or with crackers as an appetizer.

Yield: 6-8 servings

Easy Congealed Peach Salad
A "peach" of a salad

1 20-ounce can crushed pineapple, with juice
1 6-ounce box peach gelatin
2 cups buttermilk
1 8-ounce carton non-dairy frozen whipped topping

- In medium-sized boiler, heat pineapple and juice until thoroughly heated. Mix in dry gelatin. Add buttermilk and mix well.
- Fold in whipped topping and stir. Pour into an 8x8-inch square pan or individual fluted molds and refrigerate until set.
- Cut in squares to serve.

Yield: 8-10 servings

Congealed Citrus Salad

2 oranges
1 grapefruit
1 cup water
1 tablespoon unflavored gelatin
1 3.4-ounce box lemon gelatin
1 8¼-ounce can crushed pineapple with juice

- Section oranges and grapefruit and break into small pieces. Set aside.
- Soak unflavored gelatin in water for a few minutes.
- Bring water to a boil and stir in lemon gelatin until dissolved.
- Add fruit and pineapple to gelatin mixture and stir.
- Pour into greased mold and chill until set.

Fruit Aspic

2 grapefruits, sectioned
6 oranges, sectioned
1 16-ounce can of white cherries, drained, reserve juice
1 15¼-ounce can of pineapple chunks, drained, reserve juice
3 envelopes unflavored gelatin
½ cup cold water
Mayonnaise

- Combine all fruits in a large bowl.
- Dissolve gelatin in cold water and let stand 10 minutes.
- Heat gelatin in a double boiler until melted.
- Pour in reserved juices and let cool.
- Pour juice mixture over fruit and pour into molds to gel.
- Serve with mayonnaise.

Yield: 8-10 servings

Congealed Cranberry Salad

2 cups fresh cranberries, washed and picked over
1 orange
1 lemon
¾ cup sugar
½ cup pecan pieces
1 ring of pineapple, cut up
⅓ cup chopped unpeeled red apple
⅓ cup finely chopped celery
2 envelopes unflavored gelatin, dissolved in ½ cup cold water, then dissolved in 1 cup boiling water
Pinch of salt
Lettuce leaves
Mayonnaise

- Grind, don't purée, cranberries, whole orange and lemon. Old fashioned grinder does better than food processor. Add sugar and let set for 2 hours.
- Add pecans, pineapple, apple and celery. Add dissolved gelatin and salt. Chill.
- Serve on lettuce with mayonnaise.

Chili Sauce Dressing

½ cup sugar
½ cup vinegar
½ cup chili sauce
1 cup salad oil
1 teaspoon salt
Less than ⅛ teaspoon pepper
Juice of 1 lemon
⅓ cup finely chopped onion

- Mix all ingredients in a jar and shake well. Chill.
- Serve over fresh greens.

Blue Cheese Dressing

1 cup mayonnaise
1 cup sour cream
½ cup cheese: blue, Roquefort, or Gorgonzola, crumbled
½ tablespoon Worcestershire sauce
¼ teaspoon garlic powder
Salt and white pepper to taste

- Mix all ingredients; cover and chill.

Blue Cheese Tomato Dressing

1   10¾-ounce can of tomato soup
¾   cup vinegar
1   teaspoon dry mustard
½   cup salad oil
½   cup sugar
1   teaspoon paprika
1   garlic clove or ½ small onion, minced
4   ounces blue cheese

- Put all ingredients in a blender except blue cheese.
- Blend until well mixed.
- Pour into a jar and add blue cheese that has been crumbled.

Russian Dressing

¾   cup olive oil
⅛   cup red wine vinegar
⅛   cup lemon juice
½   teaspoon salt
½   teaspoon dry mustard
1   tablespoon Worcestershire sauce
2½   tablespoons sugar
½   teaspoon paprika
¼   cup ketchup
1   whole garlic clove

- Mix all ingredients together in a jar and shake until emulsified.
- Remove garlic after a few days.

Secret French Dressing

So special, they'll want the recipe

½   cup vinegar
½   cup ketchup
½   cup sugar
2-3   tablespoons fresh lemon juice
⅓   cup grated onion
1   teaspoon paprika
½   teaspoon prepared mustard
½   teaspoon salt
¼-½   teaspoon black pepper
2   cups salad oil

- Put vinegar in a blender. Add the next 8 ingredients blending well.
- With the blender running slowly, add oil in a thin stream.
- Chill.

Tangy French Dressing

¼ cup cider vinegar
¼ cup sugar
1 teaspoon salt
1 teaspoon paprika
1 teaspoon dry mustard
1 teaspoon celery seed
¼ teaspoon pepper
¼ teaspoon onion powder
¾ cup salad oil

- Put cider vinegar in a blender.
- Add next 7 ingredients and blend. With blender running, slowly add oil, in a thin stream.
- Chill.

Louis Dressing

¼ cup minced green bell pepper
¼ cup minced onion
2 tablespoons chopped green onions
1 teaspoon horseradish
1 cup mayonnaise
4 tablespoons chili sauce
1 tablespoon lemon juice
1 teaspoon Worcestershire sauce
¼-½ cup white wine
Salt to taste

- Mix ingredients and keep chilled.
Wonderful with crabmeat!

Green Goddess Salad Dressing

3-4 anchovy fillets, minced
3 tablespoons mayonnaise
5 finely chopped green onions, with tops
2 cups sour cream
3 tablespoons fresh lemon juice
3 tablespoons vinegar
1 tablespoon ground black pepper

- Mix all ingredients and refrigerate.

Glorified Italian Dressing
A unique change from the usual

½ cup vinegar
2 tablespoons water
1 6-ounce package of Good Seasons
   Italian dressing mix
1 garlic clove, pressed
1 tablespoon lemon juice
1 teaspoon lemon pepper
¼ teaspoon salt
¼ cup olive oil
¼ cup vegetable oil
1 teaspoon Dijon mustard

- Mix all ingredients together and whisk until emulsified.

Yield: About 1 cup

Poppy Seed Dressing

⅓ cup sugar
½ teaspoon dry mustard
½ teaspoon salt
½ cup oil
3 tablespoons lemon juice
1 tablespoon white vinegar
¼ cup finely chopped onion
2 teaspoons poppy seeds

- Blend first 7 ingredients in a blender.
- Add poppy seeds and stir with a fork to mix.
- Chill.

Caesar Salad Dressing

3-4 egg yolks
1 6-ounce tube of anchovy paste
3 tablespoons minced garlic
3 tablespoons Dijon mustard
2 tablespoons red wine vinegar
½ tablespoon hot pepper sauce
1 tablespoon black pepper
⅓ cup Parmesan cheese
1 cup light virgin olive oil

- Beat the egg yolks in a blender on low for 3 minutes.
- Slowly add the remaining ingredients and blend until well mixed.
- Toss with romaine lettuce, Parmesan cheese and croutons.

Salad Dressing for Fruit or Vegetables

¼ cup vinegar
¼ cup sugar, or less
½ teaspoon salt
½ teaspoon celery seed
¼ teaspoon curry powder
¼ teaspoon turmeric
½ cup salad oil
1 teaspoon prepared mustard
¼ cup ketchup
1 teaspoon grated onion
2 garlic cloves on picks

- Add dry ingredients to vinegar and blend. Add remaining ingredients except garlic. Blend well.
- Pour into jar. Put in garlic cloves on picks so they can be removed.

 ## Mayo in a Blender

2 eggs
⅛ teaspoon black pepper
⅛ teaspoon cayenne pepper
⅛ teaspoon Worcestershire sauce
1½ teaspoons salt
⅛ teaspoon paprika
1½ teaspoons dry mustard
1 teaspoon onion, thinly slivered
1 tablespoon vinegar
Juice of 1 lemon
1½ cups salad oil

- Place first 10 ingredients in a blender and turn on for about 1 minute.
- Keep blender running and add oil very slowly. Blend until oil is completely absorbed.
- Turn off blender and stir well. Mayonnaise will firm up a little when refrigerated.

Yield: About 2 cups

Breads

Ponte Vedra Innlet Banana Bread

A Heavenly Aroma

2 cups sugar
1 cup oil
4 eggs, beaten
1 pound very ripe bananas (weighed after peeling), mashed
2 cups all-purpose flour
1½ teaspoons salt
1 tablespoon soda
1 cup buttermilk
1 cup chopped pecans, optional

- Beat sugar and oil together.
- Add eggs and bananas and mix well.
- Sift together flour, salt and soda and add to banana mixture, alternating with buttermilk. Stir in pecans.
- Pour into 2 greased regular loaf pans or 4 small ones and bake in a preheated oven at 300° for 30 minutes, then at 350° for 30 minutes longer. Check to see if they are done. The large loaves may need a few more minutes.

Sweet Potato Nut Bread

1 cup cooking oil
4 eggs, slightly beaten
⅔ cup water
2 cups mashed sweet potatoes (about 3 medium)
3⅓ cups presifted all-purpose flour
3 teaspoons salt
1 tablespoon nutmeg
1 tablespoon cinnamon
1 tablespoon ginger
2 tablespoons baking soda
3 cups sugar
2 small yellow apples, peeled, cored and diced
½ cup chopped dates (raisins may be substituted)
1 cup chopped pecans
½ cup chopped walnuts

- Generously spray three 9x5-inch loaf pans with non-stick spray.
- Combine oil, eggs, water and sweet potatoes.
- In a large bowl, sift together dry ingredients.
- Make a well in the center of the dry ingredients and add the sweet potato mixture along with apples, dates and nuts.
- Stir until all dry ingredients are completely blended into the sweet potato mixture. Do not overstir.
- Turn batter into loaf pans and bake in a preheated oven at 350° for about 50 minutes.

Yield: 3 loaves

Zucchini Bread

2 eggs
½ cup oil
1 teaspoon vanilla
1 cup sugar
1½ cups all-purpose flour
½ teaspoon salt
½ teaspoon baking soda
Dash of cinnamon
1 cup grated zucchini
1 cup chopped pecans

- Grease and flour a 9x5-inch loaf pan.
- Mix eggs, oil and vanilla.
- Sift dry ingredients together and mix into egg mixture. Add zucchini and pecans.
- Pour into loaf pan and bake in a preheated oven at 350° for 1 hour.

Yield: 1 loaf

Apple Pecan Bread

1 cup unbleached all-purpose flour
1½ teaspoons baking powder
½ teaspoon baking soda
½ teaspoon salt
1 teaspoon cinnamon
½ teaspoon ground cloves
1 cup light brown sugar
¼ cup oat bran
1 cup grated carrot
1 large apple, peeled, cored and chopped
1 cup finely chopped pecans, roasted at 350° for 10 minutes
Zest of 1 orange
2 eggs
½ cup oil
1 tablespoon vanilla

- Spray a 9x5-inch loaf pan with cooking spray.
- In a medium mixing bowl, sift together flour, baking powder, baking soda, salt, cinnamon and cloves. Stir in brown sugar and oat bran.
- Mix together carrot, apple, pecans and orange zest. Stir into flour mixture.
- In a small mixing bowl, beat eggs, oil and vanilla. Stir into fruit/flour mixture until moistened.
- Spoon batter into prepared pan and bake in a preheated oven at 350° for 45 minutes or until done.

Yield: 1 loaf

Carrot Pineapple Bread

2 cups all-purpose flour
1 teaspoon baking soda
1 teaspoon salt
1½ teaspoons cinnamon
3 eggs
2 cups sugar
1 cup vegetable oil
1 cup grated carrot
1 8-ounce can crushed pineapple, undrained
2 teaspoons vanilla
1 cup chopped pecans

- Grease two 9x5-inch loaf pans.
- Combine flour, soda, salt and cinnamon. Set aside.
- Combine eggs, sugar and oil in a medium bowl. Mix well.
- Stir in carrots, pineapple and vanilla.
- Add dry ingredients, mixing well. Stir in pecans.
- Pour into prepared pans. Bake in a preheated oven at 325° for about 60 minutes.

Freezes well.

Yield: 2 loaves

Dilly Cheese Bread

Moist and oh so good!

3 cups biscuit mix
1½ cups (6 ounces) shredded sharp Cheddar cheese
1 tablespoon sugar
½ teaspoon dried whole dill weed
½ teaspoon dry mustard
1¼ cups milk
1 egg, beaten
1 tablespoon vegetable oil

- Grease a 9x5-inch loaf pan.
- Combine first 5 ingredients in a large mixing bowl; mix well.
- Add remaining ingredients, stirring just until dry ingredients are moistened.
- Spoon batter into prepared pan. Bake in a preheated oven at 350° for 50 minutes or until golden brown.

Yield: 1 loaf

Parmesan Herb Loaves

2   6 to 7-inch Italian rolls or baguettes
¼   cup softened butter or margarine
2   tablespoons grated Parmesan cheese
1   tablespoon finely chopped fresh parsley
1   teaspoon chopped chives
½   teaspoon dried thyme leaves

• Cut loaves in half lengthwise.
• Blend butter, cheese and herbs and spread about 1 tablespoon of herb mixture on cut sides of each loaf.
• Close loaves, wrap in foil and bake in a preheated oven at 350° for 15 minutes.
• Cut each loaf crosswise into 4 pieces.
  Variation: Loaves may also be placed on side of grill. Grill for 10-15 minutes or until toasted and herb mixture melts.

Yield: 4 servings

Toasted Thyme Sticks

Super with soup or salad

½   cup butter or margarine, softened
2-4   teaspoons dried thyme leaves
15   slices of thin white bread, crusts removed

• Mix butter with thyme.
• Spread butter/thyme mixture onto bread and cut each slice into three long pieces.
• Place on a greased cookie sheet and bake in a preheated oven at 300° until crisp, but not brown; about 25-30 minutes.
• Sticks may be served warm or cold.

Yield: 45 sticks

Applesauce Mini-Muffins

½ cup butter or margarine
1 cup sugar
1 egg, beaten
1 cup applesauce
1 teaspoon baking soda
2 cups all-purpose flour
½ tablespoon cinnamon
½ tablespoon allspice
1 tablespoon vanilla
1 cup chopped pecans, optional

- Cream butter and sugar. Add egg.
- Heat applesauce and stir in baking soda.
- Sift flour and spices.
- Add flour and applesauce to butter mixture, alternately. Add vanilla and pecans, if using.
- Pour into greased mini-muffin tins and bake in a preheated oven at 350° for 15-20 minutes. If using regular muffin tins, bake for 20-25 minutes.

Yield: 30 mini-muffins or 14 regular muffins

Peachy Almond Muffins

1 16-ounce can sliced peaches, drained, or 1 cup fresh chopped peaches
1½ cups all-purpose flour
½ teaspoon salt
½ teaspoon baking soda
⅔ cup sugar
2 eggs, beaten
½ cup vegetable oil
½ teaspoon vanilla
¼ teaspoon almond extract
½ cup sliced almonds, toasted

- Chop peaches, drain and set aside.
- Combine flour and next 3 ingredients in a mixing bowl.
- Make a well in the center of dry ingredients. Add eggs and oil. Stir until dry ingredients are just moistened.
- Add peaches, vanilla, almond extract and almonds. Stir until blended.
- Spoon batter into greased muffin cups. Bake in a preheated oven at 350° for 20-25 minutes.

Yield: 12 muffins

Bran Muffins

1 cup softened butter or margarine
1 13.8-ounce box All Bran cereal (Kellogg's)
2 cups boiling water
5 cups all-purpose flour
5 teaspoons baking soda
2 teaspoons salt
1 box brown sugar
1 1-pound box raisins
1 quart buttermilk
5 eggs, beaten

• Combine butter, 2 cups cereal and water, mixing well.
• Add remaining cereal and dry ingredients and mix.
• Add raisins, buttermilk and eggs and stir until blended.
• Fill greased muffin pans half full.
• Bake in a preheated oven at 400° for 15 minutes.

This batter may be stored in the refrigerator for 6 weeks and used as needed.

Yield: 48 muffins

Millionaire Muffins

1¼ cups rolled oats
1 cup buttermilk
1 egg
¾ cup brown sugar
4 tablespoons butter or margarine, melted
¾ cup all-purpose flour
1 teaspoon baking powder
½ teaspoon salt
½ teaspoon baking soda
½ cup raisins
½ cup chopped pecans

• Combine the rolled oats and buttermilk in a mixing bowl and let stand for 1 hour.
• Add the egg, sugar and butter. Mix 30 seconds. Scrape down bowl.
• Combine dry ingredients and add to mixture.
• Mix on low speed about 15 seconds or only until dry ingredients are moistened. Stir in raisins and pecans.
• Fill greased muffin cups ½ full. Bake in a preheated oven at 350° for 15 minutes.

Yield: 12 muffins

Williamsburg Blueberry Muffins
Delicious for breakfast or brunch

⅓ cup vegetable shortening
1 cup sugar
2 eggs
1¾ cups all-purpose flour
2 teaspoons baking powder
½ teaspoon salt
⅔ cup milk
1½ cups rinsed and drained blueberries
(canned, fresh or frozen)

- Cream shortening and sugar until light and fluffy.
- Add the eggs, one at a time, beating well until fluffy.
- Sift together flour, baking powder and salt.
- Add dry ingredients and milk alternately, mixing until just blended.
- Add blueberries. Do not overmix — they won't rise as well.
- Fill muffin cups ⅔ full, using cup cake liners, and bake in a preheated oven at 400° for 20-25 minutes.

Yield: 18 regular muffins

Molasses Squash Muffins

½ cup softened butter or margarine
½ cup light brown sugar
¼ cup light or dark molasses
1 large egg
1¼ cups cooked, mashed yellow squash
(about 3-4 squash)
1¾ cups unsifted all-purpose flour
1 teaspoon baking soda
½ teaspoon salt
½ cup chopped pecans

- Beat butter until fluffy, then beat in sugar and molasses until well-blended.
- Beat in egg and squash. Sift in flour, soda and salt; stir until just mixed.
- Stir in pecans.
- Spoon batter into greased muffin cups and bake in a preheated oven at 375° until lightly browned, about 20 minutes.

Yield: 12 muffins

handwritten note:
eggs
dried beef
Miracle Whip

 ## Pecan Muffins

- Break eggs in a bowl and beat slightly. Add brown sugar and mix well.
- Sift flour 3-4 times. Add a scant ½ cup flour, baking powder and salt to egg mixture.
- Stir in pecans.
- Spoon into small greased muffin cups and bake in a preheated oven at 425° for 20-25 minutes.

Yield: 12 small muffins

Melt Away Muffins

Easy, quick and delicious

...vder

...ans

...garine

- Combine all ingredients and mix with a fork until ingredients are just blended.
- Put batter in greased mini-muffin cups.
- Bake in a preheated oven at 375° for 20-25 minutes or until lightly browned.

Variation: For Cheese Melt Away Muffins: Add 1 cup grated Cheddar cheese to ingredients and bake as above.

Freezes well.

Yield: 40-48 muffins

Mexican Cornbread

1½ cups self-rising cornmeal
3 eggs
⅔ cup vegetable oil
½ cup chopped green pepper
2 pods hot pepper, finely chopped
1 cup grated sharp Cheddar cheese
1 small onion, chopped
1 8.5-ounce can cream style corn
1 cup buttermilk

- Mix all ingredients and blend well.
- Pour into a greased skillet and bake in a preheated oven at 375° for 30 minutes.

You may want to wear rubber gloves when chopping the hot peppers.

Yield: 6 servings

Sour Cream Cornbread

1 cup self-rising cornmeal
1 8.5-ounce can cream style corn
2 eggs
8 ounces sour cream
¼ cup vegetable oil

- Grease a 6x10-inch ovenproof dish.
- Mix all ingredients and spoon into prepared dish.
- Bake in a preheated oven at 375° for 25 minutes.

  Variation: May also spoon batter into muffin tin and bake for 20 minutes. Makes approximately 1 dozen medium muffins.

  Yield: 6 servings

Cricket Tea Room Cornbread

This was served at the Cricket Tea Room on Broad Street.

2 eggs
1 quart milk
2 teaspoons salt
2 cups water-ground cornmeal
2 tablespoons butter or margarine

- Preheat oven to 400° and preheat a greased 10-inch iron skillet.
- Beat eggs until light colored.
- Boil milk and add salt. Slowly stir in the cornmeal and butter. Add the beaten eggs and stir until smooth.
- Pour into prepared skillet and bake for 20-25 minutes or until brown.

Cheddar Drop Biscuits

1 cup all-purpose flour
1½ teaspoons double-acting baking powder
½ teaspoon salt
2 tablespoons cold unsalted butter or margarine, cut into bits
¼ pound grated sharp Cheddar cheese
½-¾ cup milk

- Sift the flour, baking powder and salt together into a bowl.
- Add butter and blend until it resembles coarse meal. Stir in cheese.
- Add enough milk to form a soft sticky dough.
- Drop dough by rounded tablespoons onto greased baking sheet.
- Bake in a preheated oven at 425° for 15 minutes or until they are pale golden.

  Yield: About 16

Mother's Refrigerator Rolls

1 cup scalded milk
½ cup cooking oil
½ cup sugar
1 teaspoon salt
1 package yeast
¼ cup warm water
2 eggs, slightly beaten
4 cups all-purpose flour

- Mix the first 4 ingredients and cool to luke-warm.
- Dissolve yeast in water. Add to the above mixture.
- Add eggs and flour. Knead and let rise in a warm place until double in bulk.
- Pat down and put in refrigerator overnight.
- Pinch off and roll out on a floured surface as needed. Cut out circles and fold in half.
- Place on a greased cookie sheet and let rise 30-40 minutes.
- Bake in a preheated oven at 400° for 12 minutes.

Variation: For cinnamon rolls: Ice with a mixture of melted butter or margarine, cinnamon, and powdered sugar.

Yield: About 20

Sour Dough Bread

This recipe uses a sour dough starter that must be made before you can make the bread. You can use an "Instant Starter" every time you make bread or you can "keep a starter going." Both recipes are included on these pages.

Bread:

½   cup sugar
1   cup starter, at room temperature
½   cup oil
1½   cups warm water
1½   teaspoons salt
      Approximately 6 cups bread flour

- Mix all ingredients together and knead well.
- Place kneaded dough in a bowl greased with oil
- Turn dough over in bowl so both sides are greased.
- Cover bowl with greased paper and allow dough to rise at room temperature for 8-10 hours.
- Punch down dough in the center and divide into 3 equal parts.
- Knead each part 8-10 times and place each in a greased loaf pan.
- Rub the top with oil and cover with greased paper.
- Let dough rise at room temperature for 4-5 hours.
- Bake in a preheated oven at 325° for 30-40 minutes.

Sour Dough Bread — Bread Machine
Recipe:
For a machine that uses 2 cups of flour per recipe.

½ cup warm water
⅙ cup oil
⅔ cup starter, at room temperature
⅙ cup sugar
½ teaspoon salt
2 cups bread flour
1 teaspoon active dry yeast

- Add ingredients to bread machine in order listed.
- Set machine on bread cycle and turn on.
- Bake according to machine's instructions.

Instant Starter:
¾ cup sugar
3 tablespoons instant potatoes
1 cup warm water
1 package active dry yeast

- Mix ingredients well and pour into loosely covered container.
- Keep starter at room temperature for 12 hours before making bread.

To Keep Starter Going:
- Mix instant starter recipe and keep at room temperature for 12 hours.
- Refrigerate.
- Feed the starter by adding the following every 3-5 days:
   ¾ cup sugar
   3 tablespoons instant potatoes
   1 cup warm water
- Mix well.
- Keep at room temperature 12 hours in a loosely covered container.
- Remove 1 cup and return starter to refrigerator.
- Make bread with the 1 cup of starter removed or throw it away.

Worth-the-Wait Rolls
The title says it all!

1 cup butter or margarine, divided
1 cup milk
¼ cup sugar
¼ teaspoon salt
4-5 cups all-purpose flour, divided
2 eggs
2 packages yeast
½ cup lukewarm water

- Melt ½ cup butter in milk with sugar and salt; let cool to lukewarm.
- Add 2 cups flour and eggs; stir.
- Dissolve yeast in water. Add to flour mixture. Cover and set in draft-free place to rise until it doubles in bulk, about an hour.
- Cover a large board with flour. Pour dough onto floured surface and pour about 2-3 cups of flour on top of dough.
- Knead, adding flour until dough is not sticky.
- Roll out dough about ⅛-inch thick. Cut in circles.
- Melt remaining ½ cup of butter.
- Dip one side of roll into melted butter and place, butter side down, on cookie sheet and fold in half. Place rolls side by side, touching.
- Bake in a preheated oven at 400° for 15-20 minutes or until golden.
- To freeze: Bake only 10 minutes and remove before rolls are brown. Freeze or refrigerate for future use.

Yield: About 90 rolls

Divine Dressing

3 cups crumbled cornbread
3 eggs, beaten
3 cups herb stuffing
4½ cups chicken broth
½ cup butter or margarine, melted
1 large onion, chopped
1½ cups chopped celery
½ teaspoon pepper
1½ teaspoons salt
1 tablespoon poultry seasoning

- Combine all ingredients.
- Place in a greased 3-quart baking dish and bake in a preheated oven at 350° for 1 hour.
- Remove from oven and let stand about 10 minutes before serving.

Yield: 8-10 servings

Miracle Rolls

1 package yeast
1 cup warm buttermilk
¼ teaspoon baking soda
3 tablespoons sugar
3 tablespoons butter-flavored shortening, melted
2½ cups all-purpose flour
1 teaspoon baking powder
1 teaspoon salt
½ cup butter or margarine, melted

- Place yeast in a large bowl.
- Add warm buttermilk, baking soda, sugar and shortening. Stir until yeast is dissolved.
- Add flour, baking powder and salt. Stir until dough is of proper consistency. Add more flour if needed.
- Knead well, roll out and cut with a small cutter.
- Brush with melted butter, fold in half and place on greased cookie sheet.
- Cover and put in a draft-free place. Let rise until double (about 1 hour)
- Bake in a preheated oven at 400° for 10-12 minutes.

These freeze well.

Yield: About 4 dozen

Marshmallow Cinnamon Puffs

Fun for children to make

1 8-ounce can crescent rolls
8 large marshmallows
3 tablespoons butter or margarine, melted
Cinnamon
Sugar

- Unroll crescent rolls.
- Place a marshmallow on top of each and roll up like a crescent.
- Twist ends together in a peak and fold ends over to seal in marshmallow.
- Dip into melted butter.
- Sprinkle with sugar and cinnamon.
- Place in a greased muffin tin.
- Bake in a preheated oven at 350° for 10 minutes.

Glaze (optional):
¼ cup powdered sugar
¼ teaspoon vanilla
½ teaspoon milk

- Mix all ingredients, then drizzle over warm puffs.

Yield: 8 rolls

Monkey Bread

¾ cup sugar
3 tablespoons cinnamon
4 cans buttermilk biscuits (10 per can)
¾ cup butter or margarine
1 cup sugar
⅔ cup raisins, optional
¾ cup chopped pecans, optional

- Grease a 10-inch Bundt pan.
- Combine ¾ cup sugar and cinnamon in a plastic bag.
- Cut biscuits into quarters and put into bag. Shake to coat biscuits evenly.
- Melt butter and 1 cup sugar. Bring to boil, just long enough to dissolve sugar.
- In prepared pan, drizzle a little of butter mixture in the bottom.
- Begin layering biscuits, raisins and pecans, drizzling a little of the butter mixture between each layer. Save most of the butter mixture to pour over top.
- Bake in a preheated oven at 350° for 35-40 minutes.
- Let cool about 10 minutes before inverting on a cake plate.

Yield: 8-10 servings

Breakaway Vegetable Bread

3 10-ounce cans refrigerated buttermilk biscuits
½ cup butter or margarine, melted
½ pound bacon, cooked and crumbled
½ cup grated Parmesan cheese
1 small onion, finely chopped
1 small green bell pepper, finely chopped

- Lightly grease a 10-inch Bundt pan.
- Cut biscuits into quarters and dip each piece in butter.
- Layer one third of the biscuits in prepared pan.
- Sprinkle with half of bacon, cheese, onion and green pepper.
- Repeat layers until all ingredients are used, ending with biscuits.
- Bake in a preheated oven at 350° for 45 minutes or until done.
- Serve the whole loaf, pulling off one piece at a time.

Yield: 8 servings

Flavorful French Toast

Perfect for a Sunday supper on a chilly winter evening!

6   eggs
2   tablespoons lowfat milk
2   tablespoons maple syrup
2   tablespoons orange juice, fresh or frozen
¼   teaspoon ground cinnamon
     Dash vanilla
½   teaspoon grated orange rind
8   thick slices of French bread (or raisin or cinnamon)
     Butter or margarine
1   cup maple syrup
6   tablespoons powdered sugar

- In a medium bowl, whisk eggs with milk, 2 tablespoons maple syrup, juice, cinnamon, vanilla and orange rind.
- Soak the bread in the liquid, one piece at a time, for about a minute on each side.
- In a medium skillet, heat ½ tablespoon butter over moderate heat.
- Add bread and cook for 1½ minutes or until golden brown.
- Flip and cook the other side for about 30 seconds, until golden. Add more butter to the pan as needed.
- Serve with warm maple syrup and a dusting of powdered sugar. Also great with blueberry syrup.

Sour Cream Coffee Cake

1   cup butter or margarine, softened
2   cups sugar
2   eggs
½   teaspoon vanilla
2   cups flour
¼   teaspoon baking soda
½   teaspoon salt
1   teaspoon baking powder
1   cup sour cream
2   tablespoons brown sugar
1   teaspoon cinnamon
½   cup chopped pecans

- Cream butter and sugar. Add eggs and vanilla.
- Sift together flour, baking soda, salt and baking powder; add to butter and sugar. Mix until blended.
- Fold in sour cream.
- Mix together brown sugar, cinnamon and pecans.
- Pour ⅓ of cake batter into greased and floured tube or Bundt pan.
- Sprinkle half of brown sugar mixture over batter. Pour ⅓ of batter over filling.
- Sprinkle with remaining brown sugar mixture and pour remaining batter on top.
- Bake in a preheated oven at 350° for 1 hour.

Sweet Cinnamon Quick Bread

2   cups all-purpose flour
1   cup sugar
4   teaspoons baking powder
1½   teaspoons cinnamon
1¼   teaspoons salt
1   cup buttermilk
⅓   cup oil
2   teaspoons vanilla
2   eggs
2   tablespoons sugar
1   teaspoon cinnamon
2   teaspoons butter or margarine, melted

- Grease and flour bottom only of a 9x5-inch loaf pan.
- Combine first 9 ingredients in a large bowl.
- Mix for 3 minutes at medium speed.
- Pour batter into prepared pan.
- In a small bowl, combine sugar, cinnamon and butter until crumbly.
- Sprinkle over batter and swirl lightly to marble.
- Bake in a preheated oven at 350° for 45-55 minutes, or until toothpick inserted in center comes out clean.
- Remove from pan immediately. Cool completely before slicing.

Versatile Seasoned Butter

½   cup butter or margarine
¼-⅓   cup freshly grated Parmesan cheese
1   small garlic clove, pressed
⅛   cup toasted sesame seeds
       A few dashes black pepper
½   teaspoon chopped parsley

- Process all ingredients in a food processor until smooth.
- Scrape down sides of bowl often.
- Refrigerate. This will keep several days, but the garlic will become more pungent.
- Use on toasted bread, over vegetables, for basting chicken, etc.
  Variation: For Italian style, add ¼ teaspoon basil, ¼ teaspoon oregano, and ¼ teaspoon thyme.

Honey of a Spread!

1   16-ounce tub of soft margarine
8   ounces honey
1   teaspoon cinnamon or more, according to taste

- Mix all ingredients with a hand mixer until smooth. Do not melt margarine to make it easier to mix.
- Return to tub and keep refrigerated. There will be a bit more that won't fit into tub, so just put excess in another covered container.
- Use on any bread, muffin or bagel as needed.

Pasta

Herbed Chicken and Pasta Salad

8–12 ounces fusili or rotini
¼–½ cup Glorified Italian Dressing (see Index)
4 boneless chicken breast halves
Salt and pepper to taste
Celery salt to taste
Lemon pepper to taste
3 tablespoons butter or margarine
1 tablespoon olive oil
½ tablespoon fresh oregano
1½ tablespoon fresh basil
½ teaspoon fresh rosemary
1½ tablespoon fresh lemon juice
½ cup sliced heart of palm
⅓ cup chopped onion
½ cup chopped red bell pepper
⅓ cup chopped green bell pepper
⅓ cup sliced stuffed green olives
3 tablespoons chopped fresh parsley

- Cook pasta according to package directions and toss with Glorified Italian Dressing. Set aside.
- Season chicken breasts with salt, pepper, celery salt and lemon pepper.
- Heat butter and oil in skillet and brown chicken breasts. Sprinkle chicken with oregano, basil and rosemary while cooking. When both sides are nicely browned, add lemon juice and cover. Simmer until done, turning several times.
- Allow chicken to cool, then chop into bite–size pieces.
- In a large bowl, combine chicken, pasta and chopped vegetables then toss well.
- Refrigerate until ready to serve. Check seasoning and add dressing if necessary before serving.

Yield: 8 servings

Vermicelli Salad

1 16–ounce package vermicelli, broken
6 cups salted, boiling water
¼ cup vegetable oil
3 tablespoons fresh lemon juice
1 tablespoon MSG
1 cup chopped celery
½ cup chopped onion
1 cup chopped green bell pepper
1 2–ounce jar diced pimentos, drained
1 4–ounce can pitted ripe olives, sliced
¼ cup mayonnaise
Salt to taste

- Cook vermicelli in boiling, salted water for 10 minutes. Drain.
- Mix drained pasta with oil, lemon juice and MSG. Marinate overnight.
- Add chopped vegetables, mix well with mayonnaise and serve.

Chicken-Artichoke Pasta Salad

2 chicken bouillon cubes
2 cups boiling water
4–6 boneless chicken breast halves
¼ cup chopped onions
1 cup water
8 ounces vermicelli
1 14–ounce can artichoke hearts, quartered
1 pint cherry tomatoes, halved
Herbed Dressing (recipe follows)

- Dissolve bouillon cubes in 2 cups boiling water. Add chicken and onions. Cover chicken with additional water.
- Simmer chicken and onion until done. Remove chicken, set aside and allow to cool. When chicken has cooled, chop coarsely.
- Strain broth and set aside.
- Break vermicelli into 2–inch pieces. Pour reserved broth in pot. Add enough water to cook the vermicelli according to package directions. Drain vermicelli thoroughly.
- Combine vermicelli, chicken and Herbed Dressing. Add artichoke hearts and toss.
- Refrigerate for at least 2 hours, add tomatoes and serve.

Yield: 6–8 servings

Herbed Dressing:

1½ tablespoons grated onion
⅓ cup oil
3 tablespoons red wine vinegar
3 tablespoons fresh lemon juice
1½ teaspoons seasoned salt
1½ teaspoons dried crushed basil
1½ tablespoons whole basil

- Combine all ingredients and mix well.

Crab Fettuccine

6 ounces fettuccine
¼ cup butter or margarine
2 garlic cloves, finely chopped
1 cup white lump crabmeat
1 cup half-and-half
⅛ teaspoon black pepper
½ cup Parmesan cheese

- Cook fettuccine according to package directions. Drain.
- Sauté garlic in butter over medium heat until garlic is lightly browned.
- Either break up the crabmeat into flakes or leave in bite-size chunks.
- Add half-and-half, crabmeat and pepper. Heat about 3 minutes, or until mixture just begins to bubble, stirring occasionally.
- Add Parmesan cheese; stir for 1 minute. If sauce becomes too thick, add ¼ cup water.
- Remove from heat and toss with fettuccine. Serve immediately, adding more Parmesan cheese, if desired.

Yield: 4–6 servings

Shrimp with Spinach Pasta

Guaranteed to impress your dinner guests

6 ounces spinach pasta
2 pounds shrimp, peeled and deveined
¾ cup butter or margarine
1 10¾-ounce can cream of mushroom soup
1 cup sour cream
1 cup mayonnaise
½ teaspoon Dijon mustard
4 tablespoons dry sherry
¾ cup grated sharp Cheddar cheese

- Cook pasta according to package directions.
- Line a 9x13x2-inch glass baking dish with pasta.
- In a large pan, sauté shrimp in butter until pink. Place shrimp over pasta.
- Combine soup, sour cream, mayonnaise, mustard and sherry. Pour sauce over shrimp.
- Sprinkle with Cheddar cheese and bake uncovered in a preheated 350° oven for 30 minutes.

Variation: Substitute chicken for shrimp.

Can be made ahead; freezes well.

Yield: 6–8 servings

Shrimp and Angel Hair Pasta

1 tablespoon butter or margarine
9 ounces angel hair pasta
2 eggs
1 cup half-and-half
1 cup plain yogurt
½ cup feta cheese
½ cup grated Swiss cheese
⅓ cup chopped parsley
1 teaspoon basil
1 teaspoon oregano
1 16-ounce can thick and chunky salsa
1½ pounds shrimp, peeled and deveined
½ cup grated Monterey Jack cheese

- Cook pasta in boiling water with butter for 1 minute; drain.
- Mix together eggs, half-and-half, yogurt, feta cheese, Swiss cheese, parsley, basil and oregano. Set aside.
- Place half the pasta on the bottom of a buttered 9x13x2-inch casserole dish. Cover with half the salsa, half the shrimp and half the egg mixture. Repeat.
- Sprinkle with Monterey Jack cheese and bake in a preheated 350° oven for 30 minutes or until the shrimp is tender.

Yield: 6 servings

Shrimp with Feta Sauce
Great for the Beach!

4 garlic cloves, minced
2-3 tablespoons olive oil
1 28-ounce can Italian-style peeled tomatoes, chopped
⅓ cup chopped fresh parsley
1 teaspoon oregano
Pepper to taste
½ cup sliced black olives
1 pound shrimp, peeled and deveined
5 ounces feta cheese, in chunks
7 ounces fettuccine or linguini

- Sauté garlic in olive oil in large skillet until just brown.
- Add tomatoes, parsley, oregano and pepper. Simmer until sauce is thick.
- Add olives, shrimp and feta cheese. Cook until shrimp is done.
- Cook pasta according to package directions.
- Spoon sauce over pasta and serve immediately.

Yield: 4 servings

Crawfish Fettuccine

16 ounces fettuccine noodles
1½ cups butter or margarine
1 large onion, chopped
2 celery stalks, chopped
1 green bell pepper, chopped
2 tablespoons all-purpose flour
2 tablespoons chopped parsley
1½ pounds crawfish
2 cups half-and-half
8 ounces Velveeta cheese
1½ tablespoons sliced jalapeño peppers
1 garlic clove, crushed
   Salt and pepper to taste
⅓ cup bread crumbs
⅓ cup Parmesan cheese

- Cook noodles according to package directions.
- Sauté onion, celery and bell pepper in butter for 10 minutes.
- Add flour, parsley and crawfish. Cook 20 minutes, stirring occasionally.
- Add half-and-half, Velveeta cheese, jalapeño peppers, garlic, salt and pepper and cook until cheese has melted.
- Combine cooked noodles with crawfish mixture and place in a 1½-quart baking dish. Top with bread crumbs and Parmesan cheese.
- Bake in a preheated 350° oven for 30 minutes or until bubbly.

Variation: Shrimp may be used in place of crawfish.

Yield: 6–8 servings

Chicken Marengo

Tantalizing!

½ cup all-purpose flour
1 teaspoon salt
½ teaspoon pepper
1 teaspoon tarragon
6 boneless, skinless chicken breasts, cut into strips
¼ cup oil
¼ cup butter or margarine
1 cup dry white wine
2 cups canned tomatoes with liquid
1 garlic clove, minced
¼ pound mushrooms, sliced
16 ounces fettuccine, cooked

- Season flour with salt, pepper and tarragon.
- Coat chicken with flour mixture, reserving any remaining flour.
- Brown chicken in oil and butter until done. Remove chicken and set aside.
- Add reserved flour to remaining oil and butter. Gradually whisk in wine.
- When sauce is thick and smooth, add tomatoes, garlic and mushrooms. Add chicken and heat thoroughly.
- Serve immediately over fettuccine.

Variation: Soaked sun-dried tomatoes may be added for color.

Chicken with Muscadine Sauce and Almond Pasta

4   chicken breast halves, boneless, skinless
1   tablespoon butter or margarine
    Salt and pepper to taste
2   garlic cloves, pressed
4   teaspoons balsamic vinegar
4   teaspoons cider vinegar
4   teaspoons white grape juice
¼   teaspoon honey
⅛   teaspoon thyme
1   cup heavy cream
2   tablespoons muscadine preserves
8   ounces pasta, cooked
¼   cup sliced almonds, browned in butter
    Chopped chives for garnish

- Brown chicken breasts in butter over medium heat for 5 minutes. Season with salt and pepper.
- Spread garlic over chicken and cook covered over low heat for 3 minutes.
- Prepare the sauce by mixing vinegars, grape juice, honey and thyme. Pour sauce over chicken and cook covered until barely pink in center.
- Remove the chicken and set the skillet with sauce in it aside.
- Cutting against the grain, slice the cooled chicken into ¼–½–inch slices.
- Cook the sauce on medium heat until the liquid is reduced to a glaze. Add cream and cook over high heat until the sauce thickens. Stir in the preserves and mix until well blended.
- Return the chicken to the skillet and cook until warmed.
- Toss the browned almonds with the pasta and place on serving platter.
- Pour chicken slices in sauce over pasta and top with chopped chives.

Yield: 4 servings

Rigatoni with Ham and Mozzarella

⅓ cup all–purpose flour
4 cups milk
¼ teaspoon salt
⅛ teaspoon white pepper
16 ounces rigatoni or other macaroni, cooked and drained
10 ounces frozen green English peas
1 cup diced cooked ham
8 ounces mozzarella cheese, grated

- In a 2–quart saucepan over high heat, gradually combine flour and milk.
- Add salt and pepper and heat to boiling, stirring constantly.
- Remove pan from heat and stir in the rigatoni, peas, ham and half the cheese.
- Spoon into a 13x9x2–inch casserole dish and top with remaining cheese.
- Bake covered in a preheated 350° oven for 30 minutes.

Fettuccine Carbonara

8 ounces fettuccine
¼ cup butter or margarine
1 cup chopped ham
⅓ cup sliced onion
⅓ cup chopped green bell pepper
½ cup sliced mushrooms
Salt and pepper, to taste
1 egg, beaten
½ cup half–and–half
½ cup Parmesan cheese

- Cook fettuccine according to package directions and drain.
- Melt butter then sauté ham, onion, green bell pepper and mushrooms until tender.
- Add pasta, then salt and pepper to taste.
- Stir in beaten egg, half–and–half and cheese.
- Remove from heat and serve immediately.

Yield: 4 servings

Pasta Leon

3 cups grated raw zucchini
4 tablespoons grated onion
4 tablespoons butter or margarine
⅔ cup half–and–half
¼ teaspoon dried dill weed
½ teaspoon garlic salt
Black pepper to taste
1 cup sour cream
4 ounces pasta, cooked

- Sauté zucchini and onion in butter over medium heat until golden.
- Add half–and–half, dill, garlic salt and pepper and stir constantly for 1 minute.
- Stir in sour cream and heat, but do not boil.
- Serve immediately over cooked pasta of your choice.

Yield: 2 servings

Easy Spinach Lasagna
Simply unbeatable

16 ounces ricotta cheese
2 cups shredded mozzarella
2 eggs, lightly beaten
1 10–ounce package frozen chopped spinach, thawed
1 teaspoon salt
⅛ teaspoon pepper
1 teaspoon oregano
32 ounces prepared spaghetti sauce
8 ounces lasagna noodles, uncooked
1 cup water

- Combine ricotta cheese, mozzarella cheese, eggs, spinach, salt, pepper and oregano. Stir well.
- In a greased 13x9x2–inch pan, layer ingredients 3 times in the following order: ½ cup sauce, 3 noodles and ⅓ of the cheese/spinach mixture.
- Cover the final cheese/spinach layer with the remaining sauce.
- Pour 1 cup water along edges of dish and bake in a preheated 350° oven for 1 hour. Let stand 15 minutes before serving.

Yield: 8 servings

Picante Pasta

8 ounces Mostoccoli, rotini or other pasta
1 large onion, quartered lengthwise and thinly sliced
1 green bell pepper, cut into short, thin strips
1 yellow bell pepper, cut into short, thin strips
1 red bell pepper, cut into short, thin strips
2 tablespoons minced garlic
2 tablespoons olive oil
1 teaspoon dried basil leaves
1 teaspoon oregano
⅔ cup mild Picante sauce
2 tablespoons Balsamic vinegar
¼–½ cup grated Parmesan cheese

- Cook pasta according to package directions. Drain and set aside.
- Sauté onion, peppers and garlic in oil for 5 minutes.
- Add other ingredients and heat through.
- Toss sautéed mixture with pasta and serve immediately.

Yield: 4–6 servings

Creamy Lemon-Chive Pasta with Asparagus

6   ounces fettuccine
    Cold water
    Salt
½   pound asparagus, cut into ½–inch
    pieces
2   tablespoons unsalted butter or
    margarine, softened
¼   cup heavy cream
2   large egg yolks
½   cup freshly grated Parmesan cheese
1   tablespoon fresh chives
1   teaspoon freshly grated lemon rind
2   teaspoons fresh lemon juice
    Salt and pepper to taste
    Chives
1   thin lemon slice, quartered

- Cook fettuccine until al dente. Drain and place in a large bowl of cold water.
- In a saucepan of salted, boiling water, cook the asparagus until crisp–tender. Drain and add to the pasta.
- In a large skillet, melt the butter.
- Drain the pasta and asparagus and add to the skillet. Cook over moderately low heat, stirring, until the mixture is heated through. Set aside.
- In a small bowl, whisk the cream, egg yolks and Parmesan cheese. Stir into the skillet and cook over low heat until the Parmesan cheese is just melted and pasta is coated well.
- Stir in chives, rind, lemon juice, salt and pepper to taste.
- Mound the pasta on heated plates and garnish with chives and a quartered lemon slice.

Yield: 4 servings

Noodles Supreme ✓

A wonderful pasta side dish!

5   ounces thin egg noodles
4   tablespoons butter or margarine
1   cup cottage cheese   → Ricotta
1   cup sour cream
1   medium onion, chopped
3   dashes hot pepper sauce
½   teaspoon salt
½   teaspoon garlic salt
    Freshly grated Parmesan cheese, to taste

- Cook noodles in boiling, salted water for 10 minutes. Drain. Toss noodles with butter until butter melts.
- Add remaining ingredients and stir gently until well blended.
- Bake in a preheated 350° oven for 45 minutes.

Great with steak!

Yield: 6 servings

104

Spicy Sesame Pasta

16 ounces fettuccine or other thin pasta
   Salt to taste
¼ cup vegetable oil
8–10 green onions, trimmed, sliced into
   ½-inch pieces
2 cups Sesame Mayonnaise (recipe
   follows)
   Szechuan hot chili oil, to taste

- Cook fettuccine in salted water according to package directions. Drain, rinse with cold water and toss with vegetable oil. Cool.
- Combine pasta, green onions and sesame mayonnaise then toss gently, but well. Add Szechuan hot chili oil, to taste. Cover and refrigerate.
- When ready to serve, toss the noodles again and add additional sesame mayonnaise if necessary.

Sesame Mayonnaise:
1 egg
2 egg yolks
2½ tablespoons rice vinegar
2½ tablespoons soy sauce
3 tablespoons prepared Dijon mustard
¼ cup dark Oriental sesame oil
2½ cups vegetable oil
   Szechuan-style hot and spicy oil

- In food processor fitted with steel blade, process whole egg, egg yolks, vinegar, soy sauce and mustard for 1 minute.
- With motor running, dribble in sesame oil, then vegetable oil in a slow, steady stream.
- Season with drops of Szechuan oil.

Yield: 8 servings

Penne Pasta with Fresh Tomato, Basil and Ricotta Sauce

3 cups chopped ripe tomatoes
½ cup chopped fresh basil (⅛–¼ cup dried basil)
2 tablespoons minced red onion
1 garlic clove, chopped
1 cup ricotta cheese
¼ cup olive oil
16 ounces pasta, cooked
   Salt and freshly ground black pepper, to taste

- Combine the tomatoes, basil, onion and garlic.
- Stir in the remaining ingredients except pasta and blend well.
- Toss with hot pasta and serve immediately.

Excellent on Rotelle, Fusille, Ziti or Tubetti pasta.

Yield: 3 cups (enough to cover 16 ounces of pasta)

Pesto

1 cup fresh white bread crumbs
¼ cup dry white wine
2 cups fresh basil
3 garlic cloves
½ cup pine nuts
1 teaspoon salt
1 cup oil
½ cup grated fresh Parmesan cheese
3 tablespoons grated Romano cheese

- In a saucepan, combine bread crumbs and white wine. Stir over low heat until mixture becomes a smooth paste. Cool.
- Place basil, garlic, pine nuts, salt and cooled bread mixture in blender and mix at high speed until thick and creamy.
- Add oil slowly and blend until smooth.
- Pour into bowl and gently stir in the two cheeses.

Pesto is very versatile and can be served with cold or hot pasta, potatoes or broiled fish.

Can freeze in ice cube trays and be used as needed.

Yield: 3 cups

Entrées

Seasoned Leg of Lamb
Even people who don't eat lamb love this!

Lamb:
- Salt
- Pepper
- Leg of lamb
- 2 garlic cloves

- Mix together 1 teaspoon salt and ¼ teaspoon pepper per pound of meat.
- Rub well all over leg of lamb.
- Make several slits in lamb.
- Slice peeled garlic cloves and push into slits in lamb.
- Put lamb in uncovered roasting pan.
- Bake in a preheated 350° oven for approximately 30 minutes per pound of meat. Baste lamb while cooking.
- Mix ingredients to taste to make a basting sauce. It should have a vinegar–lemon taste.

Basting Sauce:
- ¼ cup oil
- ¼ cup lemon juice
- ½ cup vinegar
- Salt
- Lemon pepper
- Dry mustard
- Garlic powder
- Onion powder
- Celery salt
- Worcestershire sauce

Gravy:
- All–purpose flour
- Kitchen Bouquet (browning and seasoning sauce)

- Remove cooked lamb from pan and scrape pan drippings out of pan. Discard fat.
- Put drippings and enough water to make 2 cups total into a skillet.
- Slowly sift 4 tablespoons of flour into the drippings and stir well.
- Cook over medium heat and continue to stir as the gravy thickens. To achieve a rich brown color, add VERY small amounts of Kitchen Bouquet as you stir.

This lamb is delicious served with wild or long grain rice.

The leftover gravy and lamb can be used to make "Lamb Curry in a Hurry".

108

Leg of Lamb

1   medium leg of lamb
    Salt (¾–1 teaspoon per pound of meat)
    Small amount of cayenne pepper
1   12–ounce bottle of ketchup
1   cup herb vinegar
1   garlic clove, crushed
1   cup water

- Rub lamb with salt and cayenne pepper and place in a roasting pan.
- Mix ketchup, vinegar, garlic and water together to form a sauce and pour over the lamb.
- Roast uncovered in a preheated 350° oven for 1½–2 hours.
- Baste occasionally and add water as needed to make sauce.
- You may thicken sauce with flour to make a gravy.

Very easy, but delicious!

Lamb Curry in a Hurry

Freezes well for a quick and elegant meal later

¼   cup butter or margarine
3   celery stalks, chopped
2   small onions, chopped
1   apple, peeled, cored and diced
2   tablespoons all–purpose flour
2   cups diced cooked lamb
2   cups beef bouillon
½   teaspoon salt
⅛   teaspoon pepper
1   teaspoon curry powder (or to taste)
½   cup raisins
⅛   teaspoon ground cloves
    Rice, cooked
    Chutney, tomatoes, bacon bits, onions, optional

- Sauté celery, onions and apple in the butter. Stir in flour. Add diced lamb and the next 6 ingredients.
- Bring to a boil, cover and reduce heat to simmer. Cook 1 hour.
- Serve over rice with a variety of condiments such as chutney, chopped and seeded tomatoes, bacon bits and chopped onions, if desired.

Freezes well.

Yield: 3–4 servings

Veal Marsala

1	pound veal, sliced thin or pounded
1	teaspoon salt
	All–purpose flour
½	cup butter or margarine
¼	cup olive oil
1	tablespoon chopped garlic
1	cup sliced mushrooms
½	cup Marsala wine
1	cup chicken stock
¼	cup lemon juice
1	tablespoon sugar
¼	cup chopped fresh parsley
	Fettuccine, cooked

- Salt and lightly flour the veal.
- Melt butter with olive oil in a skillet over medium heat.
- Sauté meat quickly without browning and transfer to serving platter.
- Sauté garlic and mushrooms in skillet and spoon over the veal.
- Add Marsala wine, chicken stock, lemon juice, sugar and parsley to skillet and bring to a quick boil. Pour over meat.
- Serve with fettuccine.

Yield: 4 servings

Veal Parmesan

1–1¼	pounds thin veal cutlet
	Salt and pepper
1	egg
2	teaspoons water
⅓	cup fine bread crumbs
⅓	cup grated Parmesan cheese
¼	cup olive oil
2	tablespoons butter or margarine
1	onion, finely chopped
1	6-ounce can tomato paste
2	cups water
½	teaspoon marjoram
½	pound mozzarella or Swiss cheese

- Cut veal into 6–8 pieces and sprinkle with salt and pepper.
- Beat egg with 2 teaspoons water.
- Combine bread crumbs and Parmesan cheese. Dip veal in egg and roll in crumb mixture.
- Heat oil in skillet and fry veal until brown on both sides. Remove veal from skillet and place in shallow baking dish.
- Pour off most of oil from skillet. Add butter and onion to skillet and cook until onion is tender.
- Add tomato paste, water and marjoram. Boil a few minutes, scraping browned bits from bottom of skillet. Pour most of sauce over veal.
- Top with thick slices of cheese. Add remaining sauce.
- Bake, uncovered, in a preheated 350° oven for 30 minutes.

Beef Tenderloin

1 beef tenderloin, room temperature
Salt and pepper
Butter or margarine

- Trim tenderloin of excess fat and place on a rack in pan. Season with salt and pepper.
- Bake tenderloin uncovered in a preheated 450° oven for 20 minutes. Reduce heat to 350° and bake an additional 15 minutes.
- Remove tenderloin from oven and spread butter over top and cover with foil.
- Allow to stand 10–15 minutes before slicing.

Cabernet Sirloin with Garlic

1 small onion, minced
3 large garlic cloves, crushed
1 tablespoon fresh grated or prepared horseradish
1¼ cups Cabernet Sauvignon
Freshly ground black pepper to taste
4 pounds sirloin steak, trimmed of excess fat
1 tablespoon light olive oil

- Combine onion, garlic, horseradish and wine in a large, shallow glass dish which is large enough to hold the steak.
- Grind black pepper over steak to taste.
- Place the steak in marinade and cover. Marinate in refrigerator 3–4 hours. Turn occasionally.
- Remove steak from marinade, pat dry and brush with olive oil on both sides.
- Place steak on broiler pan and cook in pre-heated broiler about 5 inches from heat source to rare (about 8 minutes per side for 1–inch thick steak. For each additional ½–inch thickness, add 2–3 minutes cooking time on each side. For medium doneness, add 2–3 minutes to time for 1–inch steak.)
- Steaks should be turned only once.

Great on the grill.

Olde English Prime Rib

Prime rib baked in a crust of rock salt!

1 Prime rib or standing rib (½ pound per person)
2 tablespoons Worcestershire sauce
1 teaspoon paprika
   Salt and pepper to taste
   Rock salt (ice cream salt)

- Season choice prime or standing rib by rubbing with Worcestershire sauce, paprika, salt and pepper.
- Line a roasting pan with heavy aluminum foil and pour a layer of rock salt that completely covers the bottom of the pan.
- Sprinkle salt with water until just moist.
- Place the meat onto the salt and cover it completely with more rock salt that has been moistened as above.
- Place the uncovered roast into a preheated 500° oven.
- Bake for 10–15 minutes per pound of meat. Remove the meat from oven when done.
- Create cracks in the hardened salt with a wooden mallet and carefully break the salt away from the meat.
- Slice and serve.

  This process, which does not impart a salt flavor, traps vital flavor juices and insures a minimum shrinkage of meat.

Peppered Beefsteaks with Jack Daniel's Sauce

Creates a rich, flavorful sauce

2 tablespoons minced shallots
1 tablespoon red wine vinegar
3½ teaspoons cracked black pepper, divided
2 cups beef stock or canned unsalted broth
2 8–ounce filets of beef
½ teaspoon dried thyme, crumbled
½ teaspoon dried rosemary, crumbled
½ teaspoon dried marjoram, crumbled
¼ cup olive oil
1 tablespoon Jack Daniel's whiskey

- Boil shallots, vinegar and 1½ teaspoons of pepper in a heavy saucepan until almost no liquid remains in the pan (about 1 minute).
- Add beef stock and boil until reduced to ½ cup (about 20 minutes).
- Cover and refrigerate. This can be made 1 day ahead.
- Place the steaks in a glass dish and rub the remaining 2 teaspoons pepper and the herbs onto both sides of the meat.
- Pour oil over all and turn to coat. Cover and let stand 1 hour at room temperature.
- Remove the meat from the marinade.
- Heat a heavy large skillet over medium high heat and add steaks and brown on both sides. Reduce heat to medium and cook to desired doneness (about 3 minutes per side for rare).
- Transfer steaks to plates.
- Add sauce to skillet and bring to a boil. Mix in Jack Daniel's and spoon sauce over steaks and serve.

Yield: 2 servings

Steak au Poivre

4–6 filet mignon steaks (1¼–1½ inches thick)
3 tablespoons crushed peppercorns
1½ tablespoons unsalted butter or margarine
1½ tablespoons oil
2 tablespoons chopped shallots or green onions
½ cup good brandy
¾ cup rich brown stock or canned beef broth
¾ teaspoon cornstarch, dissolved in a little stock
3½ tablespoons cream
1½ tablespoons soft butter or margarine

• Crush whole peppercorns between spoons or with mortar and pestle.
• Press crushed peppercorns into both side of steaks. Cover lightly and refrigerate at least one hour.
• Pat steaks dry. Place in hot butter and oil. Cook on medium high heat about 3–6 minutes per side, according to thickness of steaks and desired doneness. Turn only once.
• Remove from pan and put in slightly warm oven while making sauce.
• Blot up any excess fat and add shallots and brandy to pan. Flame or boil away alcohol, stirring constantly.
• Add all remaining ingredients except butter. Boil until thick enough to coat a spoon. Remove from heat.
• Swirl in butter (don't beat). Pour a bit of sauce over each steak and pass the remaining sauce.

Yield: 4–6 servings

Individual Beef Wellington
Simple, yet elegant

1 filet mignon, 1–1½ inches thick
4–5 fresh mushrooms, sliced
4–5 onion slices
¼ cup red wine
    Butter or margarine, melted
2 frozen prepared patty shells

- Brown filet in a hot skillet until almost done. Set aside to cool.
- Cook mushrooms and onions in the wine and butter in same skillet until tender and most of liquid has cooked off.
- Roll out 1 patty shell and place filet on shell.
- Spoon mushrooms and onions on top of filet.
- Place another patty shell over filet and pinch sides together to seal.
- Bake on a cookie sheet in a preheated 450° oven until brown; about 15–20 minutes.
- Serve immediately.

Pot Roast with Vegetables
Delicious!

1 3–pound chuck roast
¼ teaspoon pepper
1 teaspoon crushed rosemary
1 large onion, sliced
1 celery stalk, sliced
½ cup soy sauce
1½ cups water
6 medium potatoes, cut into wedges
6 carrots, cut into thirds
2–3 tablespoons cornstarch or all–purpose flour

- Place roast in a 3–quart casserole and season with pepper and rosemary.
- Cover roast with onion, celery and soy sauce.
- Add water and bake covered in a preheated 325° oven for 1½ hours.
- Add potatoes and carrots and continue cooking for 1½–2½ hours more or until roast is tender.
- Drain juice off and make gravy by adding 2–3 tablespoons of cornstarch or flour.
- Serve immediately.

Fantastic Flank Steak

True to its name

Flank steak
Italian dressing
3 tablespoons butter or margarine
2 ounces blue cheese
2 green spring onions, chopped

- Marinate flank steak in Italian dressing over-night or for at least 4 hours. Remove meat and discard marinade.
- Mix the butter, blue cheese and green onion together to make topping and set aside.
- Line broiler pan bottom with aluminum foil.
- Place the steak, on rack, in pan and broil for 5–6 minutes. Turn and cook 4–5 minutes more.
- Spread the cheese mixture over the meat and broil for 1 minute.
- Slice at an angle and serve while hot.

Pot Roast

1 package onion soup mix
½ cup ketchup
½ teaspoon oregano
1 teaspoon garlic salt
⅛ teaspoon pepper
½ teaspoon celery seed or celery salt
½ teaspoon marjoram
½ teaspoon thyme
2 teaspoons horseradish
1 cup water
1 4–pound beef rump roast or beef brisket roast

- Day 1:
- Combine all ingredients and pour over roast.
- Cover and bake in a preheated 300° oven for 5 hours. Cool.
- Slice thin pieces, cutting against the grain. Refrigerate.
- Day 2:
- Skim off congealed fat.
- Return roast to a preheated 325° oven and heat for 40 minutes.

Elegant Beef Tenderloin

Wonderful for special company

1   5–pound beef tenderloin, trimmed
1¼ teaspoons garlic salt
1   cup Burgundy wine
¼   cup soy sauce
¾   cup butter or margarine
1   teaspoon lemon pepper seasoning
    Grapes, optional
    Celery leaves, optional
    Lemon zest, optional

- Place tenderloin on a lightly greased, shallow roasting pan and sprinkle with garlic salt.
- Bake in a preheated 425° oven for 10 minutes.
- Combine wine, soy sauce, butter and lemon pepper in a small saucepan. Cook until mixture is thoroughly heated.
- Pour over tenderloin and bake an additional 30–40 minutes or until a meat thermometer registers 140° (rare), 150° (medium rare) or 160° (medium).
- Baste occasionally with pan drippings.
- Garnish beef with grapes, celery leaves and lemon zest if desired.
- Slice in thick pieces to serve.

Yield: 10 servings

Alfred Lunt Pot Roast

Allspice adds a pleasing change of taste

1   4–pound rump roast
2   10½–ounce cans bouillon (undiluted)
4   tablespoons vinegar
2   tablespoons Karo syrup
1   onion, quartered
16 whole peppercorns
16 whole allspice
2   bay leaves
1   teaspoon salt
    Rice or pasta, cooked

- Brown roast well on all sides in a Dutch oven. Add all ingredients and cover tightly.
- Simmer over a low flame for 4 hours.
- Thicken gravy with flour or cornstarch and serve over rice or pasta.

Beef Stir-Fry

¼ cup sugar
¼ cup soy sauce
1 medium onion, chopped
1¼ pounds flank steak, cut into strips
Lemon/lime soda or orange juice, optional
1 teaspoon cornstarch, optional
Rice, cooked

- Mix sugar and soy sauce together until blended. Stir in onion.
- Pour over steak and marinate for 2 hours or overnight in the refrigerator.
- You may add lemon/lime soda or orange juice to marinade if meat is dry or tough.
- Add steak and marinade to a hot frying pan and cook to desired doneness.
- If sauce is too thin, add 1 teaspoon cornstarch while cooking.
- Serve over rice.

Variation: You can easily add bell pepper strips, mushrooms or your favorite vegetables.

Beef Tips

3–4 pounds stew beef or sirloin tips
¼ cup soy sauce
¼ cup Worcestershire sauce
2 large onions, chopped
1 green bell pepper, chopped
1 red bell pepper, chopped
2 10¾–ounce cans golden mushroom soup
Pasta or rice, cooked

- Coat beef with soy and Worcestershire sauces and marinate for 1 hour.
- Place meat in bottom of large casserole dish. Add onion and peppers. Cover with mushroom soup. Seal tightly with aluminum foil.
- Bake 3 hours in a preheated 325° oven. The longer cooked, the better.
- Separate meat with a fork halfway through baking. Cover and return to oven.
- Serve over pasta or rice.

Can be made ahead, but does not freeze well.

Yield: 12 servings

Carnonnades Flamandes (Beef Stew)

2 pounds stew beef
  Salt and pepper
4 tablespoons olive oil
½ pound onion, sliced
1 tablespoon brown sugar
2 tablespoons vinegar
1 quart beer
  Thyme
  Bay leaves
1 large baking potato, cubed (optional)
2 cups sliced carrots (optional)
4 thick slices French bread
  Dijon mustard
  Rice, cooked

- Season meat with salt and pepper. Brown in oil. Remove meat into large kettle.
- Sauté onions in same pan. Sprinkle brown sugar over onions and cook a few minutes more.
- Deglaze pan with vinegar and pour pan contents into kettle with meat.
- Cover with beer, thyme and bay leaves to taste. Add potato and carrots if desired.
- Remove crusts from bread and coat generously with Dijon mustard. Place bread on top and bring to a boil.
- Turn down to a simmer and cook, covered, for 2 hours. When stew is stirred, bread will dissolve and thicken the stew.
- Serve over rice.

Variation: Add more Dijon mustard according to your taste. Stew can be cooked uncovered if you prefer it thicker.

Yield: 6–8 servings

119

Old Fashioned Meat Loaf

Heavenly sauce for an old–fashioned favorite

Meat Loaf:

1	cup dried bread crumbs
1½	pounds ground chuck
¼	cup finely chopped onion
1	egg
4	tablespoons ketchup
1½	teaspoons salt
½	cup milk
¼	teaspoon pepper
	Sauce (recipe below)

- Combine bread crumbs and ground chuck.
- Combine remaining ingredients, except sauce, in a bowl and mix thoroughly. Combine with ground chuck.
- Form into a loaf in a casserole dish.
- Pour sauce over meat loaf and bake in a preheated 350° oven for 1 hour.

Sauce:

4	tablespoons vinegar
4	tablespoons brown sugar
2	tablespoons Worcestershire sauce
½	cup ketchup

- Mix all sauce ingredients together and heat, but do not boil.

  Yield: 6 servings

Beef Stroganoff

1	pound round steak, cubed
1	onion, chopped
2	tablespoons butter or margarine, divided
2	tablespoons all–purpose flour
1¾	cups hot water
2	beef bouillon cubes
⅛	teaspoon hot pepper sauce
¾	teaspoon salt
¼	teaspoon pepper
1	tablespoon prepared mustard
1	tablespoon ketchup
1	tablespoon Worcestershire sauce
½	cup sour cream
	Pasta or rice, cooked

- Brown cubed meat and chopped onion in 1 tablespoon of the butter. Set aside in a 1½–quart casserole.
- Melt the rest of the butter in skillet. Add the flour and mix until smooth. Then add the water and cook until thickened, stirring constantly.
- Add remaining ingredients and mix well. Pour over the meat.
- Bake in a preheated 350° oven for 30 minutes.
- Serve over pasta or rice.

  Yield: 4 servings

Easy Swiss Steak

4 large cubed steaks
Meat tenderizer
Black pepper
All–purpose flour
Oil for browning meat
1 10¾–ounce can tomato soup
1 10¾–ounce soup can of water
3 celery stalks, chopped
1 medium onion, chopped
1 green bell pepper, chopped
Yellow rice or pasta, cooked

- Cut steak into bite–size pieces and tenderize.
- Sprinkle with pepper to taste and dredge seasoned meat in flour.
- Brown both sides of the meat in hot oil.
- Carefully wipe skillet of excess oil, but leave any remaining crumbs.
- Put all meat back in the skillet and add soup, water, celery, onion and bell pepper.
- Cover and let simmer for 15 minutes.
- Serve over yellow rice or pasta.

  This is a very easy dish and can be made ahead, refrigerated and heated when needed.

  Yield: 4 servings

Mexican Supreme
Olé

1 pound ground beef
½ cup chopped onion
1 package taco seasoning
1 cup mild salsa
½ cup canned tomatoes, drained and chopped
1 4–ounce can chopped green chilies
½ pound low fat Monterey Jack cheese, shredded
4 flour tortillas

- Brown beef and onion together in a saucepan. Drain off excess fat.
- Add taco seasoning, salsa, tomatoes and chilies to beef.
- Simmer for about 10 minutes.
- Place 2 flour tortillas on bottom of an 8–inch square casserole dish.
- Spoon ½ the meat, then ½ the cheese over the tortillas.
- Cover with last 2 tortillas and top with remaining meat, then the remaining cheese.
- Bake at 325° for 20–25 minutes.

  Good served with Mexican rice and a salad of lettuce, tomato and guacamole.

  Yield: 4–6 servings

Mexican Cornbread Casserole

1½ pounds ground beef
1 package taco seasoning
½ cup water
1 12–ounce can whole kernel corn, drained
½ cup chopped green bell pepper
1 8–ounce can tomato sauce
1 8½–ounce package corn muffin mix
1 2.8–ounce can French fried onions
½ cup shredded sharp Cheddar cheese

- Brown the beef and drain off excess fat.
- Stir in taco seasoning, water, corn, green bell pepper and tomato sauce. Pour into a 2–quart casserole.
- Prepare the corn muffin mix in a separate bowl according to package instructions. To this, add ½ can of French fried onions.
- Spoon corn muffin mix around outer edge of the casserole.
- Bake, uncovered, in a preheated 400° oven for 20 minutes.
- Top cornbread with cheese and remaining onions and bake 2–3 minutes longer.

Yield: 6 servings

Reuben Casserole

A must for Reuben fans

1½ pounds corned beef, shaved
1 8–ounce bottle Thousand Island dressing
1 16–ounce can sauerkraut, drained
10 slices Swiss cheese
½ cup butter or margarine, melted
6–8 slices rye bread, cubed
Butter or margarine

- Place beef in buttered 2–quart casserole dish.
- Spread dressing on top of meat.
- Layer drained sauerkraut on top of dressing and cover with cheese.
- Top with bread cubes that have been tossed in melted butter.
- Bake, uncovered, for 30 minutes in a preheated 350° oven.

Can be made ahead.

Yield: 6–8 servings

Spaghetti Pie

1 garlic clove, chopped
½ cup chopped onion
¼ cup chopped green bell pepper
1½ pounds ground round or lean pork sausage
1 28–ounce can whole tomatoes with juice, chopped
1 6–ounce can tomato paste
2 teaspoons dried oregano
1 teaspoon sugar
12 ounces spaghetti noodles, uncooked
4 tablespoons butter or margarine
3 eggs, beaten
⅔ cup Parmesan cheese
2 cups cottage cheese
2 cups shredded mozzarella cheese

- Cook the garlic, onion and green bell pepper with the meat in a skillet until browned and the vegetables are tender. Drain off grease.
- Stir in cut up tomatoes and juice, tomato paste, oregano and sugar. Heat thoroughly.
- Cook spaghetti in salted water for 12 minutes. Drain and rinse with water until spaghetti is just warm.
- Melt butter in the same pan the noodles were in and add the beaten eggs. Do not let the butter get so hot that the eggs cook when added.
- Stir in the Parmesan cheese and add noodles. Mix thoroughly.
- Pour noodle mixture into 2 separate 9–inch pie plates and form into a crust on bottoms and sides of plates.
- Spread 1 cup cottage cheese on top of each crust.
- Put ½ meat mixture into each pie and top with one cup mozzarella cheese.
- Bake in a preheated 350° oven for 25 minutes.

Variation: You can make one large casserole for a crowd or two separate pies for freezing.

Yield: 6–8 servings, each pie

Lasagna

1 pound Italian sausage
1 garlic clove, minced
1 tablespoon crushed dried basil
1 teaspoon salt
1 16–ounce can tomatoes
2 6–ounce cans tomato paste
8 ounces lasagna noodles
3 cups ricotta cheese
½ cup freshly grated Parmesan cheese
2 tablespoons minced fresh parsley
2 eggs, beaten
1 teaspoon salt
½ teaspoon pepper
16 ounces mozzarella cheese, thinly sliced
  or grated

- Brown meat slowly, spoon off excess fat.
- Add next 5 ingredients and simmer, uncovered, for 30 minutes, stirring occasionally.
- Cook noodles, drain, rinse and set aside.
- Combine the remaining ingredients except the mozzarella cheese in a small bowl and set aside.
- Grease a 13 x 9 x 2–inch baking dish.
- Layer the ingredients 3 times in the following order: noodles, ricotta filling, mozzarella and then the meat sauce. Save enough of the mozzarella cheese to put on the top as the final layer. If thicker layers are preferred, you can layer the ingredients two times instead of three.
- Bake in a preheated 375° oven for 30 minutes.
- Let stand 10 minutes before cutting and serving.

Yield: 10–12 servings

Soul Satisfying Chili

"Soul Satisfying" says it all

1   pound ground beef (can be ½ ground turkey)
1   white onion, chopped
1   16–ounce can red beans, drained and rinsed
1   16–ounce can tomatoes, puréed with liquid
1   cup water
1   tablespoon white vinegar
1   tablespoon sugar
3   tablespoons chili powder or to taste
    Salt and pepper to taste

• Brown meat in skillet, mashing into small bits as it cooks. Drain in colander.
• Sauté onion until tender. Cover onions with meat and cook until onions are limp.
• Stir in remaining ingredients, cover and simmer at least one hour. Correct seasonings.

Can be made in any multiple as long as you keep the ratio of sugar, vinegar and meat the same.

Additional beans are not necessary when using 2 pounds of meat.

All beef chili is better the next day.

Ground turkey needs more chili powder when reheated.

Freezes well.

Yield: 4 servings

Kentucky Bar-B-Q

1   pound ground beef
1   onion, chopped
½   green bell pepper, chopped
½   garlic clove, minced
1   cup ketchup
1   tablespoon brown sugar
1   tablespoon vinegar
½   teaspoon dry mustard
1   teaspoon Worcestershire sauce
    Hamburger buns

• Brown beef in a skillet. Add onion, pepper and garlic.
• Cook for 2 minutes, then drain off excess fat.
• Add remaining ingredients and simmer covered on low for 30–40 minutes.
• Serve on buns.

Can be made ahead and can be easily doubled.

Yield: 4 servings

Sweet Soy Marinade

4 garlic cloves, pressed
1 cup soy sauce
½ cup brown sugar
4 tablespoons olive oil
½ teaspoon ground black pepper

- Mix all ingredients and pour on either poultry or flank steak. Marinate for 4–8 hours, turning once.
- Broil or grill to desired doneness.

Midnight Marinade

½ cup black coffee
½ cup soy sauce
2 tablespoons vinegar
1 tablespoon Worcestershire sauce
1 tablespoon sesame seeds, browned in butter
1 green onion, chopped
1 green bell pepper, chopped

- Combine ingredients and pour over flank steak. Allow to marinate in refrigerator overnight.
- Steak may be grilled or broiled in the oven.

Green Peppercorn Sauce

¼ cup white wine
¾ cup heavy cream
2 teaspoons Dijon mustard
1 tablespoon green peppercorns (or to taste)

- Mix all ingredients in a small saucepan and warm over medium heat until slightly thickened.
- Serve hot over beef.

Seasoned Bar-B-Que Ribs

1 tablespoon chili powder
1 tablespoon salt
1 tablespoon celery seed
¼ cup brown sugar
1 pound ribs
½ cup vinegar
1 10¾-ounce can tomato soup

- Mix first 4 ingredients and rub over ribs.
- Broil ribs 4 minutes on each side, about 3 inches from heat. Remove from broiler.
- Mix vinegar and soup and pour over ribs.
- Bake uncovered at 350° for 1½ hours, basting every 30 minutes.

Sausage with Red Beans and Rice

1 cup dry red beans, soaked overnight
1 1-pound package smoked sausage, sliced
½ large onion, chopped
1-2 large garlic cloves, minced
1 small green bell pepper, chopped
2 tablespoons chopped fresh parsley
Salt and pepper to taste
Cayenne pepper to taste
Rice, cooked

- Brown sausage. Add onion, garlic and green bell pepper to pan just before sausage is done.
- Add parsley, salt, pepper, cayenne pepper and beans. Add water to cover beans and simmer 3-4 hours.
- Serve over rice.

Glazed Ham Steaks

Center cut ham slice
Prepared mustard
Brown sugar
⅓ cup milk

- Place ham in baking dish and liberally spread mustard over ham.
- Generously sprinkle with brown sugar, then dampen sugar by sprinkling with milk.
- Bake uncovered in a preheated 300° oven for 40 minutes per pound.

Works well with ham of any thickness.

Baked Ham

1 10–12 pound ham
   Prepared mustard
¼ teaspoon ground cloves
1 cup prepared mustard
1 cup brown sugar
1 cup sherry

- Rub surface of ham with prepared mustard.
- Place ham, covered with foil, in roasting pan and bake in a preheated 300° oven for 20 minutes per pound.
- One hour before ham is done, remove from oven.
- Cover ham again with a light coating of mustard and sprinkle with ground cloves.
- Combine 1 cup prepared mustard, brown sugar and sherry.
- Baste ham with mustard mixture and cover with foil.
- Continue cooking for remaining hour.

Pork Tenderloin with Sour Cream Sauce

Pork:

¼ cup soy sauce
¼ cup bourbon
2 tablespoons brown sugar
2 pork tenderloins

- Mix first 3 ingredients together to make marinade.
- Put pork into a ziplock bag and pour marinade over it. Let marinate for several hours.
- Bake, uncovered, in the marinade in a preheated 325° oven for 1 hour, basting several times.
- Serve with the following sauce on the side.

Sauce:

⅓ cup sour cream
⅓ cup mayonnaise
1 tablespoon dry mustard
2–3 green onions, chopped

- Mix all ingredients together and chill. This is better if made the day before.
  Variation: Can substitute low fat sour cream and mayonnaise.

Pork with Chutney Glaze

2   pork tenderloins
    Salt and pepper to taste
1   tablespoon olive oil
½   cup finely chopped onion
1   tablespoon all–purpose flour
½   cup chicken stock
¼   cup white wine
¼–½ cup chutney

- Slice the tenderloin into ½–inch slices and sprinkle with salt and pepper.
- Heat oil in skillet. Add meat and cook 6 minutes on each side. Remove meat from skillet and set aside.
- Sauté onions in skillet until tender. Sprinkle flour over onions and cook 2 minutes.
- Add chicken stock and wine and cook until slightly thickened.
- Add chutney and cook over low heat for 2 minutes.
- Return pork to skillet and warm.

Yield: 6 servings

Just Peachy Pork Chops

4   4–ounce boneless pork chops (¾–inch thick)
¼   cup low sodium teriyaki sauce, divided
1   teaspoon vegetable oil
½   cup no–sugar–added peach spread
¼   cup minced green onions
1   tablespoon lemon juice
2   fresh peaches, peeled and sliced

- Pound pork chops between sheets of waxed paper to ½–inch thickness.
- Brush with 2 tablespoons teriyaki sauce and let stand at room temperature for 15 minutes.
- Heat oil in large non–stick skillet over medium high heat.
- Add chops and cook 4–5 minutes on each side or to desired doneness. Transfer to serving platter and keep warm.
- Add remaining teriyaki sauce, peach spread, green onions, lemon juice and fresh peaches to skillet. Cook over medium heat until hot.
- Spoon over chops on platter and serve immediately.

Yield: 4 servings

Chinese Pork Tenderloin

The aroma is mouth watering

2 pork tenderloins
½ cup soy sauce
½ cup chicken broth
1 cup honey
½ cup sherry
2 garlic cloves, crushed
1 teaspoon dried ginger
1 teaspoon dry mustard
1 teaspoon paprika

- Put pork tenderloin in a glass baking dish.
- Mix together all other ingredients and simmer over medium heat until ingredients are blended.
- Let cool slightly and then pour over tenderloins. Marinate in refrigerator for about 3 hours, turning every 30 minutes.
- Place dish in oven as is and bake uncovered in a preheated 350° oven for approximately 1½ hours. Time may vary.
- Baste every 15–20 minutes and continue to bake until sauce becomes thick, dark and forms a crust.

This is a good dish to serve company and makes great leftovers. Serve with whipped potatoes or rice.

Sauce can also be used on spare ribs that have been broiled 4 minutes on each side before adding the sauce.

Yield: 8 servings

Herbed Pork Tenderloin
A real treat for pepper lovers

2 teaspoons coarse or Kosher salt
2 garlic cloves, minced
½ teaspoon white pepper
½ teaspoon coarsely ground black pepper
½ teaspoon dried thyme, crumbled
2 pinches ground allspice
1 1–pound pork tenderloin
2 tablespoons oil
½ cup whole milk
¼ cup brandy

• Combine first 6 ingredients to form a dry paste.
• Rub paste into pork and wrap it tightly in plastic wrap. Refrigerate overnight or at least 4 hours.
• Heat oil in heavy, large, oven proof skillet over medium high heat.
• Add pork and cook until brown on all sides, turning occasionally, for about 7 minutes.
• Place skillet with pork in it in preheated 325° oven and bake, uncovered, for 45 minutes.
• Transfer pork to platter and cover to keep warm.
• Add milk and brandy to skillet and bring to a boil over high heat. Continue boiling for about 8 minutes or until liquid is reduced to ¼ cup. For a thicker sauce, whisk in a small amount of cornstarch mixed with cold water.
• Slice pork and serve accompanied with sauce.

Yield: 4–6 servings

Pork with Red Plum Sauce

Roast:

1   4–pound pork loin roast
     Garlic salt to taste
     Onion salt to taste

- Sprinkle pork loin with garlic and onion salts.
- Place on a rack in a baking pan with a small amount of water added to the bottom of the pan.
- Cover pan tightly with aluminum foil.
- Bake covered in a preheated 350° oven for 3 hours.

Red Plum Sauce:

¾   cup chopped onion
2   tablespoons butter or margarine
1   cup red plum preserves
½   cup brown sugar
2   tablespoons lemon juice
⅓   cup chili sauce
¼   cup soy sauce
2   teaspoons prepared mustard
3   drops hot pepper sauce

- Sauté the onion in the butter then add the rest of the ingredients to the onion.
- Simmer for 15 minutes.
- Pour the fat off the cooked roast and place back in the pan.
- Pour half the plum sauce over the roast and continue baking, uncovered, for an additional 30 minutes. Baste often with the sauce.
- Remove from oven and allow to stand for 10 minutes before slicing.
- Serve the remaining sauce on the side.

Yield: 8–10 servings

Willie Mae's Pork Chops

6   1-inch thick pork chops
3   tablespoons oil
2   cups beef bouillon
1   cup fresh mushrooms, sliced
3   teaspoons prepared mustard
3   tablespoons minced parsley
1½ teaspoons paprika
    Salt and pepper to taste
1   onion, sliced into rings
2   tablespoons cornstarch
¾–1 cup sour cream
    Parsley, minced

- Using a skillet, brown chops in oil. While chops are browning, mix bouillon and next 6 ingredients in a bowl.
- Place browned chops in an oblong casserole and cover with bouillon mixture. Bake covered in a preheated 350° oven for 45 minutes.
- Place rings of onion on top of each chop. Cover and continue cooking for 30 minutes.
- Remove and place chops on a warm platter.
- Pour bouillon liquid into a boiler and add 2 tablespoons cornstarch. Cook until thickened, then remove from heat. Add sour cream and stir.
- Return chops to casserole and top with sour cream mixture. Sprinkle with lots of minced parsley.

Spaghetti Sauce with Italian Sausage

    Olive oil
5–6 garlic cloves, minced
2   tablespoons chopped fresh parsley
    Fresh mushrooms, sliced
1   28-ounce can crushed tomatoes
1   29-ounce can tomato purée
4–5 Italian sausages, cut in bite-size pieces
16 ounces vermicelli noodles, cooked

- Cover bottom of large pot with olive oil and sauté garlic and parsley 5 minutes. Add mushroom slices and cook until soft.
- Add crushed tomatoes and tomato purée then cook on medium low for about 20 minutes.
- Add sausage and cook an additional 20 minutes on medium low. Turn heat down and simmer for 15 more minutes.
- Serve immediately over vermicelli.

Freezes well.

Yield: 8 servings

Roasted Chicken Feast

1   large broiler-fryer chicken, whole
1   teaspoon salt
1   tablespoon lemon pepper
4   small potatoes, quartered
4   small onions, quartered
4   carrots, quartered
4   cups of water, divided

- Sprinkle outside and inside of chicken with salt and lemon pepper.
- Stuff vegetables in cavity of chicken and lace or pin cavity shut.
- Place on rack in roasting pan, breast side down. Pour 2 cups water in bottom of roaster so that water does not touch chicken.
- Roast in a preheated oven at 350° for 45 minutes.
- Turn breast side up, add 2 cups water to roasting pan and continue to roast for additional 45 minutes.

Yield: 4-6 servings

Garlic Chicken

1   3-pound chicken
⅓   cup olive oil
¼   teaspoon salt
½   teaspoon fresh pepper
1   tablespoon each of fresh chopped marjoram, oregano, thyme, rosemary and basil
20 whole garlic cloves, unpeeled
1   loaf country French bread

- Rub chicken with olive oil and sprinkle with salt and pepper. Place in a Dutch oven.
- Rub herbs on chicken and add garlic to pan.
- Cover and bake in a preheated oven at 350° for 40 minutes.
- Remove cover and bake 30 more minutes to brown chicken.
- Remove chicken to platter. Save the garlic cloves to squeeze out purée on slices of toasted French bread.

Tarragon Chicken

8 boneless chicken breast halves
¾ cup butter or margarine, melted
¼ cup all-purpose flour
3 cups chicken bouillon
⅔ cup dry sherry
1 pound fresh mushrooms, sliced
1 16-ounce can artichoke hearts, drained
  Salt and pepper to taste
1 teaspoon crumbled tarragon
  Paprika

- Sauté chicken in butter; remove chicken to large casserole, reserving butter.
- Stir flour slowly into butter. Add bouillon, stirring constantly. Add remaining ingredients, except paprika.
- Simmer 5 minutes; pour over chicken. Sprinkle with paprika.
- Bake uncovered in a preheated oven at 325° for 1 hour.

Yield: 8 servings

Hot Chicken Salad Casserole
Wonderful choice for a luncheon

4-5 cooked chicken breast halves, cut up
3 stalks celery, chopped
1 large onion, chopped
1 cup instant rice
2-1 10¾-ounce can cream of celery soup
1 cup chicken broth
1 teaspoon salt
½ teaspoon pepper
1 teaspoon lemon juice
1 cup mayonnaise
1 cup potato chip crumbs
2 cups Cheddar cheese

- Combine all ingredients except potato chips and cheese.
- Place in a greased casserole dish and top with chips and cheese.
- Bake in a preheated oven at 350° for 40-45 minutes.

Yield: 8 servings

USE STUFFING INSTEAD OF RICE

Chicken Asparagus Casserole

Impress your dinner party

4 whole chicken breasts, skinned, boned and quartered
6 tablespoons butter or margarine, divided
6 shallots, finely chopped
4 tablespoons all-purpose flour
1 teaspoon salt
½ teaspoon pepper
1½ cups light cream
½ cup dry white wine
½ cup grated Parmesan cheese, divided
24-32 asparagus spears, cooked until crisp-tender and drain

- Melt 4 tablespoons of butter in skillet. Brown chicken until cooked throughout. Drain. Set aside.
- Melt 2 tablespoons butter in saucepan. Sauté shallots. Add more butter if necessary.
- Blend in flour. Add salt and pepper.
- Gradually stir in cream and wine.
- Add ¼ cup cheese. Stir until melted.
- Arrange asparagus in a buttered, shallow baking dish.
- Put chicken on top and cover with sauce. Sprinkle with remaining cheese.
- Bake in a preheated oven at 375° for 20-25 minutes.

Yield: 6 servings

Poppy Seed Chicken

A great family dish

6-8 chicken breast halves
2 10¾-ounce cans cream of chicken soup
1 8-ounce carton sour cream
1 roll Ritz crackers, crushed
½ cup butter or margarine, melted
2 teaspoons poppy seeds

- Boil, debone and cut up chicken. Place in 13x9x2-inch dish.
- Mix soup and sour cream and pour over chicken.
- Mix crushed crackers and butter and spoon over chicken mixture. Sprinkle poppy seeds on top of crackers.
- Bake in a preheated oven at 375° for 30 minutes or until bubbly.

Yield: 6-8 servings

Chicken Soufflé with Mushroom Sauce

2 tablespoons butter or margarine
1 tablespoon all-purpose flour
1 cup milk
1 cup chicken stock
½ cup soft bread crumbs
½ teaspoon salt
½ teaspoon pepper
Few grains celery salt
½ teaspoon minced parsley
2 cups finely chopped, cooked chicken
3 egg yolks, beaten
3 egg whites, stiffly beaten
Mushroom sauce (recipe follows)

Mushroom Sauce:
½ cup chicken stock
½ cup milk
2 tablespoons all-purpose flour
2 tablespoons butter or margarine
Salt and pepper
1 4.5-ounce jar whole mushrooms

- Melt butter, add flour and blend well.
- Add milk and chicken stock and stir until smooth and creamy.
- Add bread crumbs, salt, pepper, celery salt and parsley. Mix well.
- Add cooked chicken and well beaten egg yolks. Fold in stiffly beaten egg whites.
- Turn into a buttered mold, and set in a pan of hot water.
- Bake in a preheated oven at 350° until firm in the center, about 40-45 minutes.
- Serve on a hot platter with hot mushroom sauce.

- Make a white sauce with chicken stock, milk, flour, butter, salt and pepper.
- Cook until thick.
- Drain mushrooms, cut in half and add to white sauce. Serve hot.

Lemon Mushroom Chicken with Parsley

8 ounces fresh mushrooms, sliced
2 tablespoons olive oil
3 tablespoons lemon juice
3 tablespoons chopped fresh parsley
Salt to taste
Lemon pepper to taste
4-6 chicken breast halves, skinned and boned
Rice, cooked

- Sauté mushrooms in olive oil, lemon juice, parsley, salt and lemon pepper.
- Place chicken in 13x9x2-inch glass dish. Cover with mushroom mixture.
- Bake, covered, in a preheated oven at 350° for 30 minutes, then uncover and bake 15 more minutes. Baste often.
- Serve over long grain white rice or wild rice.
Yield: 4-6 servings

137

Italian Boneless Chicken

4-5 whole chicken breasts, boned and
     skinned
     Salt
3 tablespoons olive oil or vegetable oil
3 garlic cloves, finely minced
1 onion, minced
2½ cups whole tomatoes
1¼ teaspoons salt
¼ teaspoon pepper
1 8-ounce can tomato sauce
¼ teaspoon dried thyme
¼ cup packed dried bread crumbs
¼ cup grated Parmesan cheese
1 egg, beaten
3 tablespoons olive oil or vegetable oil
½ pound sliced mozzarella cheese
½ cup grated Parmesan cheese

- Cut chicken into 8 pieces. Salt lightly.
- Sauté garlic and onions in 3 tablespoons of olive oil until golden.
- Add tomatoes, salt and pepper. Break up tomatoes with spoon and simmer, uncovered, for 10 minutes.
- Add tomato sauce and thyme; simmer, uncovered, for 20 minutes.
- Combine crumbs with ¼ cup Parmesan cheese. Dip each piece of chicken into egg, then into crumbs.
- Sauté chicken in 1 tablespoon of olive oil in skillet until golden brown, turning once. Add more oil if necessary. Repeat until all pieces are done.
- Set pieces of chicken side by side in a 13x9x2-inch baking dish.
- Pour ⅔ of tomato mixture over chicken, straining if necessary. Arrange slices of mozzarella on top.
- Spoon rest of tomato mixture over chicken and sprinkle with Parmesan cheese.
- Bake uncovered, in a preheated oven at 350° for 30 minutes.

Yield: 8-10 servings

Baked Chicken Parmesan

1 cup dry bread crumbs
⅓ cup grated Parmesan cheese
¼ teaspoon ground oregano
¼ teaspoon pepper
  Salt to taste
1 garlic clove, minced
¾ cup butter or margarine, melted
6 boneless chicken breast halves

- Combine in plastic bag the bread crumbs, cheese, oregano, pepper and salt. Set aside.
- Sauté garlic in 2 tablespoons of butter. Add remaining butter.
- Dip chicken in garlic butter and roll in crumb mixture.
- Place chicken in casserole dish and sprinkle with remaining bread crumbs. Pour on remaining butter.
- Bake in a preheated oven at 350° for 55 minutes.

  Yield: 6 servings

Apricot Chicken

12 chicken breast halves, boned and skinned
1 12-ounce can apricot nectar
1 teaspoon ground allspice
½ teaspoon salt
¼ teaspoon ground ginger
¼ teaspoon pepper
¾ cup apricot preserves
½ cup chopped pecans

- Place chicken breasts in 13x9x2-inch baking dish.
- Combine apricot nectar, allspice, salt, ginger and pepper. Pour over chicken. Cover and chill for 8 hours.
- Remove chicken. Let stand at room temperature for 30 minutes.
- Bake, covered, in a preheated oven at 350° for 30 minutes. Uncover and drain liquid from dish.
- Heat preserves in a small saucepan until warm. Brush over chicken.
- Bake, uncovered, 25 minutes. Baste occasionally.
- Sprinkle with pecans.

  Yield: 12 servings

139

Chicken Parmigiana

4 boneless chicken breast halves
2 eggs, beaten
1 cup Italian bread crumbs
¼ cup olive oil
1 16-ounce jar meat flavored spaghetti sauce
½ cup grated Parmesan cheese
5 ounces mozzarella cheese cut into 8 slices

- Flatten chicken to ¼-inch thickness.
- Dip chicken into eggs, then bread crumbs.
- Brown chicken on both sides in olive oil.
- Pour spaghetti sauce in 11x7x2-inch dish. Place chicken on top.
- Sprinkle grated Parmesan over chicken, and top with the mozzarella cheese slices.
- Bake in a preheated oven at 400° for 15 minutes or until cheese is lightly brown.

Yield: 4 servings

Chicken in Dill Sauce

6-8 chicken breast halves, boned
2 shallots, chopped
1 tablespoon butter or margarine
1 cup sour cream
1 10¾-ounce can cream of mushroom soup
1 tablespoon Worcestershire sauce
1 teaspoon dill weed
½ cup sherry
3 cups shredded Cheddar cheese
Rice or noodles, cooked

- Place chicken in 13x9x2-inch dish.
- Sauté shallots in butter.
- Mix shallots, sour cream, cream of mushroom soup, Worcestershire sauce, dill weed and sherry. Pour over chicken.
- Sprinkle with cheese and bake in a preheated oven at 350° for 1 hour.
- Serve over rice or noodles.

Yield: 6-8 servings

Pecan Chicken

4 tablespoons butter or margarine
1 cup buttermilk
1 egg, slightly beaten
1 cup all-purpose flour
1 cup ground pecans
1 tablespoon salt
1 tablespoon paprika
⅛ teaspoon pepper
¼ cup sesame seeds
4-5 pounds fryer parts or chicken breast halves
¼ cup pecan halves

• Melt butter in 10x15-inch baking dish.
• In a separate dish combine buttermilk and egg.
• In a third dish combine flour, ground pecans, seasonings and sesame seeds.
• Dip chicken in buttermilk, then flour.
• Place chicken skin side down in melted butter. Turn to coat and leave skin side up. Sprinkle with pecan halves.
• Bake, covered, in a preheated oven at 350° for 45 minutes. Uncover and bake for 30 minutes more or until done.

Sesame Chicken

8 chicken breast halves with skin
2 teaspoons salt
Black pepper to taste
½ cup all-purpose flour
2 teaspoons paprika
¼ cup butter or margarine
¼ cup vegetable oil
3 tablespoons sesame seeds, divided
½ cup minced green onions
1 cup Sauterne

• Sprinkle chicken breasts with salt and pepper. Dredge in mixture of flour and paprika.
• Melt butter and oil in baking dish. Place chicken skin side down.
• Sprinkle with 1½ tablespoons of sesame seeds.
• Bake in a preheated oven at 400° for 30 minutes. Turn chicken and sprinkle with green onions and remaining sesame seeds.
• Add Sauterne. Reduce heat to 375° and bake 20 minutes or until done.

Yield: 8 servings

Sweet and Sour Chicken

2   cut up fryers or breast halves if preferred
    Italian dressing
½   cup water
½   cup raisins
½   cup brown sugar
1   teaspoon garlic powder
2   medium onions, thinly sliced
1   12-ounce bottle chili sauce
1   tablespoon Worcestershire sauce
1   16-ounce can Bing cherries, with juice

- Marinate chicken in Italian dressing for 2 hours. Drain and place in casserole dish.
- Combine water, raisins, brown sugar, garlic powder, onions, chili sauce and Worcestershire sauce in saucepan. Heat until boiling. Pour over chicken.
- Bake, covered, in a preheated oven at 325° for 1½ hours. Add cherries and bake an additional 20-30 minutes.

Cranberry Chicken

1   8-ounce bottle French dressing
⅓   cup brown sugar
¼-½ teaspoon curry powder, optional
1   16-ounce can whole cranberry sauce
4-6 chicken breast halves, boned and skinned

- Mix dressing and sugar in saucepan. Heat; stir in curry powder and cranberry sauce.
- Place chicken in baking dish and pour sauce over.
- Bake, uncovered, in a preheated oven at 350° for 30-45 minutes.

Yield: 4-6 servings

Chicken Diablo

4   tablespoons butter or margarine
½   cup honey
¼   cup prepared mustard
1   teaspoon curry powder
1   teaspoon salt
½-1 cup white wine
8   chicken breast halves, boned and skinned

- Melt butter in shallow baking pan. Stir in remaining ingredients except chicken.
- Roll chicken in mixture to coat both sides.
- Arrange chicken in a single layer in same pan.
- Bake in a preheated oven at 375° for 1 hour, basting once.

Yield: 6-8 servings

Oven Barbecued Chicken
The family will rave

1 cup vinegar
⅓ cup vegetable oil, optional
2 tablespoons Worcestershire sauce
1 teaspoon grated onion
2 garlic cloves, minced
1½ teaspoons salt
½ teaspoon paprika
3 tablespoons tomato paste
½ tablespoon dry mustard
6-8 chicken breast halves, boned and skinned
1 lemon, sliced very thin

- Bring first 9 ingredients to a boil and simmer for 10 minutes.
- Place chicken breasts in glass dish and pour barbecue sauce over them. Top with lemon slices.
- Bake, uncovered, in a preheated oven at 350° for 1½ hours. Baste every 15 minutes.

Yield: 6-8 servings

Crunchy Chicken Cheese Bake

8 chicken breast halves, boned and skinned
8 slices Swiss or American cheese
1 10¾-ounce can cream of chicken soup
¼ cup sherry, optional
8 thin slices of tomato
2 tablespoons butter or margarine, melted
½ cup seasoned stuffing or bread crumbs
Rice, cooked

- Place chicken in 13x9x2-inch dish. Top with cheese.
- Mix soup and sherry and spread over cheese. Top with tomato slices.
- Combine butter and stuffing and sprinkle over tomatoes.
- Bake in a preheated oven at 400° for 25 minutes.
- Serve over rice.

Yield: 8 servings

143

 # French Chicken

1   5 or 6 pound hen
2   cups chopped green bell peppers
2   cups chopped onion
2   bunches of celery, chopped
1   garlic clove, chopped fine
1   pound wide noodles
2   10¾-ounce cans tomato soup
1   6-ounce (dr. wt.) can pitted ripe olives, drained and sliced
2   4-ounce cans sliced mushrooms
1   cup fine chopped parsley
1   5-ounce bottle Worcestershire sauce, less 1 tablespoon

- Cook hen in boiling, seasoned water until it falls from the bone. Reserve strained stock. Cut hen into bite size pieces.
- Cook peppers, onions, celery and garlic in half of broth until tender.
- Cook noodles in remaining broth according to directions on package. Be careful not to over cook.
- Combine hen, vegetables and noodles and remaining ingredients, adding Worcestershire last.
- Heat but do not cook.

This recipe can be made ahead of time, put in casserole, and frozen until ready to use.

Yield: 14 servings

Pineapple Chicken

4-6   chicken breast halves, boned and skinned
⅓   cup all-purpose flour
½   teaspoon salt
⅛   teaspoon pepper
⅛   teaspoon paprika
6   tablespoons oil, divided
1   garlic clove, minced
¼   cup chopped onion
⅓   cup chopped green bell pepper
½   teaspoon dry mustard
¾   teaspoon soy sauce
⅓   cup chili sauce
1½   cups pineapple juice

- Cut chicken into bite-sized chunks. Roll in flour that has been seasoned with salt, pepper and paprika.
- Sauté in 5 tablespoons of oil until light brown. Place in a 2-quart greased casserole dish.
- Add 1 tablespoon of oil to pan and sauté garlic, onion and green pepper for 5 minutes. Add mustard, soy sauce, chili sauce and pineapple juice. Bring to a boil and simmer for 5 minutes.
- Pour over chicken and bake, covered, in a preheated oven at 350° for 45 minutes.

Yield: 4-6 servings

144

Use Rotisserie Chickens

Chicken Tetrazzini

2 large hens or 1 turkey breast
Salt, celery leaves, bay leaves and onions
¾ cup butter or margarine
¾ cup all-purpose flour
3 cups half-and-half
4 cups milk
1½ cups Parmesan cheese, divided
Salt, cayenne pepper, hot pepper sauce to taste
3 large onions, sliced
½ cup butter or margarine, separated
1 pound mushrooms, sliced
1 8-ounce box thin spaghetti
Sherry to taste, optional

- Boil hen or turkey in water to which salt, celery leaves, bay leaves and chopped onions have been added.
- After meat has finished cooking strain broth and set aside. When cool, cut meat into bite-size pieces.
- Combine butter, flour, half-and-half and milk in a double boiler to make cream sauce. Cook over medium heat stirring constantly until thickened.
- Remove cream sauce from heat. Add 1 cup Parmesan cheese and seasonings to taste. Set aside.
- Sauté onion in four tablespoons of butter until soft. Set aside.
- Sauté mushrooms in remaining four tablespoons of butter for about five minutes.
- Cook spaghetti in reserved broth, drain. Combine spaghetti, meat, sauce, onions and mushrooms.
- Adjust seasonings to taste, add sherry if desired, and put mixture in a 13x9x2-inch baking dish.
- Sprinkle top with ½ cup Parmesan cheese and bake in a preheated oven at 350° until it bubbles.

Freezes well.

Yield: 12 servings

Country Captain

When General George Patton was en route through Columbus, Georgia, he wired ahead, "If you can't give me a party and have Country Captain, put some in a bucket and bring it to the train."

1   2-3 pound fryer or frying pieces
2   onions, finely chopped
2   green bell peppers, chopped
1-2 garlic cloves, crushed
1   good teaspoon salt
½   teaspoon white pepper
2   teaspoons curry powder
2   16-ounce cans tomatoes
1   teaspoon chopped parsley
½   teaspoon powdered thyme
    Black pepper to taste
2   cups cooked rice
3   or more tablespoons currants
¼   pound slivered almonds, toasted

- Season chicken well and fry as usual. Remove from pan but keep chicken hot; this is a secret of the dish's success.
- Pour off most of the grease; add onions, green peppers and garlic cloves. Cook very slowly, stirring constantly.
- Season with salt, white pepper and curry powder.
- Add tomatoes, chopped parsley, thyme and black pepper to taste.
- Place chicken in roaster and pour sauce over it. Bake, covered, in a preheated oven at 350° for 45 minutes.
- Place chicken in middle of platter and pile rice around chicken.
- Mix currants with sauce and pour over rice. Scatter almonds over top.

Yield: 4 servings

Hunter's Chicken

4 tablespoons butter or margarine
4 tablespoons oil
2 fryers, cut up
6 peeled shallots
1 onion, coarsely chopped
1⅓ cups sliced fresh mushrooms
  Salt and freshly ground pepper to taste
1 16-ounce can stewed tomatoes, drained
1 teaspoon crushed dried thyme
⅛ teaspoon cayenne pepper
¼ cup dry white wine
1 tablespoon plus 1 teaspoon fresh lemon juice
  Chopped parsley

- Heat butter and oil in large deep skillet or Dutch oven over medium heat.
- Sauté chicken pieces until brown on all sides.
- Sauté shallots, onion and mushrooms until golden brown.
- Add salt, pepper, tomatoes, thyme and cayenne, stirring well. Stir in wine and bring to a boil.
- Reduce heat, cover and simmer 30-45 minutes until chicken is cooked. Transfer chicken to a platter and keep warm.
- Remove mushrooms and onions with a slotted spoon and set them aside. Cool sauce slightly.
- Skim off surface fat and bring sauce to a boil again. Cook uncovered until reduced by a third.
- Return chicken, onion and mushrooms to pan.
- Add lemon juice. Heat thoroughly and top with parsley.

Variation: Chicken broth or bouillon may be substituted for dry white wine.

Yield: 4-6 servings

Baked Chicken Breasts with Scallions and Lime

4 chicken breast halves, boned and skinned
½ cup all-purpose flour
4 tablespoons unsalted butter or margarine
⅔ cup minced scallions (white and tender green)
1 large garlic clove, minced
½ cup dry white wine
½ teaspoon salt
¼ teaspoon freshly ground pepper
1 tablespoon fresh lime juice
1 tablespoon chopped parsley
2 teaspoons grated lime zest
1 tablespoon butter or margarine
1 tablespoon fine, dry bread crumbs

- Pound chicken to an even thickness.
- Dredge chicken in flour; shake off excess.
- Melt 4 tablespoons of butter over moderately high heat in large skillet.
- Add chicken and sauté, turning once until golden brown. Remove chicken from skillet.
- Reduce heat to low. Add scallions and garlic and cook until soft.
- Increase heat to moderately high. Add wine and bring to a boil, scraping up browned bits until reduced by half, 2-3 minutes.
- Spread ½ the scallion sauce in buttered baking dish. Add chicken and season with salt and pepper.
- Drizzle on lime juice. Cover with remaining sauce.
- Sprinkle on the parsley, lime zest and bread crumbs and dot with 1 tablespoon butter.
- Bake chicken in a preheated oven at 400° for 15 minutes or until chicken is tender.

Yield: 4 servings

Balsamic Chicken and Peppers

4 chicken breast halves, boned and skinned
½ teaspoon salt
¼ teaspoon pepper
2 tablespoons all-purpose flour
1 tablespoon olive oil
2 garlic cloves, minced
1 small red bell pepper, cut into short thin strips
½ cup chicken broth
½ cup tomato sauce
2 tablespoons balsamic vinegar, divided
1½ teaspoons dried basil or about 3 tablespoons fresh basil, minced
3 cups long grain white rice, cooked (when cooking add ¼ cup thinly sliced green onions with tops)
Freshly ground black pepper

- Cut each chicken breast in half as if fileting them and sprinkle with salt and pepper. Rub with flour.
- Brown chicken in oil over medium heat until golden brown. Remove and set aside.
- Combine garlic, red bell pepper, broth, tomato sauce, 1 tablespoon of vinegar and the basil in skillet and heat.
- Return chicken to skillet and spoon sauce over. Cover and cook over low heat for 8 minutes.
- Stir in remaining tablespoon of vinegar and cook, uncovered, over high heat until sauce has thickened.
- Serve chicken over rice and top with sauce. Sprinkle with pepper.

Yield: 4 servings

Devilish Chicken

1 pound boneless chicken breast halves
Salt
Pepper
2 tablespoons vegetable oil
⅓ cup finely chopped onion
1 large garlic clove, minced
5 ounces dry white wine
5 ounces chicken broth
1 teaspoon cornstarch or all-purpose flour
1 tablespoon Dijon mustard
2 teaspoons capers
Salt
Pepper
Chopped parsley
Noodles, cooked

- Season chicken with salt and pepper and brown in oil, removing when fully cooked.
- Sauté onion and garlic in remaining oil until clear.
- Add wine and chicken broth and bring to a boil.
- Mix a little of the broth with cornstarch and add back to the skillet.
- Add mustard, capers, salt and pepper and heat thoroughly.
- Spoon over chicken and garnish with parsley.
- Serve with buttered egg noodles.

Yield: 4 servings

Chicken Pie

A hearty meal in itself

1   chicken or 4-6 chicken breast halves, cooked and boned
2   cups chopped mixed vegetables, may use canned
1¾-2   cups chicken broth
1   10¾-ounce can cream of celery or cream of chicken soup
    Salt
    Pepper
½   cup butter or margarine, softened
1   cup self-rising flour
¾   cup milk or buttermilk

• Place chicken and vegetables in a 13x9x2-inch glass dish.
• Pour broth over chicken. Spoon soup over broth and sprinkle with salt and pepper.
• Mix butter, flour and milk and pour over top layer.
• Bake in a preheated oven at 350° for 40 minutes or until crust browns.

Yield: 6 servings

Chicken Breast Lombardy

Supper club will love it

8   chicken breast halves, skinned and boned
½   cup all-purpose flour
½   cup butter or margarine
2   cups sliced mushrooms
½   cup Marsala wine or ½ cup white wine plus 2 tablespoons brandy
⅓   cup chicken broth
½   cup shredded Fontina or mozzarella cheese
½   cup grated Parmesan cheese

• Place chicken between two sheets of waxed paper and flatten to ⅛-inch thickness using meat mallet or rolling pin.
• Dredge chicken lightly in flour.
• Melt butter in a large skillet and cook chicken over low heat 3-4 minutes on each side until golden brown.
• Place chicken, overlapping edges, in a 13x9x2-inch baking dish.
• Sauté mushrooms in skillet, adding butter if necessary, and sprinkle evenly over chicken.
• Stir wine and chicken broth into pan drippings. Simmer 10 minutes, stirring occasionally.
• Spoon sauce over chicken and bake in a preheated oven at 400° for 10 minutes.
• Combine cheese and sprinkle over chicken. Bake an additional 5 minutes.

Yield: 8 servings

Royal Chicken Crêpes

12   crêpes (recipe follows)
¼   cup butter or margarine
1½   cups sliced fresh mushrooms
¼   cup chopped onion
⅛   teaspoon thyme
2   cups cooked, diced chicken
¼   cup chopped fresh parsley
1   10¾-ounce can cream of chicken soup
¼   teaspoon salt
⅛   teaspoon pepper
¼   cup light cream or half-and-half
2   tablespoons dry white wine

- In a large skillet melt butter. Add mushrooms, onion and thyme and cook and stir over medium heat 2-3 minutes.
- Stir in chicken, parsley, ¾ cup of the soup, salt and pepper.
- Bring to a boil, reduce heat and simmer, stirring occasionally, until heated through. Set aside.
- Combine remaining soup, cream and wine in a saucepan. Cook and stir over medium heat until hot and bubbly.
- Spoon about ¼ cup chicken mixture down center of each crêpe. Roll up the crêpe and place in a glass dish.
- Top each crêpe with about 1 tablespoon sauce.
- Heat in a preheated oven at 350° until hot — about 15 minutes. These may also be stored in refrigerator for a day or two until ready to use and then heated.

Crêpes:
1½   cups milk
3   eggs
2   tablespoons butter or margarine, melted
1   cup all-purpose flour
½   teaspoon salt

- Combine milk, eggs and butter in a mixing bowl and beat together.
- Add flour and salt, beating until smooth. Refrigerate for 1 hour. Be sure to stir batter before using.
- Lightly grease a 6-inch skillet.
- Heat skillet and pour in ¼ cup batter. Rotate skillet to spread the batter evenly over the bottom. When slightly brown on the bottom turn the crêpe over and cook the other side until slightly brown.
- Stack the crêpes between waxed paper. These may be used now for filling or stored in refrigerator a couple of days until ready to use.

151

Chicken Divan

6   chicken breast halves
2   10-ounce packages frozen broccoli
    spears
1   cup sour cream
2   10¾-ounce cans cream of chicken soup
1   cup mayonnaise
1   cup shredded sharp Cheddar cheese
1   teaspoon curry powder
1   tablespoon lemon juice
½-¾ cup grated fresh Parmesan cheese
    Paprika

- Boil chicken breasts in water until done and then cut into small pieces.
- Cook broccoli according to directions on package and drain.
- Mix together sour cream, chicken soup, mayonnaise, Cheddar cheese, curry powder and lemon juice.
- Layer in a 13x9x2-inch dish the broccoli, chicken and then the sauce sprinkling each layer with ⅓ of the Parmesan cheese.
- Top with a dusting of paprika.
- Bake in a preheated oven at 350° until bubbly, about 30 minutes.

Yield: 6-8 servings

Individual Chicken Pockets

1   boneless chicken breast
1   teaspoon Dijon mustard
1   slice mozzarella cheese
    Raw vegetables — whatever you might have — broccoli, mushrooms, squash, onion, cherry tomatoes, potatoes, carrots
¼   teaspoon basil
¼   teaspoon garlic powder
⅛   teaspoon salt
⅛   teaspoon pepper
½   teaspoon lemon juice

- Spray a square of foil with non-stick spray.
- Place chicken on foil and spread with mustard. Top with mozzarella cheese.
- Add raw vegetables and sprinkle with remaining ingredients.
- Seal foil tightly and bake on cookie sheet in a preheated oven at 350° for 1 hour.

Yield: Make as many as you need.

White Chili

1 pound white beans
6 cups chicken broth
2 garlic cloves, minced
2 medium onions, chopped, divided
1 tablespoon oil
2 4-ounce cans mild green chilies, chopped
2 teaspoons cumin
1½ teaspoons oregano
¼ teaspoon ground cloves
¼ teaspoon cayenne pepper
4 cups cooked, diced chicken
3 cups grated Monterey Jack cheese
Salsa
Sour cream or plain non-fat yogurt
Green onions, chopped

- Combine beans, chicken broth, garlic and half of the onions in a large soup pot. Bring to a boil.
- Reduce heat; simmer until beans are soft (3 hours or more) adding more broth if necessary.
- Sauté remaining onions in oil until tender.
- Add chilies and seasonings and mix thoroughly. Add to bean mixture.
- Add chicken and simmer one hour. Serve topped with grated cheese, salsa, sour cream and green onions.

  Yield: 8-10 servings

Stir-Fry Chicken and Vegetables

1 pound chicken breast strips
2 tablespoons vegetable oil
4 cups vegetables — broccoli flowerets, green bell pepper strips, sliced water chestnuts — or any others you have
1½ cups chicken broth
3 tablespoons soy sauce
2 tablespoons cornstarch
2 teaspoons brown sugar
1 teaspoon garlic powder
¾ teaspoon ground ginger
Rice

- Stir-fry chicken in hot oil in large skillet until browned.
- Add vegetables; stir-fry until crisp-tender.
- Mix remaining ingredients, except rice, and add to skillet. Cook for one minute.
- Serve over rice.

  Yield: 4 servings

Southwest Chicken

2 chickens, about 3½-pounds each
Salt and pepper
½ pound feta cheese
2 tablespoons chopped fresh chives
1 tablespoon grated red onion
1 egg
Lemon-garlic jalapeño sauce (recipe follows)
2 tablespoons finely chopped red bell pepper, optional
2 tablespoons sunflower seeds, optional

Lemon-Garlic Jalapeño Sauce:
½ cup butter or margarine
⅔ cup chopped onion
2 jalapeño chili peppers, seeded and sliced
3 garlic cloves, peeled and chopped
Zest and juice of 1 lemon
3 tablespoons tequila
½ cup unbleached all-purpose flour
3-4 cups chicken stock or canned chicken broth
3 tablespoons balsamic vinegar
Salt and pepper to taste
Pinch cayenne, optional

• Cut chicken in half, discarding backbone.
• Salt and pepper lightly.
• Place skin side up in shallow baking pan and roast in a preheated oven at 400° for approximately 30 minutes. Birds should be slightly underdone.
• Remove and set aside to cool.
• In a bowl combine feta cheese, chives, red onion and egg.
• Remove breast bone and thigh bones from chicken halves.
• Carefully lift skin and insert cheese mixture between meat and skin. Pull skin tight and pat to spread mixture evenly.
• Approximately 25 minutes before serving, preheat oven to 375°.
• Return stuffed chickens to baking pan, skin side up. Roast until warmed through, about 20-30 minutes.
• Place one chicken half on each plate and pour ½ cup lemon-garlic jalapeño sauce over each. Garnish with red bell pepper and sunflower seeds.
• Heat butter until foaming and sauté onion, peppers, and garlic until onions are softened, about 5 minutes.
• Stir in lemon zest and juice.
• Deglaze pan with tequila. Stir in flour and cook over low heat for 2 or 3 minutes.
• Gradually whisk in 2 cups chicken stock, adding remainder if necessary to thin sauce to desired consistency.
• Stir in balsamic vinegar and add salt and pepper to taste. Taste sauce and adjust seasonings, adding cayenne pepper if a spicier sauce is desired.

Yield: 4 servings

154

Orange Glazed Cornish Hens

4 Cornish hens
   Salt
   Melted butter or margarine
½ cup orange juice
½ cup butter or margarine, melted
4 tablespoons white wine
   Orange marmalade
   Orange rice, cooked

- Remove giblets and rinse hens with cold water. Pat dry and sprinkle cavities with salt.
- Secure with wooden pins and truss.
- Place hens, breast side up, in a shallow baking pan. Brush with melted butter.
- Bake in a preheated oven at 325° 1½ hours, basting several times with mixture of orange juice, butter and white wine.
- Five minutes before removing from oven, spoon orange marmalade over hens.
- Serve with orange rice.

Yield: 4 servings

Ed's Frozen Turkey Breast

1 turkey breast, unthawed
   Salt and pepper
   Butter or margarine
1 onion, chopped
3 celery stalks with leaves, chopped
1 cup chicken bouillon

- Salt, pepper and butter turkey breast.
- Place in roaster on top of onions and celery. Pour in bouillon.
- Bake uncovered in a preheated oven at 350° until light brown, approximately 1 hour.
- Reduce heat to 250°, cover breast with foil and baste every 20 minutes. Total cooking time will be about 4 hours.

Holiday Turkey with No Basting

Turkey
Lemon juice
Salt and pepper
Butter or margarine
Other seasonings of your preference
Kitchen Bouquet
Bacon
Butter or margarine
¼ cup water

- Wash turkey and pat dry.
- Squeeze juice of lemon into cavity of turkey. Season with salt and pepper. Stuff with favorite dressing, if desired.
- Add a lump of butter to the cavity to keep moist.
- To skin of turkey, rub in your choice of seasonings such as garlic juice, seasoned salt and soy sauce.
- Rub turkey generously with Kitchen Bouquet.
- Across the breast and legs, crisscross strips of bacon.
- Add a lump of butter and ¼ cup water to pan.
- Cover turkey loosely with foil, to allow steam to escape.
- Bake 25 minutes to the pound in a preheated 350° oven. Remove foil the last hour to allow the turkey to brown.
- Check pan during cooking time and add water and/or butter if necessary to keep bottom from burning. Use drippings for gravy.

Mamie's Quail or Dove

12 birds
    Salt
    Pepper
    All-purpose flour
    Paprika
    Butter or margarine
½ cup butter or margarine
½ cup all-purpose flour
1 quart warm water or chicken stock
½ teaspoon Kitchen Bouquet
    Instant beef bouillon
    Juice of 1 lemon plus a few lemon slices

- Place birds in roaster and sprinkle with salt, pepper, flour and paprika.
- Dot each with a thin slice of butter.
- Cover with light weight aluminum foil and cook on lower rack of a preheated oven at 450° for 45 minutes.
- Remove birds to make gravy in the roaster.
- Scrape bottom of roaster, add butter and flour and stir until smooth.
- Add warm water, or chicken stock, and Kitchen Bouquet. Cook until thick.
- Place birds back in roaster, breast side up, and baste a few times. Be sure to have enough gravy to half cover the birds.
- Shake some instant beef bouillon on top of birds, add lemon juice and lemon slice and cover with foil.
- Return to oven and bake at 350° for 30 minutes.

Southern Quail

    Quail
    Salt, pepper and paprika
1 tablespoon all-purpose flour
½ lemon
½ cup butter or margarine

- Split birds. Place in roaster and sprinkle with salt, pepper, paprika, flour and lemon juice. Dot with butter.
- Place in oven under flame so that birds are about 8 inches below flame. Brown.
- Add enough water to half cover birds. Cover and let steam until birds are tender.
- Keep basted, as the thickened gravy gives them a glazed look.

  Serve with wild rice or baked grits and be sure to have plenty of gravy.

Venison Chili

2 pounds ground deer meat
¼ cup vegetable oil
1 cup chopped onion
2 garlic cloves, minced
1 green bell pepper, chopped
3 tablespoons chili powder
2 teaspoons sugar
3 16-ounce cans whole tomatoes
1 16-ounce can tomato sauce
1 cup water
2 cans kidney beans
½ teaspoon salt
2 tablespoons all-purpose flour
4 tablespoons water

• Brown meat in oil. Add onion, garlic and bell pepper. Cook 5 minutes. Drain.
• Add chili powder, sugar, tomatoes, tomato sauce, water, beans and salt. Simmer 1 hour.
• Add flour and water mixture and add to meat mixture stirring until thickened.

Yield: 8-10 servings

Ground Venison Casserole

1 pound ground deer meat
½ cup chopped green bell pepper
1 cup chopped onion
2 teaspoons chili powder
2 teaspoons garlic salt
1 8-ounce package noodles, cooked
1 10¾-ounce can cream of mushroom soup
1 10¾-ounce can tomato soup
1 10¾-ounce can water
¾-1 cup shredded Cheddar cheese

• Mix meat, pepper, onion, chili powder and garlic salt thoroughly.
• Spread into a 13x9x2-inch baking dish.
• Layer noodles over meat mixture.
• Combine mushroom soup, tomato soup and water and mix thoroughly. Pour over noodles.
• Sprinkle cheese over casserole and bake in a preheated oven at 375° for 1 hour.

Yield: 6 servings

A Sauce for Venison, Dove or Duck

Transforms game meats to a gourmet status!

5 ounces red currant jelly
½ cup butter or margarine
Pinch of cornstarch
5 ounces dry sherry

• Heat jelly, butter and cornstarch in top of a double boiler until jelly is liquid.
• Add sherry and serve hot.

Yield: 8-10 servings

Venison

Venison
Buttermilk, enough to cover meat
1 cup butter or margarine
Cointreau
Orange juice
Juice of 1 lemon

- Cover venison in buttermilk and soak overnight in the refrigerator.
- Drain and dry when ready to put into oven.
- Insert meat thermometer. Place butter on top and allow to melt in oven.
- Pour sauce of 3 parts Cointreau to 1 part orange juice and juice of 1 lemon over roast.
- Bake in a preheated oven at 325° basting frequently, until thermometer registers desired amount of rareness or doneness.

Poultry Marinade

½ cup olive oil
⅓ cup dry white wine (vermouth or chablis)
¼ cup white wine vinegar
⅛ cup lemon juice
1 garlic clove, minced
1 teaspoon dry mustard
½ teaspoon poultry seasoning
½ teaspoon celery salt
1 teaspoon salt
¼ teaspoon black pepper
½ teaspoon Accent

- Shake all ingredients in a jar.
- Pour over poultry and let stand for three hours in refrigerator, turning chicken several times.
- Baste chicken with marinade while cooking either in the oven or on the grill.

Yield: 6-8 servings

Mustard Sauce

⅓ cup plain yogurt
¼ cup mayonnaise
3 tablespoons Dijon mustard
2 tablespoons sweet pickle relish
1 tablespoon minced onion
2 teaspoons white wine vinegar

- Combine all ingredients and stir well.
- Cover and chill thoroughly.
  Serve with fish, shellfish or chicken.
  Yield: ¾ cup

Scallops

2 cups white wine
1 teaspoon salt
1 bay leaf
4 tablespoons chopped green onion
2 pounds scallops
Water, if necessary

Cream Sauce:
4 tablespoons butter or margarine
4 tablespoons all-purpose flour
½ cup cream
½ cup grated Gruyère cheese

- Simmer wine, salt, bay leaf and onion for 5 minutes.
- Add scallops; add water, if necessary, to barely cover.
- Simmer 5 minutes.
- Remove scallops. Set aside.
- Boil down liquid to two cups. Set aside.

- Combine butter and flour and cook over low heat for two minutes.
- Add reserved liquid and cream.
- Melt cheese into sauce. Heat thoroughly.
- Arrange scallops in serving dish and top with sauce.
- Broil until bubbly and lightly browned.
- Sprinkle with chopped parsley and serve. Do not overcook.
  Yield: 4-6 servings

Out of This World Oysters

½ cup plus 2 tablespoons butter or margarine
1½ cups finely chopped celery
1 small bunch parsley, chopped fine
4 green onions, chopped fine
1 quart oysters, drained & chopped (reserve ¼ cup liquid)
6 slices toasted bread, crumbled
1 egg, slightly beaten
¼ cup oyster liquid
¼ teaspoon dry mustard
Pinch of salt
1½ teaspoons black pepper or more to taste
Parmesan cheese

- Cook celery, parsley, and onions, in butter until soft.
- Add oysters. Bring to a simmer and add bread crumbs, egg, oyster liquid, dry mustard, salt and pepper.
- Remove to a casserole dish and sprinkle with Parmesan cheese.
- Bake in a preheated oven at 350° for 30 minutes.

Scalloped Oysters

½ cup butter or margarine, melted
1 cup cracker crumbs
½ cup stale bread crumbs
1 pint oysters
 Salt and black pepper
3 tablespoons oyster liquor
3 tablespoons cream

- Mix melted butter, cracker and bread crumbs.
- Line bottom of buttered shallow baking dish with ⅓ of the crumb mixture. Top with a layer of ½ of the oysters, sprinkle with salt and black pepper, and add ½ each of the oyster liquor and cream.
- Repeat and cover top with remaining crumbs. Never allow more than two layers of oysters for scalloped oysters.
- Bake in a medium oven until crumbs are golden brown, 20-30 minutes.
- During the last 10 minutes of cooking time, take a peek and if they seem to be getting dry, add a little more cream.

Yield: 4 servings

Crab Au Gratin
For Special Company

1 pound white lump crabmeat
1½ tablespoons fresh lemon juice
 Salt and lots of cayenne pepper
½ teaspoon onion juice
1 tablespoon butter or margarine
1 tablespoon all-purpose flour
1 cup coffee cream
½ cup sherry or white wine
1 cup grated sharp Cheddar cheese
1 egg yolk, beaten
 Paprika

- Pick crabmeat. Sprinkle lemon juice, salt, pepper and onion juice over crab and let stand while making sauce.
- Melt butter in top of double boiler. Blend in flour and add cream and sherry. Stir until thickened.
- Add ½ cup of grated cheese.
- Pour hot sauce over beaten egg yolk and let cool slightly.
- Mix carefully with crabmeat.
- Fill 6-8 ramekins; sprinkle rest of cheese on top. A sprinkle of paprika will make it brown well.
- Bake in a preheated oven at 450° until hot and bubbly.

161

Crab Cakes

3-4 tablespoons all-purpose flour
1 pound fresh crabmeat
  Mayonnaise, to taste
  Lemon juice, to taste
  Salt and pepper, to taste
2 tablespoons green onions
  Bread crumbs
3 tablespoons butter or margarine
3 tablespoons olive oil

ADD "OLD BAY"

Sauce:
1 tablespoon Dijon mustard
1 tablespoon mayonnaise
2 tablespoons sour cream
1 tablespoon lemon juice
  Garlic powder (dark)
1 teaspoon curry powder

- Sprinkle flour over crabmeat. Mix in mayonnaise, lemon juice, salt, pepper, and green onions until stiff enough to form cakes.
- Make ¾-inch thick cakes. These need to be patted together gently; not too much flour.
- Lightly pat cakes in bread crumbs and refrigerate several hours (this makes them firm).
- Sauté in olive oil and butter until light brown.
- Serve with the following sauce.

- Mix all ingredients together, blending well.
  Yield: 4 cakes

Julia's Crabmeat

½ cup butter or margarine
½ cup all-purpose flour
1 pint half-and-half
  Worcestershire sauce to taste, about 1 tablespoon
  Salt and pepper to taste
2 pounds white lump crab meat
8 large scallop shells

- Melt butter, add flour to make a roux.
- Add half-and-half and stir over low heat until thickened.
- Add Worcestershire, salt, pepper, and crabmeat.
- Place in 8 large scallop shells, and bake in a preheated oven at 350° for approximately 30 minutes.

Delicious with melon balls and cold salad. May be reheated.

🍍 *Baked Red Snapper*

1 onion, chopped
2 tomatoes, peeled and chopped
2 stalks celery, chopped
1 garlic clove, crushed
 Salt and pepper to taste
2 bay leaves
1 lemon, cut in thin slices
2-3 pounds red snapper
3 tablespoons olive oil
3 tablespoons butter or margarine, melted
½ cup white wine
½ tablespoon Pernod, optional

- Lay about ⅔ of chopped vegetables, herbs and lemon slices in bottom of baking dish. Place fish on top and stuff fish with remaining vegetables.
- Pour olive oil, melted butter, white wine and Pernod over all.
- Cover pan with aluminum foil and bake in a preheated oven at 350° for about 45 minutes.
- If desired, you may remove foil during last 10 minutes and brown the fish.
Yield: 3-4 servings

Pan Fried Snapper

2 fillets of red snapper or other mild fish
 Cayenne pepper
 Lemon pepper
 All-purpose flour
4 tablespoons margarine or cooking oil
3 tablespoons white wine
¾ teaspoon ground garlic

- Lightly season both sides of fillets with cayenne and lemon pepper.
- Dip fillets in flour.
- Melt margarine and heat with garlic and wine.
- Pan fry fillets approximately 7-8 minutes or until meat is flaky.
Yield: 2 servings

Fish with Crumbs

2 pounds fish fillets, bass or other fresh fish
1 cup milk
1 tablespoon salt
1 cup bread crumbs
4 tablespoons butter or margarine

- Cut fish fillets into serving pieces.
- Add salt to milk and soak fish for ½ hour.
- Roll fillets in soft crumbs and place in well buttered baking dish.
- Pour some melted butter over top of fillets.
- Place pan on rack near top of a very hot, 500° oven.
- Bake 10-12 minutes, or until fish flakes easily when tested with a fork, and is nicely browned on top.

  Yield: 4 servings

Grouper Greco

6 grouper fillets
⅛ teaspoon salt
⅛ teaspoon pepper
¼ teaspoon paprika
1½ teaspoons Cavender's Greek seasoning
8 ounces fresh mushrooms
⅛ inch pat of butter or margarine on each fillet
1 lime
10 green onions, chopped
2 tablespoons chopped parsley
1 tablespoon butter or margarine

- Sprinkle fish with salt, pepper, paprika, and Greek seasoning.
- Top with mushrooms and butter pats. Squeeze fresh lime juice over fish.
- Bake, covered with foil, in a preheated 350° oven for 15-30 minutes, depending on size of fish.
- Remove foil and cook 5 more minutes.
- Sauté green onions and parsley in butter and pour over fish just before serving.

Cheesy Broiled Flounder

Simple and tasty

2 pounds flounder fillets
2 tablespoons lemon juice
½ cup grated Parmesan cheese
¼ cup butter or margarine, softened
3 tablespoons mayonnaise
3 green onions, chopped
¼ teaspoon salt
  Dash of hot pepper sauce

- Place fillets in a single layer on rack of greased broiler pan.
- Combine remaining ingredients in a small bowl and set aside.
- Broil fillets 4-6 minutes or until fish flakes easily when tested with fork.
- Remove from oven; spread with cheese mixture.
- Broil an additional 30 seconds or until cheese is lightly browned and bubbly.
  Yield: 6 servings

Orange Roughy with Cucumber and Dill

½ cup mayonnaise
¼ cup unpeeled, chopped cucumber
½ teaspoon fresh dill (or ¼ teaspoon dry dill)
2 green onions, chopped
2 drops hot pepper sauce
  Salt to taste
1 pound orange roughy
1 lemon

- Combine mayonnaise, cucumber, dill, onions, hot pepper sauce, and salt.
- Spray 13x9x2-inch baking dish with non-stick spray. Place fish in baking dish. Spread cucumber mixture on fish.
- Broil 3-5 inches from heat for 7-10 minutes, until lightly brown.
- Garnish with lemon slices.
  Yield: 2 servings

Shrimp Jambalaya

¼ cup chopped onion
¼ cup chopped green bell pepper
¼ cup butter or margarine, melted
1 tablespoon all-purpose flour
2 teaspoons chili powder
½ teaspoon salt
¼ teaspoon garlic powder
¼ teaspoon pepper
⅛ teaspoon cayenne pepper
¼ teaspoon Worcestershire sauce
1 tablespoon vinegar
2 cups peeled and chopped tomatoes
1 10-ounce package frozen sliced okra, thawed
1½ pounds shrimp, uncooked, peeled and deveined
2 cups cooked rice

- Sauté onion and green pepper in butter until tender.
- Combine flour and all dry seasonings, blend into onion mixture.
- Stir in Worcestershire sauce and vinegar until smooth.
- Add tomatoes and okra, stirring constantly until thickened.
- Add shrimp and simmer uncovered for 15 minutes.
- Stir in rice.

Easily doubled and can be made ahead.
Yield: 6 servings

Shrimp and Wild Rice Casserole

½ cup butter or margarine, divided
½ cup sliced onion
¼ cup sliced green bell pepper
½ pound fresh mushrooms, sliced
1 2-ounce jar pimientos, chopped
4 tablespoons all-purpose flour
1 cup whole milk
1 cup chicken broth
1 tablespoon Worcestershire sauce
1 teaspoon curry powder
4 drops hot pepper sauce
½ teaspoon salt
2 cups cooked wild rice
1 pound shrimp, cooked and cleaned

- In 4 tablespoons butter, sauté onions and bell pepper lightly until limp.
- Add mushrooms and pimientos and cook 2-3 minutes. Set aside.
- In another saucepan, melt remaining 4 table-spoons butter, add flour, then stir in milk and chicken broth and cook until white sauce is smooth and slightly thickened.
- Add Worcestershire, curry powder, hot pep-per sauce and salt to white sauce.
- Combine cooked vegetables, cream sauce, wild rice, and shrimp and place in 1½-quart casserole.
- Heat at 325° until hot.

Yield: 6 servings

Low Country Boil

Serve with plenty of napkins.

1 bay leaf
1 teaspoon salt
1 teaspoon black pepper
1 large onion, chopped
½ garlic clove
3 pounds Polish sausage, cut in 1-inch pieces
½ cup butter or margarine
12 ears of corn, fresh or frozen
24-30 new potatoes
4 pounds raw shrimp, unpeeled
1 lemon, sliced
1 packet crab boil

- Fill a 5-quart stock pot a little more than halfway with water.
- Add bay leaf, salt, pepper, onion, garlic, and sausage.
- Bring to a boil and cook 10 minutes.
- Add butter, corn and potatoes.
- Cook 10-15 minutes or until vegetables are tender.
- Add shrimp, lemon and crab boil.
- Bring to a boil and cook for 2 minutes or until shrimp are pink.
- Drain water and serve in a large bowl or on a platter.
- Serve with cocktail sauce and plenty of napkins

Yield: 10-12 servings

Sea Captain

A close cousin to Southern Country Captain

2 onions, finely chopped
2 green bell peppers, chopped
2 garlic cloves, chopped
1 tablespoon oil
1 heaping teaspoon salt
½ teaspoon white pepper
2 teaspoons curry powder
2 16-ounce cans tomatoes
1 teaspoon chopped parsley
½ teaspoon powdered thyme
Black pepper to taste
1½ teaspoons horseradish, or to taste
1 tablespoon lemon juice
1 pound shrimp, peeled and cooked

- Sauté onion, bell peppers and garlic cloves in oil. Cook slowly, stirring constantly. Season with salt, white pepper and curry powder.
- Add tomatoes, chopped parsley, thyme, black pepper, horseradish, and lemon juice.
- Add cooked shrimp and heat thoroughly.
- Serve over rice.

Yield: 2-3 servings

Creole Shrimp

A superb dish!

¼ cup bacon grease
¼ cup all-purpose flour
1½ cups chopped onions
1 cup chopped green onions
1 cup chopped green bell pepper
1 cup chopped celery
1 pound fresh mushrooms, sliced
1 6-ounce can tomato paste
1 16-ounce can chopped tomatoes
1 8-ounce can tomato sauce
1 cup water
5 teaspoons salt
1 teaspoon pepper
2 garlic cloves, minced
½ teaspoon cayenne pepper
⅛ teaspoon hot pepper sauce, or more to taste
2-3 bay leaves
1 teaspoon sugar
1 teaspoon thyme
1 teaspoon curry powder
1 teaspoon Worcestershire sauce
3 teaspoons lemon juice
4 pounds fresh shrimp, peeled and deveined
½ cup chopped parsley

- Make a roux of flour and bacon grease.
- Add onion, green onions, bell pepper, celery and mushrooms and sauté, until tender, 20-30 minutes.
- Add tomato paste, tomatoes, tomato sauce, water, salt, pepper and other seasonings and simmer, covered for 1 hour.
- Add shrimp and cook until done, 5-15 minutes.
- This dish needs to be made early in the day or the day before so the flavors will blend. Correct the seasoning and serve over rice garnished with parsley.

Seafood Medley

½	¾	cup butter or margarine
7	13	tablespoons all-purpose flour (¾ cup plus 1 tablespoon)
1½	3	cups half-and-half
3/4	1½	teaspoons salt, or more to taste
¼	½	teaspoon cayenne pepper
1	2	cups grated sharp Cheddar cheese
1½	3	teaspoons onion juice
3/4	1⅓	cups sherry
½	1	pound crabmeat (preferably claw meat)
½	1	pound shrimp, peeled, cleaned and steamed in butter until pink
½	1	pound scallops, steamed 2-3 minutes in own juice
1 -	2	8½-ounce cans water chestnuts, sliced
1 -	2	14-ounce cans artichoke hearts, halved
½	1	cup slivered almonds
		Parmesan cheese

- Melt butter and add flour. Stir over heat for 3 minutes, then add cream, salt and cayenne. Stir constantly and continue cooking until thickened.
- Add Cheddar cheese and stir until cheese melts.
- Add onion juice and sherry and stir.
- Line 2 large buttered casseroles with crabmeat, shrimp, scallops, water chestnuts and artichoke hearts.
- Pour in cream sauce and sprinkle with almonds and Parmesan cheese.
- Bake in a preheated oven at 325° for 30 minutes.

Yield: 16-20 servings

Chicken Shrimp Artichoke Casserole

2	8½-ounce cans artichokes, drained
2	pounds shrimp, peeled, deveined and cooked
4	whole chicken breasts, cooked and boned
1½	cups fresh mushrooms, sliced
1½	tablespoons butter or margarine
¾	cup melted butter or margarine
¾	cup all-purpose flour
3	cups milk
1	tablespoon Worcestershire sauce
	Salt and pepper to taste
½	cup sherry
¼	cup grated Parmesan cheese
	Paprika
	Parsley, chopped

- Place artichokes in bottom of buttered casserole.
- Add shrimp and chicken.
- In large skillet, sauté mushrooms in 1½ tablespoons butter. Drain and add to casserole.
- In a saucepan, combine ¾ cup butter, flour and milk. Heat until creamy.
- Add Worcestershire, salt, pepper and sherry. Pour over casserole.
- Sprinkle with cheese and dust with paprika and sprinkle parsley.
- Bake uncovered in a preheated oven at 375° for 50 minutes.

Crab may be substituted for shrimp.

Yield: 4-6 servings

169

Dill Shrimp

2 tablespoons chopped onion
1 tablespoon butter or margarine, melted
1½ pounds medium shrimp, peeled and deveined
¾ cup Chablis or other dry white wine
1 garlic clove, pressed or ⅛ teaspoon garlic powder
3 tablespoons butter or margarine
3 tablespoons all-purpose flour
1⅓ cups skim milk
2 tablespoons lemon juice (or to taste)
1 tablespoon chopped fresh dillweed or 1 teaspoon dried whole dillweed
¼-½ teaspoon salt
Hot cooked rice

- Sauté onion in 1 tablespoon butter in a large skillet until tender.
- Add shrimp, wine and garlic. Bring to a boil.
- Cook 5 minutes, stirring constantly. Remove from heat and set aside.
- Melt 3 tablespoons butter in a saucepan over low heat; add flour, stirring until smooth. Cook 1 minute.
- Gradually add milk; cook over medium heat, stirring until thickened and bubbly.
- Add lemon juice, dillweed, and salt. Add to shrimp mixture.
- Cook 5 minutes, stirring well. Serve over rice.
Yield: 4 servings

New World Shrimp

2 tablespoons butter or margarine
1 cup chopped green bell pepper
¼ cup chopped onion
1 14½-ounce can whole tomatoes
1 bay leaf
½ teaspoon sugar
¼ teaspoon ground allspice
¼ teaspoon salt
⅛ teaspoon cayenne pepper
1 pound medium shrimp, peeled and deveined
1 tablespoon fresh lime or lemon juice

- Heat butter in large skillet until hot.
- Add green bell pepper and onion; cook, stirring until almost crisp tender, about 3 minutes.
- Add tomatoes, bay leaf, sugar, allspice, salt, and cayenne, breaking tomatoes up with a spoon.
- Bring to a boil, reduce heat and simmer, uncovered until slightly thickened, about 20 minutes.
- Add shrimp; cook and stir until pink; 3-5 minutes. Stir in lime juice.
- Remove bay leaf before serving. Serve over rice.
Yield: 2-4 servings

Curried Scallops and Shrimp

3½ cups raw scallops, fresh or frozen
4 cups shrimp, cooked
4 tablespoons butter or margarine
2-3 garlic cloves, finely minced
½ cup butter or margarine
¾ cup all-purpose flour
2 tablespoons curry powder
2 tablespoons vinegar
⅔ cup milk
4½ more cups whole milk
½ cup dry sherry, optional
½ teaspoon ginger
¼ teaspoon nutmeg
¼ teaspoon cayenne pepper
3 envelopes chicken bouillon powder or 3 bouillon cubes
2 teaspoons salt
5 tablespoons chopped parsley
   Cooked rice

- Cut scallops into small pieces.
- Use small shrimp or cut large ones into chunks.
- Melt 4 tablespoons butter in a skillet; add scallops and garlic and cook 5 minutes, stirring often.
- Melt ½ cup butter or margarine in large saucepan and stir in flour.
- Stir curry powder with vinegar in a measuring cup. Fill cup with milk and add this and 4½ cups more whole milk to saucepan. If you like, ½ cup dry sherry may be substituted for ½ cup milk.
- Add ginger, nutmeg, cayenne, bouillon powder and salt. Cook, stirring constantly, until sauce has boiled 1 minute.
- Add shrimp, scallops and liquid that has cooked out of them, and parsley. Taste, and add more seasoning if necessary. Curry taste should be fairly strong and garlic taste faint but definitely there.
- Make day before and reheat.
- Serve over rice, with additional parsley; or serve in chafing dish with crisp buttered toast points.

Yield: 10-12 servings

171

Barbecue Shrimp

1   cup butter
½   cup margarine
4   garlic cloves
2   teaspoons paprika
6   tablespoons chili powder
½   cup white wine
    Juice of one lemon
⅛   teaspoon oregano
⅛   teaspoon hot pepper sauce
    Salt and pepper to taste
    Shrimp - up to 6 pounds, unpeeled

• Combine all ingredients except shrimp in saucepan and cook until butter melts.
• Place uncooked shrimp in sauce and marinate for six hours or more in refrigerator.
• Place in shallow baking pan and bake in a preheated oven at 325° for 30 minutes, stirring shrimp occasionally.

Greta Sauce

3   garlic cloves
1   tablespoon black pepper
2   tablespoons sugar
¼   cup vinegar or lemon juice
½   cup ketchup
½   cup olive oil

• Process all ingredients except the olive oil in a blender or food processor until garlic is chopped.
• Add the olive oil and continue blending until smooth.

This is wonderful on all seafood and can also be used as a salad dressing.
Yield: 1¼ cups

Grilling

Savory Grilled Potatoes

3 baking potatoes cut into ¼-inch slices
½ cup mayonnaise
3 garlic cloves, minced
½ teaspoon paprika
¼ teaspoon salt
¼ teaspoon pepper
1 large onion, sliced

- Cook potatoes in boiling salted water for 10 minutes. Drain.
- Combine mayonnaise and seasonings until well blended.
- Stir in potatoes and onions to coat.
- Divide potato mixture evenly between 4 square pieces of heavy duty foil. Seal each to form a packet.
- Place foil packets on grill over medium-hot coals.
- Cook for about 30 minutes or until potatoes are tender.

Yield: 4-6 servings

Grilled Vegetables

2 tablespoons olive oil
2 garlic cloves, blanched and puréed
Juice of 1 lemon
1 tablespoon Worcestershire sauce
1 red bell pepper, cubed
1 zucchini, sliced ½-inch thick
1 yellow summer squash, halved lengthwise and sliced ½-inch thick
4 green onions, cut in 1-inch pieces
24 snow pea pods
2 carrots, pared, blanched and sliced on the bias ½-inch thick
1 yellow pepper, cubed
1 red onion, in wedges
Salt and ground black pepper

- Preheat barbecue grill on high.
- Mix oil, garlic, lemon juice and Worcestershire sauce together in a bowl.
- Add vegetables and toss to coat. Season with salt and pepper.
- Arrange vegetables in barbecue grilling basket.
- Place basket on barbecue grill and partly cover. Cook 9 minutes on each side. Serve.

Butterflied Lamb

2 cups orange juice
1 cup honey
1 cup soy sauce
2 tablespoons grated fresh ginger
2 tablespoons chopped fresh mint
3-4 garlic cloves
Leg of lamb (butterfly cut)

- Combine all ingredients, except lamb, in a large bowl and mix well.
- Place lamb in pan and pour marinade over. Cover and refrigerate overnight.
- When ready to cook, drain lamb and reserve marinade.
- Remove to grill. Cook over hot coals 20 minutes on each side.
- Heat marinade on stove and use for gravy on rice, if desired.
  Yield: 6 servings

Grilled Lamb Chops

4 loin or rib lamb chops, 1½-inches thick
⅓ cup vegetable oil
⅓ cup lemon or lime juice
1 tablespoon tarragon wine vinegar
2 teaspoons minced fresh thyme or ½ teaspoon crumbled dry thyme
1 garlic clove, minced
⅔ cup dry red wine
1 tablespoon honey

- Trim chops of excess fat and arrange in a shallow dish.
- Combine remaining ingredients, stirring well to blend and pour over chops. Cover and refrigerate overnight or for several hours.
- When ready to cook, drain chops and reserve marinade.
- Cook chops on grill over hot coals, about 5 inches from the heat, basting occasionally.
- Turn chops and cook a total of 10 minutes, or until rare or medium rare, as desired.
- Let stand on platter a few minutes before serving.
  Yield: 4 servings

Grilled Lamb Roast

1   cup olive oil
     Garlic powder to taste
⅛   teaspoon of red wine vinegar
⅛   teaspoon Worcestershire sauce
½   cup red wine
     Salt and pepper to taste
½   teaspoon onion powder
½   teaspoon thyme
     Lamb roast

- Mix all ingredients and pour over lamb roast.
- Cover and marinate overnight in refrigerator. Drain, reserving marinade.
- Grill over medium coals until desired doneness, basting frequently with reserved marinade.

Yield: 6-8 servings

Oriental Beef

1½   pounds flank steak or rump roast
2   tablespoons sesame oil
3   tablespoons sugar
⅓   cup soy sauce
     Garlic powder to taste
     Black pepper to taste
     Onion powder to taste (or one green onion, chopped)

- Cut beef at angle in strips and place in shallow baking dish.
- Combine remaining ingredients and pour over meat.
- Marinate overnight in refrigerator, turning occasionally.
- Grill over medium coals until desired doneness.

Yield: 4-6 servings

Bourbon Steaks
Tender and delicious!

4   slices of bacon
4   filets, 2 inches thick
¼   cup bourbon
1   cup red wine
½   cup soy sauce
     Garlic powder to taste
     Black pepper to taste

- Wrap bacon around filets, securing with toothpicks.
- Combine remaining ingredients, pour over filets and marinate at least 1 hour.
- Cook on grill over medium-hot coals until desired doneness.

Yield: 4 servings

Zesty Marinated Flank Steak

6 tablespoons frozen orange juice
 concentrate
¼ cup vinegar
½ cup vegetable oil
2 tablespoons soy sauce
1 small onion, sliced
½ teaspoon rosemary, optional
½ teaspoon celery salt
½ teaspoon leaf thyme
1 small garlic clove, sliced
2½-3 pounds flank steak (can use top round or
 sirloin)

- Combine marinade ingredients and pour over meat.
- Marinate in refrigerator at least 8-12 hours.
- Cook on grill over medium-hot coals.
- Baste frequently with marinade while grilling.
 Yield: 6 servings

Fabulous Flank Steak

1 cup vegetable oil
⅔ cup dry Burgundy wine
6 tablespoons minced green onions with
 tops
2 garlic cloves, minced
2 teaspoons dry mustard
½ cup soy sauce
4 teaspoons red wine vinegar
2-4 tablespoons brown sugar
1 teaspoon basil
½ teaspoon cracked black pepper
¼ teaspoon marjoram
1½ pounds flank steak

- Combine all ingredients except steak and mix well.
- Pour half of the marinade over the steak, cover and refrigerate overnight. Reserve the remaining marinade and refrigerate for later use.
- Remove steaks from marinade and grill over medium coals until desired doneness. (For rare — no more than 5 minutes per side.)
- Cut into thin diagonal strips.
- Warm reserved marinade over medium heat and serve with meat.
 Yield: 4-6 servings

Marinated Beef Tenderloin

1⅓ cups red wine vinegar
1 cup ketchup
½ cup vegetable oil
½ cup soy sauce
¼ cup Worcestershire sauce
4 teaspoons prepared mustard
4 teaspoons monosodium glutamate, optional
4 teaspoons salt
2-4 teaspoons garlic powder
3 teaspoons onion powder
1 teaspoon pepper
1 7-9 pound beef tenderloin
6-8 strips bacon

- Combine all ingredients except tenderloin and bacon and mix well. Set aside.
- Remove fat from beef.
- Marinate tenderloin 48 hours in refrigerator, turning twice daily.
- Remove from marinade and wrap with bacon.
- Place in shallow pan and insert meat thermometer.

To Grill:
- Place coals in one end of grill.
- When coals are ready, place pan containing meat on grill at opposite end of grill from coals.
- Cover and cook by indirect method to temperature indicated for "rare", about 1½ hours.
- Baste occasionally with marinade.

To Oven Cook:
- Place tenderloin in a foil-lined pan.
- Bake in a preheated oven at 450° for 20 minutes.
- Reduce heat to 350° and cook 15 minutes more or until meat thermometer indicates "rare."
- Remove from oven and let stand 15 minutes before slicing.

Yield: 12 servings

Beef Shish Kabobs

1½ cups vegetable oil
¾ cup soy sauce
¼ cup Worcestershire sauce
2 tablespoons dry mustard
2¼ teaspoons salt
1 teaspoon coarsely ground pepper
1½ teaspoons parsley flakes
2 garlic cloves, minced
⅓ cup lemon juice
2½ pounds sirloin steak, cut in 1½ inch cubes
3 green bell peppers cut in 1-inch squares
5 small firm tomatoes, quartered
5 small onions, quartered
20 mushrooms, stems removed

- Blend first nine ingredients in a blender.
- Pour over meat, cover and refrigerate at least 4 hours.
- Drain meat, reserving marinade.
- Alternate meat, peppers, tomatoes, onions, and mushrooms on skewers.
- Grill over medium heat until desired doneness, about 15-20 minutes, basting occasionally with reserved marinade.
Yield: 6 servings

Marinated Orange Roughy

2 orange roughy fillets (fresh or thawed)
Lemon juice
Lemon dill seasoning

- Place fillets in shallow pan and cover with lemon juice. Sprinkle with lemon dill seasoning and allow to marinate 30 minutes.
- Coat grill with cooking spray.
- Grill over medium to medium-low coals until flaky, turning once.
Yield: 2 servings

Grilled Catfish Fillets

Olive oil
Garlic powder
Lemon pepper
Creole seasoning
Catfish fillets

- Coat grill or fish basket with cooking spray.
- Rub fish with olive oil and sprinkle with remaining ingredients.
- Grill over medium-hot coals, about 10 minutes per side.

Grilled Salmon Steaks

4 6-ounce salmon steaks
   Cavender's Greek seasoning to taste
   Salt and pepper to taste
2 green onions, chopped
½ cup butter or margarine, melted
4 lemons plus 1 for garnish

- Season salmon with Greek seasoning, salt and pepper.
- Place salmon on hot grill and sprinkle with about ½ of the green onions.
- Spoon melted butter over onions, covering salmon well.
- Add the juice of 2 lemons.
- Close grill and cook about 5-7 minutes.
- Turn salmon over and repeat process of toppings over salmon (remaining onions, melted butter and juice of 2 lemons).
- Close grill and cook 5-7 minutes, or until salmon flakes with a fork.
- Garnish with a slice of lemon.

  Can microwave additional onions, butter and lemon juice to serve with salmon steaks.
  Yield: 4 servings

Apple Cider Salmon

¾ cup apple cider
6 tablespoons soy sauce
1 large garlic clove, minced
2 tablespoons butter or margarine
6 salmon fillets

- Combine apple cider and soy sauce in heavy saucepan and bring to a boil over medium heat.
- Add garlic and butter and cook until it is reduced by ⅓.
- Remove from heat and let cool to room temperature.
- Pour over salmon and marinate 30 minutes.
- Grill salmon to desired doneness.
  Yield: 6 servings

Grilled Shrimp

Tangy and flavorful

½ cup butter or margarine, melted
½ cup vegetable oil
½ cup white wine
3 garlic cloves, minced
¼ teaspoon oregano
3-4 bay leaves
2 tablespoons Worcestershire sauce
1 tablespoon soy sauce
1 teaspoon seasoned salt
1 teaspoon pepper
2 pounds large shrimp, unshelled

- Combine all ingredients except shrimp, mixing well. Pour over shrimp and marinate in refrigerator 4 hours or overnight.
- Place in oiled grill basket or thread on skewers and grill over hot fire until bright orange, about 7 minutes on each side. Brush with marinade while grilling.

Yield: 4-5 servings

Sesame Ginger Chicken

Great for summer supper guests

½ cup soy sauce
¼ cup water
¼ cup vegetable oil
2 tablespoons instant minced onion
2 tablespoons sesame seeds
1 teaspoon ground ginger
1 teaspoon garlic powder
⅛ teaspoon cayenne pepper
6 boneless chicken breast halves, skinned

- Combine all ingredients, except chicken, in a large bowl. Mix well.
- Place chicken in container and pour marinade over. Marinate overnight, turning occasionally.
- Grill over medium coals until done (approximately 20-25 minutes).

Yield: 4-6 servings

Chicken Fajitas

1   cup white wine vinegar
1   cup vegetable oil
1   tablespoon minced garlic
2   tablespoons minced fresh cilantro
1   teaspoon ground cumin
    Salt and pepper to taste
4   boneless chicken breast halves
    Tortillas
    Guacamole
    Picante sauce
    Sour cream

- Combine marinade ingredients and pour over chicken breasts in a glass dish.
- Cover and chill at least 4 hours or overnight.
- Grill until done.
- Serve sliced in flour tortillas with guacamole, picante sauce and sour cream.

Yield: 4-6 servings

Honey Mustard Chicken

The number one choice of the family

½   cup mayonnaise
2   tablespoons Dijon mustard
1   tablespoon honey
4   boneless chicken breast halves, skinned

- Mix together mayonnaise, mustard and honey.
- Coat grill with cooking spray.
- Baste chicken with half of the honey mustard mixture and grill 8-10 minutes over medium-hot coals.
- Turn chicken, brush with remaining mixture and continue grilling 8-10 minutes or until done.

Make extra honey mustard for dipping.
Yield: 4 servings

Ranch Style Chicken

2 garlic cloves, crushed
1 tablespoon vegetable oil
8 ounces sour cream
1 cup prepared Ranch salad dressing
8 ounces plain yogurt
10 chicken breast halves

- Sauté crushed garlic in oil for 3 minutes.
- Combine sour cream, dressing and yogurt in a bowl. Add the oil and garlic.
- Place chicken in shallow dish and cover with sour cream mixture.
- Cover and refrigerate at least 12 hours.
- Grill over medium coals, brushing chicken with sauce.
  Yield: 10 servings

Hawaiian Chicken

8 boneless chicken breast halves, skinned
⅓ cup vegetable oil
⅓ cup soy sauce
3 garlic cloves, minced
¾ cup finely chopped onion
3 tablespoons brown sugar
3 tablespoons fresh lemon juice
  Stuffing (recipe follows)
½ cup chopped macadamia nuts
8 lemon slices

- Flatten chicken breasts and place in a large bowl.
- Combine vegetable oil, soy sauce, garlic, onion, brown sugar, and lemon juice.
- Pour mixture over chicken. Cover and marinate in refrigerator for at least 8 hours.
- Remove chicken breasts from marinade and lay flat on work surface.
- Top with stuffing, dividing evenly. Fold chicken over stuffing and secure with toothpicks.
- Grill slowly over low heat, turning occasionally and basting with marinade.
- Garnish with nuts and lemon slices.

- Heat oil in skillet. Add onion and celery and sauté. Stir in remaining ingredients, blending well. Remove from heat.
  Yield: 8 servings

Stuffing:
⅓ cup oil
¾ cup finely chopped onion
2 cups chopped celery
2 tablespoons brown sugar
3 tablespoons lemon juice
2 8-ounce cans pineapple chunks
1 teaspoon salt
¼ teaspoon black pepper

Rotisserie Chicken
Simply delicious for family or company!

2 teaspoons salt
1 teaspoon pepper
¾ teaspoon cayenne pepper
½ teaspoon onion powder
½ teaspoon thyme
¼ teaspoon white pepper
¼ teaspoon garlic powder
¼ teaspoon black pepper
1 3-pound chicken
1 cup chopped onions

• Combine thoroughly the first 8 ingredients in a small bowl.
• Rub mixture into chicken, inside and out, patting mixture into skin to make sure it is evenly distributed and deep into skin.
• Place chicken in plastic bag and refrigerate overnight.
• When ready to cook, stuff cavity of chicken with chopped onions.
• Grill, using rotisserie, over medium fire or at 250° to 300° for 2½-3 hours until golden brown.
Yield: 4 servings

Lime Chicken with Honey Butter

6 chicken breast halves, boned and skinned
3 small limes
2-3 garlic cloves, minced
4 tablespoons butter or margarine, softened
2 tablespoons honey
Salt, optional

• Place chicken in shallow glass baking dish.
• In a separate bowl, grate peel and squeeze juice from 2 limes. Add minced garlic to lime juice, blend well and pour over chicken.
• Cover with plastic wrap and marinate overnight, turning occasionally.
• Grill 7-10 minutes per side, depending on heat and thickness of chicken.
• While chicken is cooking, blend butter and honey.
• To serve, place chicken on heated platter and top with honey butter. Salt if desired.
• Slice remaining lime and use as garnish.
Yield: 6 servings

Basil Chicken

4 chicken breast halves, skinned
¾ teaspoon coarsely ground pepper
⅓ cup butter or margarine, melted
¼ cup fresh chopped basil

- Press pepper into chicken breasts.
- Combine melted butter and chopped basil and stir well.
- Brush chicken lightly with melted butter mixture.
- Grill chicken over medium heat 8-10 minutes on each side, basting frequently with remaining melted butter mixture.
- Serve with Basil Butter Spread.

Basil Butter Spread:
½ cup butter or margarine, softened
2 tablespoons chopped basil
¼ cup grated Parmesan cheese
  Garlic powder, salt and pepper to taste

- Combine ingredients in small bowl and beat at low speed until mixture is well blended and smooth. Set aside.

Basil butter is delicious on toasted bread.
Yield: 4 servings

Texas Style Game Hens

4 1¼-pound Cornish hens
½ teaspoon salt
½ teaspoon garlic powder
½ teaspoon chili powder
½ cup apple jelly
½ cup ketchup
1 tablespoon vinegar
½ teaspoon chili powder

- Rinse hens with cold water and pat dry. Split hens in half.
- Combine salt, garlic powder and ½ teaspoon chili powder. Sprinkle hens with seasonings.
- Grill over medium coals 45 minutes, turning occasionally.
- Combine apple jelly, ketchup, vinegar and ½ teaspoon chili powder in a saucepan.
- Cook over medium heat, stirring constantly, until jelly melts.
- Brush hens with sauce and grill an additional 15 minutes, turning and basting frequently with the sauce.

Yield: 6-8 servings

Rosemary Marinated Pork Tenderloin

3 tablespoons olive oil
1 tablespoon white wine vinegar
3 teaspoons chopped fresh rosemary or
   1 ½ teaspoons crushed dried rosemary
½ teaspoon salt
¼ teaspoon pepper
2 garlic cloves, crushed
2 pork tenderloins

- Combine first six ingredients, stirring well.
- Place tenderloins in an oblong baking dish and brush with marinade.
- Cover and refrigerate at least 3 hours.
- Grill, covered, over medium-hot coals, turning occasionally, for 12-15 minutes or until meat thermometer registers 160°.

You may want to double the recipe for the marinade mixture so as to have enough to brush over tenderloins while grilling.
Yield: 6 servings

Sesame Pork Tenderloin

½ cup soy sauce
¼ cup water
1 tablespoon sugar
½ teaspoon pepper
¼ cup sesame seeds
1 tablespoon vegetable oil
½ tablespoon ground ginger
2 garlic cloves, pressed
2 green onions, chopped
2 pork tenderloins

- Mix all ingredients except for the pork.
- Roll pork in the sauce and marinate overnight. (Can use a plastic bag.)
- Grill over medium coals for about 25 minutes, turning occasionally.

Yield: 6-8 servings

Grilled Dove Breasts

¾ cup olive oil
2 tablespoons balsamic vinegar or red wine vinegar
1 tablespoon snipped cilantro
1 tablespoon crushed dried oregano
3-4 garlic cloves, minced
1 teaspoon crushed dried marjoram
½ teaspoon crushed dried thyme
1 teaspoon ground cumin
12 whole dove breasts, cleaned and boned
4 ounces Monterey Jack or Cheddar cheese, cut into 24 small pieces
3 fresh jalapeño peppers, seeded and sliced into 24 strips
12 slices bacon

- Combine olive oil, vinegar, cilantro, oregano, garlic, marjoram, thyme and cumin.
- Place dove breasts in a plastic bag and pour marinade over. Marinate in the refrigerator for 4 hours, turning bag occasionally to distribute marinade.
- Drain dove breasts.
- Cut a pocket in the meaty part of each breast half and tuck a piece of cheese and a strip of jalapeño pepper into each pocket.
- Wrap a bacon slice around each breast; secure with a toothpick.
- Place dove breasts on grill and cook, uncovered, directly over medium coals for 10-15 minutes or until dove is tender and bacon is well-cooked.

Yield: 6 servings

Smoked Turkey

1 cup soy sauce
½ cup honey
1 cup sherry
1 teaspoon cinnamon
1 teaspoon pepper
½ teaspoon ground cloves
½ cup strong tea
1-2 garlic cloves, minced, optional
Turkey
½ cup red currant jelly
1 cup sour cream
1 tablespoon horseradish

- Make a marinade of the first eight ingredients.
- Place turkey in smoker — the kind with a water pan.
- Brush generously with marinade every 45 minutes.
- Smoke for 7-8 hours.
- Make a sauce by melting the currant jelly over low heat. Blend in sour cream and horseradish.
- Serve at room temperature.

Teriyaki Pork Chops
So easy and so good

4-6   pork chops
      Honey
      Teriyaki sauce

- Rub honey on one side of each pork chop and place, honey side up, in a shallow baking dish. Pour teriyaki sauce over pork chops.
- Refrigerate for at least two hours.
- Apply honey and teriyaki sauce to the other side and refrigerate for two more hours.
- Grill over medium coals to desired doneness.
  Yield: 4-6 servings

Barbequed Ribs
An all-time favorite

2   large sets pork ribs
2   quarts water
⅔   cup salt
3   lemons
2   quarts apple cider vinegar
⅔   cup black pepper
⅓   cup diced red bell pepper

- Mix the salt and water together and baste ribs for 1½ hours over an indirect fire. Cook at 250° with the top down on the grill. You may wish to add oak or hickory to your fire for a smoked flavor.
- Combine the vinegar, juice of 3 lemons and peppers and baste the ribs for 2 hours at the same temperature.
- Serve with your favorite barbeque sauce.
  Yield: 6-8 servings

Zesty Barbecue Sauce

1 14-ounce bottle ketchup
¾ cup chili sauce
¼ cup prepared mustard
½ tablespoon dry mustard
¾ cup firmly packed brown sugar
1 tablespoon pepper
¾ cup red wine vinegar
½ cup lemon juice
¼ cup Heinz 57 sauce
½ teaspoon hot pepper sauce
¼ cup Worcestershire sauce
½ tablespoon soy sauce
1 tablespoon vegetable oil
¾ cup beer

- Blend all ingredients together.
- Pour into glass jar, cover and refrigerate.
  Keeps well for several weeks in refrigerator and also freezes.
  Yield: 6 cups

Quick Barbecue Sauce

⅔ cup ketchup
⅓ cup red currant jelly
2 tablespoons Worcestershire sauce
¼ teaspoon hot pepper sauce

- Combine all ingredients and simmer for 10 minutes.
  Great for dipping chicken fingers.

189

Barbecue Sauce

¼   cup diced onion
2   cups apple cider vinegar
4   cups ketchup
1¼ cups prepared mustard
½   cup plus 2 tablespoons Worcestershire
    sauce
    Juice of 2 lemons
¼   cup butter or margarine
2   teaspoons cayenne pepper (can be
    adjusted to taste)
2   teaspoons black pepper

- Put onion and vinegar in a blender or food processor and blend to liquify.
- Mix this with remaining ingredients in a saucepan and simmer for one hour.

Can be used for poultry, beef or pork.
Yield: 2½ quarts

Chicken Marinade

1   cup vegetable oil
½   cup lemon juice
1   tablespoon salt
1   teaspoon paprika
½   teaspoon onion powder
2   teaspoons basil
½   teaspoon thyme
½   teaspoon garlic powder
⅛-¼ teaspoon soy sauce
⅛-¼ teaspoon Worcestershire sauce

- Mix all ingredients together and marinate chicken pieces as long as possible in refrigerator.
- Grill chicken slowly until done.

Vegetables

Asparagus Caesar

3   pounds fresh asparagus, trimmed and peeled
¼   cup butter or margarine, melted
¼   cup fresh lemon juice
¼   cup fresh grated Parmesan cheese
    Paprika
    Lemon slices

- Steam or boil asparagus until crisp-tender and place in a baking dish.
- Combine butter and lemon juice and pour over asparagus. Sprinkle with cheese and paprika.
- Place under broiler until browned and bubbly.
- Garnish with lemon.
  Yield: 12 servings

Marinated Asparagus

2   pounds fresh asparagus, trimmed and peeled
2   tablespoons oil
¼   cup cider vinegar
¼   cup soy sauce
¼   cup sugar
⅛   teaspoon pepper
¾   cup finely chopped pecans

- Steam or boil asparagus until crisp-tender, then drench in ice bath.
- Whisk together oil, vinegar, soy sauce, sugar and pepper.
- Stir in pecans.
- Pour marinade over asparagus and chill for at least 2 hours or overnight.
  Yield: 8-12 servings

Asparagus and Pea Casserole

4   slices fresh bread, processed in blender until fine crumbs
6   tablespoons butter or margarine, melted
1   15-ounce can very small early peas, drained
1   pound fresh asparagus, trimmed and boiled or steamed, or 1 15-ounce can asparagus, drained
1   10¾-ounce can cream of mushroom soup
1   cup grated Cheddar cheese

- Mix bread crumbs with melted butter. Set aside.
- In a greased 13x9x2-inch casserole dish layer peas, asparagus, soup and then cheese.
- Top with crumb mixture.
- Bake in a preheated oven at 350° for 30 minutes.
  Yield: 6 servings

Three Bean Bake

Nice accompaniment for outdoor summer supper

2 tablespoons butter or margarine
1 large onion, chopped
1 16-ounce can kidney beans
1 15-ounce can pork and beans
1 15-ounce can lima beans
1 8-ounce can tomato sauce
1 tablespoon vinegar
1 tablespoon prepared mustard
½ cup brown sugar
1 teaspoon pepper
4 slices of bacon, partially cooked

• Brown onions in butter and place in large mixing bowl.
• Partially drain kidney beans, pork and beans, and lima beans; then add to browned onion.
• Add remaining ingredients except bacon and mix well.
• Place in baking dish and top with bacon.
• Cook in a preheated oven at 325° for 1 hour.
  Yield: 8-10 servings

Spicy Black-eyed Peas

3 slices of bacon
1 17-ounce can black-eyed peas
1 16-ounce can tomatoes, undrained and chopped
1 cup chopped onion
1 large green bell pepper, chopped
⅛ teaspoon garlic powder
1 teaspoon ground or dry mustard
½ teaspoon curry powder
½ teaspoon chili powder
1 teaspoon salt
½ teaspoon pepper
   Parsley, finely chopped

• Cook bacon until crisp in large skillet and crumble into small pieces.
• Stir the crumbled bacon and remaining ingredients into bacon grease.
• Simmer covered for 20 minutes.
  Yield: 6-8 servings

 ## Cauliflower

1   head of cauliflower
½   cup water
1   teaspoon rosemary
1   tablespoon dried parsley flakes
2   tablespoons butter or margarine
½   cup half-and-half
    Salt and pepper
    Cayenne pepper

- Cut cauliflower buds into small flowerets, about ½ to ¾ inches in size.
- Place cauliflower in frying pan with ½ cup water (just enough to cover bottom of pan), rosemary and parsley.
- Cover and cook over high heat for approximately 5-7 minutes, shaking pan occasionally.
- Pour off any water that remains in pan, add butter, half-and-half and salt and pepper to taste.
- Cook, stirring, a few minutes longer. Just before serving, sprinkle with cayenne.

Be careful, the cream will curdle if cooked too long.
Yield: 6-8 servings

Cauliflower Bloom

1   cup water
1   medium head cauliflower
¾   cup mayonnaise
½   cup Parmesan cheese
1   teaspoon dry mustard
¼   teaspoon salt
¼   teaspoon cayenne pepper

- Bring water to boil and add cauliflower, head side down. Return to boil then simmer for 15 minutes until tender. Drain well.
- Combine mayonnaise, cheese, mustard, salt and cayenne.
- Place cauliflower, head side up in a 3-quart casserole. Spread cauliflower with mayonnaise mixture.
- Bake for approximately 8-10 minutes in a preheated oven at 375° until browned.

Grated sharp Cheddar cheese can replace Parmesan cheese.
Yield: 4 servings

Broccoli Lorraine

1 bunch broccoli
3 slices bacon, cooked and crumbled
  Salt and pepper to taste
⅛ teaspoon nutmeg
½ teaspoon dry mustard
2 eggs
1 cup half-and-half
2 tablespoons grated Parmesan cheese
1 tablespoon lemon juice

- Trim tough ends from broccoli stems. Cut off flowerets and reserve.
- Slice stems in ⅓-inch pieces. Cook in boiling, salted water for 5 minutes.
- Add flowerets and cook 2-3 minutes longer. Drain well.
- Turn into a 10-inch round baking dish and sprinkle with bacon.
- In a bowl combine salt, pepper, nutmeg and mustard.
- Add eggs and beat lightly.
- Stir in half-and-half, Parmesan cheese and lemon juice. Pour over broccoli.
- Sprinkle with additional Parmesan cheese and set dish in a pan of hot water.
- Bake in a preheated oven at 350° for 25-30 minutes.

Yield: 4 servings

Broccoli Soufflé

2 tablespoons butter or margarine
2 tablespoons all-purpose flour
1 cup heated milk
1 cup grated Cheddar cheese
¼ teaspoon salt
¼ teaspoon pepper
¾ cup mayonnaise
3 eggs, beaten
⅛ teaspoon hot pepper sauce
1 tablespoon diced onion
1 10-ounce box chopped frozen broccoli, blanched and drained
¼ cup fresh, fine bread crumbs

- Make a cream sauce with butter, flour and milk. Add cheese, salt, pepper, mayonnaise, eggs, hot pepper sauce and onion. Mix well.
- Fold in broccoli. Place in buttered casserole dish and top with bread crumbs.
- Place dish in a large pan and fill with water to come half way up the side of the casserole.
- Bake in a preheated oven at 350° for 30 minutes or until knife comes out clean.

This can be made using low-fat milk, cheese and mayonnaise.

Yield: 6-8 servings

Cheesy Broccoli and Rice

2   cups uncooked rice
2   10-ounce packages chopped frozen broccoli, cooked and drained
¼   cup butter or margarine
1   cup mixture of chopped onion, green bell pepper and celery
1   16-ounce jar pasteurized processed cheese spread
1   10¾-ounce can cream of mushroom soup
1   8-ounce can sliced water chestnuts, drained
½   cup grated Cheddar cheese

- Cook rice according to package directions. Combine with broccoli.
- In heavy skillet melt butter and sauté onion, green bell pepper and celery until crisp-tender. Add to rice and broccoli.
- Fold in processed cheese spread, mushroom soup and water chestnuts mixing thoroughly. Place in a 13x9x2-inch casserole dish and sprinkle with grated Cheddar cheese.
- Bake in a preheated oven at 350° until bubbly.

Yield: 8-10 servings

Cool Dill Carrots

2   pounds carrots, peeled and cut into ¼-inch rounds (about 5 cups)
½   cup water
⅓   cup finely chopped onions
1   tablespoon butter or margarine
½   cup mayonnaise
½   teaspoon salt
¼   teaspoon pepper
2   tablespoons prepared brown mustard
1½ teaspoons finely chopped fresh dill or ½ teaspoon dry dill

- Put carrots and water in a 2-quart microwave safe dish. Cover with plastic wrap and vent. Microwave on high for 10-14 minutes or until just tender.
- Place onions and butter in microwave safe dish. Cover and vent. Microwave on high 1-2 minutes.
- Stir mayonnaise, salt, pepper, mustard and dill into onion mixture. Add mixture to carrots and toss well. Can be served hot or cold.

Yield: 8 servings

Company Carrots

2 pounds carrots, cut into strips
¼ cup water, reserved from cooked carrots
½ cup mayonnaise
1 tablespoon minced onion
2 tablespoons prepared horseradish
Salt and pepper to taste
6 saltine crackers, crumbled
1 tablespoon parsley flakes
Paprika
2 tablespoons butter or margarine

- Cook carrots in boiling water until tender. Drain, reserving ¼ cup of water.
- Arrange carrots in a shallow 1½-quart baking dish.
- Combine mayonnaise, reserved water, onion, horseradish, salt and pepper. Pour over carrots.
- Sprinkle with cracker crumbs, parsley flakes and paprika. Dot with butter.
- Bake, uncovered, in a preheated oven 375° for 20 minutes.

Yield: 6-8 servings

Glazed Carrots

1 medium bunch carrots, peeled and sliced
½ cup butter or margarine
⅓ cup packed light brown sugar
1 teaspoon nutmeg
3 tablespoons orange juice
¼ cup honey

- Steam carrots until slightly tender.
- Sauté carrots in butter; add sugar, nutmeg, honey and orange juice.
- Cook and stir until sugar melts and carrots are glazed.

Corn Pudding

6 ears corn
½ cup butter or margarine, melted
5 eggs
2 cups half-and-half
1 tablespoon sugar
Salt and pepper to taste

- Grate corn and add to melted butter. Beat eggs and fold into corn. Add remaining ingredients; stir and place in casserole.
- Place in oven in a pan of water and cook in a preheated oven at 300° for 1 hour and 15 minutes.

Yield: 6-8 servings

Corn Tomato Zucchini Casserole

1 medium onion, chopped medium fine
1 green bell pepper, chopped medium fine
2 tablespoons butter or margarine
6 ears corn or frozen cut corn
4 medium zucchini, sliced thin
5 medium tomatoes, sliced thick
  Salt and pepper
  Lots of butter or margarine
  Buttered bread crumbs

- Sauté onion and pepper in 2 tablespoons butter for 5 minutes. Cut corn from ears and put half in a 2-quart buttered casserole.
- Layer on top of the corn, half each of the zucchini, tomatoes, onion and green bell peppers. Salt and pepper generously. Dot with plenty of butter.
- Repeat layers and cover with bread crumbs. Bake in a preheated oven at 350° for 40 minutes.
  Yield: 6 servings

Fried Green Tomatoes

So southern and so good!

2 firm green tomatoes
1 egg, beaten
¼ cup cracker meal
½ teaspoon salt
¼ teaspoon pepper
3 tablespoons oil or bacon grease

- Slice tomatoes, dip in egg and then in cracker meal mixed with salt and pepper.
- Cook in hot skillet with oil until golden brown on both sides, turning once.
  Yield: 4 servings

Okra and Tomatoes

3 pounds fresh young okra
12 slices bacon
2 medium onions, chopped
2 teaspoons salt
8 medium ripe tomatoes, peeled and chopped (or 1 16-ounce can whole tomatoes, chopped)
½ teaspoon pepper

- Wash, dry and cut okra into 1-inch pieces.
- Fry bacon in skillet until crisp. Remove and set aside.
- Add okra, onion and salt to bacon drippings in skillet and cook for 10 minutes over high heat.
- Lower heat and add tomatoes and pepper and cook for 3 minutes, stirring constantly.
- Reduce heat and simmer 30-45 minutes, stirring frequently.
- Top with crumbled bacon.
  Yield: 10-12 servings

Oven Fried Eggplant

1 eggplant
Mayonnaise
½ cup crushed buttery crackers or bread crumbs
¼ cup fresh grated Parmesan cheese
Salt and pepper

- Peel and slice eggplant in ½-inch thick rounds. Coat both sides of eggplant with mayonnaise.
- Mix together crumbs and Parmesan cheese. Dip coated eggplant in crumb mixture and sprinkle with salt and pepper to taste.
- Place on baking sheet and bake in a pre-heated 425° oven for 15 minutes or until brown on both sides. Serve immediately.

Yield: 4 servings

Tomato and Eggplant Casserole

2 medium eggplant, peeled and cut into ½-inch slices
Salt
All-purpose flour
½ cup olive oil
4 garlic cloves, minced
1 tablespoon olive oil
2 cups chopped fresh or canned tomatoes
1 teaspoon sugar
1 teaspoon dried basil
Salt and pepper to taste
1 cup fresh bread crumbs
3 tablespoons butter or margarine, melted
½ cup fresh grated Parmesan cheese

- Sprinkle eggplant with salt and set aside for 30 minutes. Wipe salt off slices, dredge in flour and fry in oil, browning both sides. Place in large casserole dish.
- Sauté garlic briefly in 1 tablespoon olive oil. Add tomatoes, sugar and basil and pour over eggplant.
- Add salt and pepper to taste. Top with bread crumbs, butter and cheese and bake in a preheated oven at 350° until bubbly.

Yield: 6 servings

Eggplant Patrice

1 small eggplant
2 medium tomatoes, sliced
1 medium onion, chopped
1 green bell pepper, chopped
 Salt, pepper and garlic salt
1½ cups grated sharp Cheddar cheese

- Slice unpeeled eggplant ¼-inch thick; parboil slices until partially tender.
- In a casserole dish, layer eggplant, sliced tomatoes, chopped onion and green bell pepper. Sprinkle with salt, pepper, garlic salt and ½ of the grated cheese. Repeat layers, ending with cheese.
- Cover and bake in a preheated oven at 400° until mixture is steaming. Remove cover, reduce heat to 350° and bake 30-45 minutes or until eggplant is tender and sauce is thick and golden brown.

Yield: 6 servings

Baked Oranges

A special touch for a special meal

6 oranges
6 apples
1 8¼-ounce can crushed pineapple in heavy syrup
1 cup sugar
¼ cup butter or margarine
¼ cup brown sugar
¼ cup pecan halves

- Halve oranges and scoop out pulp, reserving pulp, juice and orange shells. Peel apples, core and chop.
- Place orange pulp and juice, apples, pineapple and sugar in Dutch oven. Cook over slow or medium heat until cooked down, stirring often.
- Clean orange shells and fill with fruit mixture. Dot with butter, sprinkle with brown sugar and place pecan halves on top.
- Bake in a preheated 375° oven for 15-20 minutes or until heated through.

Yield: 12 servings

Hot Pineapple Casserole

1 20-ounce can pineapple chunks, drained, reserving 3 tablespoons juice
3 tablespoons all-purpose flour
½ cup sugar
1 cup grated Cheddar cheese
1 cup butter-flavored cracker crumbs
½ cup butter or margarine, melted

- Place pineapple chunks and reserved juice in a greased casserole dish.
- Mix flour and sugar and sprinkle over pineapple. Sprinkle cheese on top.
- Top with cracker crumbs and drizzle melted butter over all.
- Bake in a preheated 350° oven for 30 minutes. Serve while hot.
  Yield: 4-6 servings

Hot Curried Fruit

A sensational side dish to accompany any meal

1 29-ounce can pears, drained
1 16-ounce can apricots, drained
1 29-ounce can peaches, drained
1 8½-ounce can pineapple chunks, drained
1 16-ounce can seedless Bing cherries, drained
6 tablespoons butter or margarine
1 cup brown sugar
2 teaspoons curry powder
½ teaspoon ground ginger
½ cup sherry, optional

- Cut fruit into pieces and place in greased 3-quart baking dish.
- In a saucepan melt butter, adding sugar, curry powder and ginger. Stir until blended and pour over fruit. Add sherry if desired.
- Bake in a preheated 350° oven for 1 hour.
  Yield: 6-8 servings

Cranberry Relish

2 oranges, quartered and seeds removed
1 pound cranberries
1 cup pecans
2 cups sugar
¼ cup bourbon, optional

- Grind oranges including peel in a food processor.
- Add cranberries, pecans and sugar and continue to grind but do not pulverize.
- Mix in bourbon and refrigerate overnight.
  This will keep 3 weeks in the refrigerator.
  Yield: 12 servings

Drunken Beans

1 pound dried pinto beans
2 jalapeño peppers, chopped
¼ cup chopped cilantro
1 cup chopped green onions
3 tomatoes, peeled and chopped
1 cup beer
1½ tablespoons salt
4 tablespoons olive oil
1 garlic clove, chopped

- Wash beans; put into large pot with 2 quarts of water.
- Bring beans to a boil; cover and remove from heat. Let stand 40 minutes.
- Drain and wash beans; discard water.
- Combine beans with remaining ingredients in a large pot. Add enough water to cover beans; bring to a boil.
- Reduce heat; cover and cook until beans are tender, about 1 hour. Add more water as needed.
  Yield: 8 servings

Marinated Green Beans and Artichokes

2 pounds fresh green beans, ends trimmed
1 14-ounce can artichoke hearts, drained and chopped
1 cup sugar
1 cup oil
1 cup cider vinegar
2 garlic cloves, minced
1 tablespoon salt

- Cook green beans in salted, boiling water 7-8 minutes or until crisp-tender.
- Rinse with cold water, pat dry and place in a bowl. Add artichoke hearts.
- Mix together sugar, oil, vinegar, garlic and salt. Heat mixture until sugar is dissolved.
- Pour over beans and artichokes, toss well and cover. Refrigerate at least 4 hours (the longer the better) turning several times. Serve hot or cold.
  Yield: 8-12 servings

Sautéed Green Beans

1 pound fresh, crisp green beans
3 tablespoons butter or margarine
¼ cup freshly grated Parmesan-Reggiano cheese
Garlic salt to taste
White pepper

- Trim beans. Soak in cold water 2-3 minutes.
- Boil in 4 quarts salted water (1 tablespoon salt) 6-7 minutes if young and tender, 10-12 minutes if not. Drain when just tender to the bite.
- Put beans and butter in a skillet over medium heat. As butter melts and begins to foam, turn the beans to coat them well.
- Add cheese, turning beans to coat. Add white pepper and correct seasoning if necessary.
- Turn beans once or twice again, transfer to a warm platter and serve at once.
Yield: 4-6 servings

Stuffed Vidalias

6 large Vidalia onions
1 10-ounce package frozen chopped broccoli, cooked
1 cup grated Cheddar cheese
1 10¾-ounce can cream of mushroom soup
¾ cup crushed buttery crackers
1 egg, beaten

- Slice off top ⅓ of onions and scoop out center.
- Mix the broccoli, cheese, soup, crackers and egg and fill onions generously.
- Place onions in a greased baking dish and bake in a preheated 350° oven for 45 minutes.
Yield: 6 servings

Vidalia Onion Pie

2 pounds Vidalia onions, sliced thin
½ cup butter or margarine
3 eggs, beaten
1 cup sour cream
¼ teaspoon salt
½ teaspoon pepper
⅛ teaspoon hot pepper sauce
2 9-inch pie crusts
½ cup grated Parmesan cheese

- Sauté onions in butter.
- Combine eggs and sour cream and add to onion mixture.
- Add salt, pepper and hot pepper sauce to mixture and pour into the two pie crusts.
- Sprinkle the Parmesan cheese over each pie.
- Bake in a preheated 350° oven for 20 minutes, then reduce heat to 325° for 20 more minutes. You may want to cover edges of pie crust to prevent burning.
Yield: 6-8 servings per pie

 ## Tomato Bacon Cheese Onions

8 Spanish onions
16 slices bacon
Salt and pepper
1 1-pound can stewed tomatoes, drained
4 ounces grated New York sharp Cheddar cheese

- Cut a thick slice from the top of onions, leaving the stem end intact. Boil onions in salted water for 30 minutes.
- Drain and scoop out center, leaving a ¼-inch shell.
- Partially cook bacon. Lay 2 slices of bacon in a cross and place an onion in the center of each.
- Salt and pepper inside of onion and stuff with the tomatoes and cheese.
- Bring the ends of the bacon up around onion and secure at the top with a toothpick.
- Place onions on a rack in a pan and bake in a preheated oven at 350° for 20-30 minutes, until bacon is brown.
Yield: 8 servings

Parmesan Vidalias
Truly tasty

5 jumbo Vidalia onions
Salt and pepper to taste
14 buttery crackers
½ cup butter or margarine
1 cup grated Parmesan cheese
1 tablespoon milk

- Peel and cut onions into ½-inch thick slices. Cook in salted, boiling water until only half done. Drain in a colander.
- Place ⅓ of onions in a buttered 8-inch square casserole dish. Sprinkle with salt and pepper.
- Layer ⅓ each of the cracker crumbs, butter and Parmesan cheese. Repeat twice.
- Drizzle milk on top and bake in a preheated 350° oven for 20-25 minutes or until onions are cooked.

Yield: 4-6 servings

Gourmet Potatoes

6 medium baking potatoes
½ cup butter or margarine
2 cups grated Cheddar cheese
1½ cups sour cream
¼ teaspoon pepper
½ teaspoon celery salt
½ teaspoon onion salt

- Cook potatoes in oven with skin on. Cool. Peel and shred with a hand grater.
- Combine butter and cheese in large saucepan. Heat, stirring until cheese is melted.
- Remove from heat and add sour cream, salt and pepper. Fold in potatoes and spoon mixture into greased 2-quart casserole dish.
- Bake in a preheated 300° oven for 25 minutes.

Yield: 8 servings

New Potatoes with Basil Cream Sauce
An elegant addition

2 pounds new potatoes, unpeeled and sliced
2 tablespoons dry white wine
2 tablespoons finely chopped shallots
1½ cups whipping cream or half-and-half
¼ cup chopped fresh basil
¼ teaspoon salt
⅛ teaspoon white pepper

- Cook potatoes in boiling salted water for 10-15 minutes or until tender. Drain and keep warm.
- Combine wine and shallots in saucepan. Bring to a boil and cook 1 minute.
- Add cream, reduce heat and simmer 20 minutes, stirring occasionally. Stir in basil, salt and pepper.
- Arrange potatoes on a warmed platter, spoon sauce over potatoes and serve immediately.
Yield: 8 servings

Thyme Potatoes

5 medium potatoes, thinly sliced but not peeled
¼ cup butter or margarine, melted
¼ cup oil
2 garlic cloves, minced
½-1 teaspoon salt
1½-2 teaspoons fresh thyme or ½ teaspoon dried thyme

- Place a layer of sliced potatoes in a greased 13x9x2-inch casserole dish.
- In a small bowl combine butter, oil, garlic, salt and thyme. Brush mixture over potatoes and continue to layer and brush until every potato slice is covered well.
- Bake in a preheated oven at 400° for 25-30 minutes or until brown and tender.
Yield: 8-10 servings

Microwave New Potatoes

10-12 small new potatoes, quartered
1 medium onion, coarsely chopped
1 medium green bell pepper, coarsely chopped
3 tablespoons butter or margarine, melted
Seasoned salt to taste
Pepper to taste

- Layer quartered new potatoes in casserole dish.
- Add chopped onions and green bell pepper.
- Pour melted butter over vegetables and sprinkle with seasoned salt and pepper.
- Cover and microwave on high approximately 15 minutes or until potatoes are tender.
- Serve as is or top with grated Parmesan cheese.

Yield: 4 servings

Casserole Arroz

3 cups cooked rice
¾ pound Monterey Jack cheese, cut in strips
2 cups sour cream
1 4.5-ounce can chopped green chilies
½ cup grated Cheddar cheese

- Stir Monterey Jack cheese into hot rice. Add sour cream and green chilies.
- Put mixture into a 11x7x2-inch casserole dish and sprinkle with Cheddar cheese.
- Bake in a preheated 350° oven for 30 minutes or until heated through.

Yield: 6-8 servings

Highland Gourmet's Marinated Rice

1 6-ounce package long grain and wild rice
½ cup toasted broken pecans
3 stalks celery, chopped
3 tablespoons lemon juice
1 tablespoon white vinegar
⅓ cup oil
Salt and pepper to taste

- Prepare rice according to directions, leaving out butter. Cool. Add toasted pecans and celery.
- In small bowl whisk together lemon, vinegar, oil, salt and a generous amount of pepper. Add dressing to rice and toss well.

This improves with age.

Yield: 6 servings

Orange Rice

¼ cup butter or margarine
½ cup chopped celery
½ cup chopped onion
1¼ cups chicken broth
1 cup orange juice
¼ cup lemon juice
2 tablespoons grated orange rind
1 teaspoon salt
2 teaspoons sugar
1 cup uncooked rice

- Melt butter in saucepan and sauté celery and onion until translucent.
- Add chicken broth, orange juice, lemon juice, orange rind, salt and sugar and bring to a boil. Add rice and reduce heat.
- Simmer 20-25 minutes or until rice is tender and fluffy.

Yield: 6 servings

Plantation Rice

8 slices bacon, diced
1 medium onion, chopped
¼ cup butter or margarine
1 cup coarsely chopped pecans
1¼ cups uncooked long grain white rice
1 teaspoon salt
2¼ cups cold water
2 tablespoons chopped fresh parsley

- Sauté bacon in large saucepan until almost crisp. Add onions and sauté lightly.
- Remove bacon and onions and set aside, leaving 2 tablespoons grease in pan.
- Add butter to pan, and sauté pecans over medium heat. Remove pecans and set aside.
- Add rice and salt to pan, coating well. Add cold water, stir, bringing to a boil. Cover and simmer 25-30 minutes.
- Stir in bacon, onions, pecans and parsley.

Yield: 6-8 servings

Easy Brown Rice

1 cup uncooked long grain white rice
1 10½-ounce can French onion soup
1 10¼-ounce can beef consommé
¼ cup butter or margarine, melted
1 4-ounce can mushrooms

- Combine all ingredients.
- Pour into casserole dish.
- Cover and bake in a preheated 350° oven for 1 hour.

Yield: 6 servings

Artichoke and Spinach Casserole

2 10-ounce packages chopped frozen
   spinach
½ cup butter or margarine, melted
1 8-ounce package cream cheese,
   softened
   Juice of ½ lemon
   Salt and pepper
   Seasoned salt
   Nutmeg to taste
1 16-ounce can artichoke hearts
   Round buttery crackers, crumbled

- Cook spinach according to directions on package and drain well.
- To spinach add butter, cream cheese, lemon juice and seasonings. Blend.
- Place artichokes, cut in quarters, in bottom of a greased casserole. Add spinach mixture. Top with cracker crumbs and dot with butter.
- Bake in a preheated 350° oven for 25 minutes.

Yield: 6 servings

Butternut Squash Puff

2 cups butternut squash, seeds removed,
   peeled, cubed and boiled until tender
5 tablespoons butter or margarine, melted
½ cup sugar
½ teaspoon ground ginger
½ cup heated milk
3 eggs, beaten
2 tablespoons flaked coconut, optional

- Mash cooked squash. Add butter, then blend in sugar and ginger.
- Stir in milk. Fold in eggs and mix well.
- Pour into lightly buttered 1½-quart soufflé or casserole dish and bake in a preheated oven at 350° for 1 hour or until center is firm.

Yield: 6-8 servings

Baked Squash Casserole
A committee favorite

2   pounds squash, diced
1   large onion, chopped
2   eggs
6   tablespoons butter or margarine, melted
½   cup milk
2   tablespoons brown sugar
1   teaspoon salt or to taste
2½ cups bread, torn in small pieces
1½ cups grated sharp Cheddar cheese

- Cook squash and onion. Drain well.
- In a separate bowl, beat eggs and add next 4 ingredients. Stir in squash and onions.
- In a buttered 2-quart shallow casserole, layer bread, then squash mixture and then cheese. Repeat layers. Dot with butter and bake uncovered in a preheated oven at 350° for 45 minutes.

Sweet Potato Casserole

3 cups sweet potatoes, peeled, cubed and boiled until tender
½ cup sugar
½ cup butter or margarine, melted
½ cup heated milk
1 teaspoon vanilla
½ teaspoon salt
2 eggs, beaten

Topping:
½ cup brown sugar
⅓ cup all-purpose flour
1 cup finely chopped pecans
½ cup butter or margarine, melted

- Drain potatoes and mash while still very warm. Add sugar, butter, milk, vanilla, salt and eggs and cream well.
- Mix topping and spread over top or bake as is and use alternate topping.
- Bake in a preheated oven at 350° for 30 minutes or until firm.
- Alternate Topping: After baking, top with marshmallows and place under broiler until marshmallows turn golden brown.

Yield: 6 servings

Berry Mallow Yambake

⅓ cup all-purpose flour
⅓ cup firmly packed brown sugar
⅓ cup uncooked old fashioned or quick oats
½ teaspoon cinnamon
¼ cup butter or margarine
4 cups yams, peeled, sliced and boiled until fork tender
2 cups fresh cranberries
1½ cups miniature marshmallows

- Combine flour, sugar, oats and cinnamon; cut in butter until mixture resembles coarse crumbs.
- Arrange yams and cranberries in 16x10x2-inch casserole dish and sprinkle with crumb mixture.
- Bake in a preheated oven at 350° for 30 minutes.
- Remove from oven, sprinkle with marshmallows and broil until lightly browned, being careful not to let burn.

Yield: 6 servings

Italian Tomato Pie

1 9-inch deep dish pie crust
3 tomatoes, thick sliced
1 teaspoon salt
1 teaspoon pepper
1 teaspoon basil
1 tablespoon chives
1 cup mayonnaise
8 ounces sharp Cheddar cheese, grated

- Bake pie crust 5-7 minutes in a preheated oven at 350°.
- Place layer of tomatoes on bottom of pie crust and sprinkle with salt, pepper, basil and chives.
- Place another layer of tomatoes on top.
- Combine mayonnaise and cheese and spread over tomatoes, sealing all edges.
- Bake in a preheated oven at 350° for 35-40 minutes.

Variation: A Bacon Tomato Pie can be made by adding 6 strips of fried and crumbled bacon and leaving out the basil and chives. You may also want to decrease the amount of salt and pepper.

Zucchini Casserole

1 pound zucchini, sliced and cooked until crisp-tender
½ cup grated extra sharp Cheddar cheese
¼ cup sour cream
1 egg, slightly beaten
2 teaspoons sugar
¼ cup minced onion
½ teaspoon salt
¼ teaspoon pepper

- Combine the warm zucchini with half of the cheese.
- Mix sour cream and egg. Whisk in sugar.
- Add onion, salt and pepper.
- Fold in zucchini/cheese combination and pour into a greased baking dish.
- Bake in a preheated oven at 325° for 30 minutes.
- Top with the remaining cheese after removing from the oven.

Yield: 4 servings

Patti Howard's Zucchini and Tomatoes

2 tablespoons olive oil
1 medium onion, sliced
½ green bell pepper, cut into strips
2 small to medium zucchini, sliced
½ teaspoon salt
¼ teaspoon pepper
1 tomato, chopped, or handful of cherry tomatoes
1 cup shredded mozzarella cheese

- Stir-fry onion and pepper in olive oil for 2 minutes.
- Add zucchini and mix well. Sprinkle with salt and pepper.
- Cover and cook for 3-4 minutes, stirring occasionally.
- Remove from heat, add tomatoes and sprinkle with cheese.
- Cover and let sit for several minutes before serving.

Yield: 4-6 servings

Zucchini in Garlic Butter

2 tablespoons olive oil
1 garlic clove, finely chopped
1 shallot, finely chopped
1 pound zucchini, julienned
2 tablespoons chopped fresh parsley
½ teaspoon dried thyme
Black pepper

- Heat oil over low heat and sauté garlic and shallot for 1 minute.
- Add remaining ingredients and cook 5-8 minutes, stirring occasionally, until zucchini is crisp-tender.

Yield: 4 servings

Delightful Zucchini

1 pound zucchini
½ onion, thinly sliced
4 eggs
1½-2 cups grated Swiss cheese
Salt and pepper
½ teaspoon oregano
½ teaspoon basil

- Steam zucchini and onion; do not overcook.
- Beat eggs and add cheese.
- Mash (do not purée) zucchini and onions and add to eggs. Add salt, pepper, oregano and basil.
- Pour into greased baking dish and bake, covered, in a preheated oven at 325° until set, approximately 45 minutes to 1 hour.

Red Cabbage

Head of red cabbage, shredded
2 tablespoons butter or margarine
2 onions, chopped
4 whole cloves
2 apples, peeled and chopped
½ cup red wine vinegar
1 cup water
2 tablespoons sugar
Salt

• Combine ingredients in a pan and simmer for 3-4 hours.

Yield: 3-4 servings

Swiss Cheese Grits

Delightful for brunch

1 quart milk
½ cup butter or margarine
1 cup quick grits
1 cup grated Swiss cheese
Salt and pepper to taste
⅓ cup grated Parmesan cheese

• Bring milk and butter to a slow boil and slowly add grits, stirring until thick.

• Put grits into a large bowl and beat for 5 minutes until creamy. Add Swiss cheese, salt and pepper, mixing with a wooden spoon.

• Pour into a 2-quart greased casserole and sprinkle with Parmesan cheese.

• Dot with butter and bake in a preheated oven at 375° for 35-40 minutes.

Yield: 8 servings

Baked Grits

1 cup grits
2 cups water
2 cups milk
¼ cup butter or margarine
4 beaten eggs
½ teaspoon baking powder
Salt and pepper to taste

- Cook grits in mixture of water and milk as directed on package. Stir constantly to keep smooth. (The longer grits are cooked, the better they are, but you may have to add more liquid.)
- When grits are done, remove from heat and add butter. Allow to cool.
- Add beaten eggs, baking powder, salt and pepper, mixing well.
- Pour into a well-greased casserole dish and bake in a preheated oven at 350° for 1 hour.

Louisiana Grits

1½ cups grits
6 cups water
½ cup butter or margarine
3 teaspoons Lawry's seasoned salt
8 ounces Velveeta cheese
8 ounces sharp cheese
3 eggs, beaten
½ cup slightly browned onions
2 tablespoons chopped pimentos, optional

- Cook grits in water, as directed on box. Do not add salt to water at this time.
- Add remaining ingredients, cutting up butter and cheese into small pieces. Blend well and place in a buttered baking dish.
- Cook, uncovered, in a preheated oven at 350° for 1 hour. If not ready to serve, cover with foil and let stand.

Sweets

Chocolate Chip Pound Cake

4 eggs
1 18.25–ounce yellow cake mix
1 3.4–ounce box vanilla instant pudding
½ cup oil
1 cup water
1 6–ounce package chocolate chips
1 4–ounce bar German chocolate, grated

- Beat eggs well and add other ingredients except German chocolate and chocolate chips.
- Fold in chocolate chips and ⅔ of German chocolate.
- Pour batter into a greased and floured 10–inch tube pan and bake in a preheated 350° oven for 1 hour or until done.
- Cool slightly and turn out of pan.
- While still warm, sprinkle with remaining German chocolate.

Chocolate Pound Loaf Cakes

A great gift idea!

1½ cups butter or margarine
3 cups sugar
5 eggs
3⅓ cups all–purpose flour
½ cup cocoa
¼ teaspoon salt
1 teaspoon baking soda
1 cup sour cream
1 cup water, boiling
1 teaspoon vanilla

- Cream butter. Gradually add sugar and beat for at least 10 minutes.
- Add eggs, one at a time, mixing well after each.
- Sift dry ingredients 5 times.
- Add dry ingredients alternately with sour cream to butter and sugar mixture (beginning and ending with the dry ingredients).
- Stir in boiling water and vanilla.
- Pour into 2 greased and floured 9x5x3–inch loaf pans.
- Bake in a preheated 325° oven for 1 hour 10 minutes.
- Cool 10 minutes in pans.
  Yield: 2 9–inch loaves

Brown Sugar and Cinnamon Pound Cake

Cake:

1   18.25–ounce yellow cake mix
½   cup sugar
¾   cup butter–flavored cooking oil
1   cup sour cream
4   eggs
1   cup chopped pecans
2   tablespoons brown sugar
3   tablespoons cinnamon

Glaze:

1   cup powdered sugar
2   tablespoons butter or margarine, melted
2   tablespoons milk

- In large bowl, combine cake mix, sugar, oil and sour cream.
- Add eggs one at a time, mixing well. Batter will be very thick.
- In a separate bowl, mix together pecans, brown sugar and cinnamon.
- Pour batter and nut mixture alternately in a greased 10–inch tube pan.
- Bake in a preheated 350° oven for 1 hour. Cool, then remove from pan.

- Mix all ingredients and pour over cake.
  Variation: May use vegetable oil instead of butter–flavored cooking oil.

Sour Cream Cinnamon–Nut Pound Cake

What a treat!

1½   teaspoons sugar
1   teaspoon cinnamon
1   cup butter or margarine, softened
2   cups sugar
2   eggs
1   8–ounce carton sour cream
2   cups all–purpose flour, unsifted
1   rounded teaspoon baking powder
¼   teaspoon salt
1   cup finely chopped pecans
1   teaspoon vanilla

- Combine sugar and cinnamon. Set aside.
- Cream butter and sugar. Add eggs one at a time.
- Beat in sour cream.
- Mix together flour, baking powder and salt. Slowly add to batter, mixing well.
- Stir in pecans and vanilla.
- Pour ⅓ batter into well–greased 10–inch tube pan.
- Sprinkle with sugar and cinnamon mixture.
- Pour in remaining batter.
- Bake in a preheated 325° oven for 1 hour 20 minutes or until done.

217

Cream Cheese Pound Cake

1½ cups butter or margarine
1 8–ounce package cream cheese, softened
3 cups sugar
3 cups cake flour, sifted
6 large eggs, room temperature

- Cream butter and cream cheese together.
- Add sugar and beat until light.
- Add flour and eggs alternately, beating after each addition.
- Pour batter into a greased and floured 10–inch tube pan.
- Bake in a preheated 300° oven for 90 minutes.
- Cool on a wire rack for 20 minutes, then remove from pan.

 ## Chocolate Dish Cake

Cake:
1 cup water
½ cup butter or margarine
½ cup vegetable oil
3 tablespoons cocoa
2 cups all–purpose flour, sifted twice
½ teaspoon salt
2 cups sugar
2 eggs
½ cup buttermilk
1 teaspoon baking soda

Chocolate Icing:
½ cup butter or margarine
4 tablespoons cocoa
6 tablespoons milk
1 teaspoon vanilla
1 1–pound box powdered sugar
  Chopped pecans, optional

- Bring the first 4 ingredients to a boil, stirring constantly. Remove from heat.
- In a large mixing bowl combine flour, salt and sugar. Add the hot cocoa mixture.
- Mix the eggs, buttermilk and soda in a separate bowl. Add to the above mixture.
- Pour into a greased 13x9x2–inch glass dish and bake in a preheated 350° oven for approximately 30 minutes.
- Leave in dish and ice while still warm.

- Bring first 3 ingredients to a boil and remove from heat.
- Add vanilla and sugar, mixing well.
- Stir in pecans, if desired.
  Yield: 24 2–inch squares

Chocolate Praline Cake
Sensational!

Praline Sauce:
- ½ cup butter or margarine
- ¼ cup whipping cream
- 1 cup brown sugar
- ¾ cup chopped pecans

Cake:
- 1 18.25–ounce devil's food cake mix
- 1¼ cups water
- ⅓ cup oil
- 3 eggs

Frosting:
- 1¾ cups whipping cream
- ¼ cup powdered sugar
- ¼ teaspoon vanilla

  Pecans, finely chopped, optional

- Heat butter, whipping cream and brown sugar just until butter melts.
- Pour evenly into two 9–inch cake pans.
- Sprinkle with pecans.

- Mix cake mix, water, oil and eggs on low speed for 1 minute, then 2 minutes on high speed.
- Carefully spoon batter over praline mixture, dividing evenly into pans.
- Bake in a preheated 325° oven for 45 minutes.
- Begin to prepare frosting 10 minutes before layers complete baking.

- Beat whipping cream until soft peaks form.
- Add powdered sugar and vanilla and continue beating until soft peaks reappear.

Assembly:
- Remove cake layers from oven when done.
- Immediately turn one layer onto cake stand.
- Spread ½ frosting onto layer.
- Immediately place second layer on first layer and frost the top of the cake.
- Keep refrigerated until 15 minutes before serving.

  If desired, sprinkle top of cake with finely chopped pecans.

Oreo Cheesecake
Worth the time to prepare!

Crust:

1¼ cups graham cracker crumbs
⅓ cup unsalted butter or margarine, melted
¼ cup firmly packed light brown sugar
1 teaspoon cinnamon

Cheesecake:

4 8–ounce packages cream cheese, softened
1¼ cups sugar
2 tablespoons all–purpose flour
4 extra large eggs
2 large egg yolks
⅓ cup whipping cream
1 teaspoon vanilla
1½ cups coarsely chopped Oreos

Sour Cream Topping:

2 cups sour cream
¼ cup sugar
1 teaspoon vanilla

Fudge Glaze:

1 cup whipping cream
1 8–ounce package semi–sweet chocolate, chopped
1 teaspoon vanilla
5 Oreos, halved crosswise
1 cherry, halved

- Blend all ingredients in bottom of a 9- or 10–inch springform pan, then press onto bottom and sides.
- Refrigerate about 30 minutes.

- Beat cream cheese on lowest speed until smooth. Beat in sugar and flour until well blended.
- Beat in eggs and yolks until mixture is smooth.
- Stir in cream and 1 teaspoon vanilla.
- Pour half batter into crust and sprinkle with chopped Oreos. Pour remaining batter over Oreos, smoothing with spatula.
- Bake in a preheated 425° oven for 15 minutes. Turn oven down to 225° and bake an additional 50 minutes. Cover with foil if browning too quickly. Remove from oven.
- Increase oven temperature to 350°.

- Blend sour cream, sugar and vanilla until smooth.
- Spread over cake and return to oven.
- Bake for 7 minutes.
- Refrigerate immediately. When cool, cover with plastic wrap and chill overnight.

- Scald cream in a heavy saucepan over high heat.
- Add chocolate and vanilla and stir for 1 minute. Remove from heat and stir until all chocolate is melted.
- Refrigerate glaze for 10 minutes.

Continued on next page

Oreo Cheesecake (Continued)

Assembly:
- Put cake on platter and remove springform pan.
- Pour glaze over top of cake, smoothing with a pastry brush.
- If desired, arrange Oreo halves cut side down around outer edge of cake and place cherry halves in center.
- Refrigerate until ready to serve.

...tter Chocolate Chip Cheesecake

Crust:
- 1¼ cups fi... ...m crackers
- ⅓ cup sugar
- ¼ cup cocoa
- ⅓ cup butter or margarine, melted

Filling:
- 3 8–ounce packages cream cheese, softened
- 1 14–ounce can sweetened condensed milk
- 1 10–ounce package peanut butter chips, melted
- 2 teaspoons vanilla
- 4 eggs
- 1 cup mini semi–sweet chocolate chips

- Stir together graham cracker crumbs, sugar, cocoa and butter.
- Press into bottom of 9–inch springform pan.

- In a large mixing bowl, beat cream cheese until fluffy.
- Gradually add sweetened condensed milk and peanut butter chips, beating until cream cheese is smooth.
- Add vanilla, then eggs, one at a time. Beat well.
- Stir in mini semi–sweet chocolate chips.
- Pour into crust.
- Bake in a preheated 300° oven for 55–65 minutes or until center is set.
- Cool on counter top.
- Refrigerate 1 hour before serving.

Sour Cream Cheese Cake

Crust:

1¾ cups finely crushed honey–made graham crackers
6 tablespoons butter or margarine, melted
¾ cup sugar
1 teaspoon ground cinnamon

- Blend all ingredients.
- Press in bottom of a 9- or 10–inch springform pan.

Filling:

4 eggs, room temperature
1 cup sugar
3 8–ounce packages cream cheese, room temperature
7 tablespoons milk, room temperature

- Beat eggs. Add sugar and mix until smooth.
- Add cream cheese and beat until creamy.
- Blend in milk.
- Pour over crust and bake in a preheated 300° oven for 1 hour 10 minutes. Center will not be firm.
- Prepare the topping while the cake is cooling 5 minutes.

Sour Cream Topping:

2 cups sour cream
¾ cup sugar
1 teaspoon vanilla

- Mix together and pour over cake.
- Return to oven and bake 5 minutes.
  Variation: Serve with a fresh fruit topping.

Chocolate Cake

1 12–ounce package semi–sweet chocolate chips
5 tablespoons strong coffee
1 cup butter or margarine
2 cups sugar
6 eggs, separated
1 cup all–purpose flour

- In a double boiler, melt chocolate chips in coffee. Cool and set aside.
- Cream butter and sugar.
- Add egg yolks one at a time to creamed mixture. Add flour.
- In a separate bowl, beat egg whites until stiff.
- Mix chocolate into egg whites. Fold into flour mixture.
- Pour into a greased and floured 9–inch springform pan and bake in a preheated 350° oven for 60–70 minutes. When done, the cake top will be crusty and cracked and the middle will be slightly moist.

Hershey Chocolate Cake

1 cup all-purpose flour
1 teaspoon baking powder
½ teaspoon salt
½ cup butter or margarine, softened
1 cup sugar
4 eggs, beaten
1 1-pound can Hershey's chocolate syrup
1 teaspoon vanilla

Icing:
¾ cup cocoa
½ cup butter or margarine, melted
1 1-pound box powdered sugar
½ cup evaporated milk
½ teaspoon salt
1 teaspoon vanilla

- Sift first three ingredients together and set aside.
- Cream butter and sugar until smooth and lemon colored.
- Add eggs, chocolate syrup, dry ingredients and vanilla, mixing well.
- Pour into 3 waxed paper lined 8-inch round pans or a 13x9x2-inch glass casserole dish that is well greased and floured.
- Bake in a preheated 350° oven for 25 minutes in round pans, or 45-60 minutes in oblong pan.
- Cool cake 15 minutes, then remove from pans.
- Ice when completely cooled.

- Mix all ingredients and spread on cake.
  Variation: For Kahlúa icing, delete salt and add ¼ cup Kahlúa. When using Kahlúa icing, keep cake in refrigerator or freezer.

Banana Nut Cake

Cake:
- 1 cup butter or margarine
- 2 cups sugar
- 2 eggs
- 3 cups all–purpose flour
- 2 teaspoons baking soda
- ¾ cup milk
- 1½ cups mashed very ripe bananas

- Cream butter and sugar.
- Add eggs.
- Alternately add flour, soda and milk.
- Fold in bananas.
- Pour into two 9–inch round pans or one 13x9x2–inch baking pan, greased and floured.
- Bake in a preheated 350° oven for 25 minutes.

Icing:
- 1 8–ounce package cream cheese
- 1 1–pound box powdered sugar
- 6 tablespoons butter or margarine
- Milk
- 2 teaspoons vanilla
- 1 cup chopped pecans

- Mix cream cheese, powdered sugar and butter until blended well. Add very small amounts of milk until icing is smooth.
- Add vanilla, then pecans.
- Ice cooled cake.

Carrot Cake

Cake:
- 2 cups sugar
- 4 eggs
- 1½ cups oil
- 2 cups all–purpose flour
- 2 teaspoons baking soda
- 2½ teaspoons cinnamon
- 3 cups grated carrots

- Mix together sugar, eggs and oil until creamy.
- In a separate bowl, sift together flour, soda and cinnamon. Add to creamed mixture.
- Blend in carrots.
- Pour in 3 greased and floured 9–inch round cake pans.
- Bake in a preheated 325° oven for 30 minutes.

Icing:
- 1 8–ounce package cream cheese, softened
- 1 1–pound box powdered sugar
- 1 cup chopped pecans
- 6 tablespoons butter or margarine
- 2 teaspoons vanilla

- Cream together all ingredients.
- Ice cooled cake.

Favorite Jam Cake

1 cup butter or margarine
1½ cups dark brown sugar
3 cups all–purpose flour
½ teaspoon salt
1 teaspoon baking soda
½ teaspoon nutmeg
1 teaspoon cinnamon
1 teaspoon allspice
1 cup buttermilk
3 eggs
1 cup jam, any flavor

- Cream butter and sugar.
- Mix dry ingredients and add alternately with buttermilk.
- Add eggs and blend well.
- Fold in jam.
- Pour into a greased and floured 10–inch tube pan.
- Bake in a preheated 350° oven for 45 minutes or until done to touch.

Blackberry jam makes a delicious cake!

Plum Cake

Cake:
2 cups self–rising flour
2 cups sugar
1 teaspoon cinnamon
1 teaspoon ground cloves
1 cup vegetable oil
3 eggs
2 4–ounce jars of baby food plums
1 cup chopped pecans, optional

Glaze:
1 cup powdered sugar
3 tablespoons fresh lemon juice

- Combine all ingredients in a bowl and beat well on medium speed. Stir in pecans, if desired.
- Pour into a greased and floured 10–inch Bundt pan.
- Bake in a preheated 350° oven for 50 minutes.
- Cool cake in pan for 10 minutes, then glaze with the following.

- Combine powdered sugar and lemon juice.
- Drizzle over cake while hot.

Freezes well.

Apple Pecan Cake
Moist and delicious!

Cake:

- 2 cups sugar
- 3 eggs, beaten
- 1½ cups oil
- 3 cups all–purpose flour
- 1 teaspoon baking soda
- 1 teaspoon salt
- 1 teaspoon vanilla
- ½ teaspoon cinnamon
- 3 cups chopped apples
- 1 cup chopped pecans
- ½ cup wheat germ
- 3 tablespoons lemon juice

- Mix sugar, eggs and oil.
- Add remaining ingredients and mix thoroughly.
- Pour into a 10–inch greased and floured Bundt pan.
- Bake in a preheated 350° oven for 45–55 minutes.
- Glaze with one of the following:

Powdered Sugar Cinnamon Glaze:

- 1 cup powdered sugar
- 2 tablespoons butter or margarine, melted
- ½ teaspoon cinnamon
  Orange juice

- Combine powdered sugar, butter and cinnamon.
- Add enough orange juice to thin the mixture.
- Pour over hot cake.

Brown Sugar Glaze:

- 1 cup dark brown sugar
- ¼ cup evaporated milk
- ½ cup butter or margarine
- 1 teaspoon vanilla

- Combine all ingredients in saucepan.
- Boil 5 minutes.
- Pour over warm cake.

Buttermilk Glaze:

- ¾ cup sugar
- ½ cup buttermilk
- ½ teaspoon baking soda
- 2 tablespoons corn syrup
- ½ cup butter or margarine
- ½ teaspoon vanilla

- Begin preparing the glaze 15 minutes before cake completes baking.
- Combine all ingredients in saucepan and cook over low heat until sugar melts. Using medium heat, bring to rolling boil and boil 10 minutes, stirring often.
- Pour over hot cake while cake is still in pan. Cool.
- Remove to cake plate, cover with foil and chill.
- Store refrigerated.

Cake in a Pan

½ cup butter or margarine
1¼ cups all–purpose flour, sifted
1 cup sugar
1 cup chopped pecans
2 teaspoons cinnamon
1 teaspoon baking soda
½ teaspoon salt
1 egg
1 teaspoon vanilla
1 8¾–ounce can crushed pineapple, with juice
1 4–ounce jar baby food sweet potatoes

• Melt butter in 9–inch baking pan.
• Add remaining ingredients, mixing with a fork until smooth.
• Bake in a 350° preheated oven for 30 minutes or until cake tests done.

Poppy Seed Cake

Cake:

¼ cup poppy seeds
1 cup unsweetened pineapple juice
1 18.25–ounce yellow cake mix
1 3.4–ounce package instant vanilla pudding
5 eggs, slightly beaten
½ cup vegetable oil
1 tablespoon almond extract

Glaze:

¼ cup sugar
¼ teaspoon poppy seeds
2 tablespoons orange juice
¼ teaspoon almond extract
¼ teaspoon butter flavoring

• Soak poppy seeds in pineapple juice for 1 hour.
• Using electric mixer, mix together remaining ingredients. Add pineapple juice and poppy seeds and blend.
• Spray a 10–inch Bundt or tube pan with non–stick vegetable spray. Pour batter into pan.
• Bake in a preheated 350° oven for 1 hour.
• Test cake to make sure center is done. Cool.

• Combine all ingredients until smooth and pour over cooled cake.

Lemon Cake

Cake:

1 3–ounce box lemon gelatin
¾ cup boiling water
4 eggs
¾ cup oil
1 18.25–ounce yellow cake mix
1 teaspoon vanilla

Icing:

6 tablespoons freshly squeezed lemon
   juice
2 cups powdered sugar
   Grated rind from 1 lemon

- Mix gelatin with boiling water, then let cool.
- Beat eggs and oil, then add cake mix and vanilla.
- Stir in gelatin.
- Pour in a greased and floured 10–inch Bundt pan and bake in a preheated 300° oven for 1 hour.

- Mix lemon juice, powdered sugar and rind until smooth.
- Spread icing over hot cake.
  Yield: 1 10–inch Bundt cake or 3 small loaf cakes

Orange Blooms

Too wonderful to eat just one

Cupcakes:

1 18.25–ounce yellow cake mix
4 eggs
1 3.4–ounce package instant lemon
   pudding
¾ cup orange juice
¾ cup oil

Glaze:

2 tablespoons oil
⅓ cup, plus 2 tablespoons orange juice
2 cups powdered sugar

- Mix all ingredients and pour into mini–muffin pans sprayed with non–stick vegetable oil.
- Bake in a preheated 350° oven for 8–10 minutes.

- Mix all ingredients until smooth.
- Dip top of cupcakes in glaze and set on wire rack.
  Yield: 48 cupcakes

Gran's Lemon Cheese Cake

Cake:

- 3 cups all–purpose flour, sifted
- 3½ teaspoons baking powder
- 1 cup butter or margarine, softened
- 1¾ cups sugar
- ¾ cup milk
- 6 egg whites
- 1 teaspoon vanilla

Lemon Cheese Filling:

- ¾ cup sugar
- 4 tablespoons butter or margarine
- 1 tablespoon cornstarch
  Juice and grated rind from 2 large lemons
- 6 egg yolks, well beaten

- • Sift flour and baking powder together.
- • Cream butter and sugar. Add flour and milk alternately.
- • In a separate bowl, beat egg whites, then fold into batter. Add vanilla.
- • Grease pans and line with waxed paper. Divide batter into 3 pans and bake in a preheated 350° oven for 25 minutes.

- • Mix sugar, butter, cornstarch, lemon juice and rind in top of double boiler. Add well–beaten egg yolks and cook until thick.
- • Let this cool completely before spreading. Do not spread too near the edge of cake.

Easy Chocolate Frosting

- ½ cup butter or margarine, softened
- ½ cup cocoa
- ¼ cup plus 2 tablespoons hot water
- 1 teaspoon vanilla
- 1 1–pound box powdered sugar, sifted
- 1 cup chopped pecans, optional

- • Combine first 4 ingredients and blend until smooth.
- • Gradually add powdered sugar, mixing well.
- • Stir in chopped pecans.

 *Mary's Caramel Icing*

3   cups sugar
1   cup evaporated milk
½   cup butter or margarine
1   teaspoon vanilla
¼   cup sugar
¼   cup boiling water

- Combine first 4 ingredients in a saucepan and heat on low to melt butter.
- Put remaining sugar in a heavy skillet and cook on medium high until sugar has melted and turned a caramel color.
- Add boiling water and stir well.
- Pour melted sugar into milk mixture in saucepan; turn heat to medium and bring to a slow boil.
- Boil about 8–10 minutes or until it reaches soft ball stage. Stir occasionally.
- Remove from heat; cool slightly, then beat to spreading consistency.
- Quickly spread on cake. If icing should harden too quickly, keep a glass of warm water handy to dip spatula in.

 *Never Fail White Icing*

2   cups sugar
½   cup water
2   egg whites
8   large marshmallows, cut up
1   teaspoon vanilla

- Combine sugar and water in a saucepan and place on cold burner.
- Beat egg whites with electric mixer. When eggs are almost stiff, add marshmallows.
- At this time, turn heat on under sugar and water. When sugar water starts to boil (making a syrup), add 6 tablespoons of the syrup to the egg mixture as it is mixing.
- Turn mixer off until syrup on stove spins a thread or reaches 238° on candy thermometer.
- Turn mixer back on and pour in the remaining syrup. Beat until spreading consistency.
- Add vanilla, being careful not to overbeat.

Joyce Christie's Fudge Pie

2   9–inch deep dish pie crusts
6   ounces chocolate chips
¼   cup butter or margarine
2   eggs
1½ cups sugar
⅛   teaspoon salt
3   heaping teaspoons cornstarch
1   14–ounce can sweetened condensed
    milk
1   5–ounce can evaporated milk
⅓   cup pecans or almonds, slightly toasted

• Bake pie crusts for 6 minutes at manufacturer's suggested temperature.
• Melt chocolate chips and butter in the micro-wave oven.
• Mix remaining ingredients, except pecans, and add to the chocolate mixture.
• Divide evenly in pie crusts then top with pecans or almonds.
• Bake in a preheated 350° oven for 40 minutes.
• Serve warm or refrigerate for fudge–like texture.

Brownie Pie

2   squares unsweetened chocolate
½   cup butter or margarine
1   cup sugar
2   eggs
¼   cup all–purpose flour
1   teaspoon vanilla
¼   cup chopped pecans, optional
    Whipped cream or ice cream

• Melt chocolate and butter in medium sauce-pan.
• Add remaining ingredients, except pecans, and mix well. Stir in pecans, if desired.
• Pour into a well–greased 9–inch pie plate and bake in a preheated 350° oven for 30 minutes.
• Serve with whipped cream or ice cream.

Mom's Chocolate Pie

¼   cup butter or margarine, melted
2   eggs, slightly beaten
2   tablespoons all–purpose flour
1½ cups sugar
4   tablespoons cocoa
1   teaspoon vanilla
½   cup evaporated milk
1   9–inch unbaked pie crust

• Mix all ingredients together and pour into pie crust.
• Bake in a preheated 350° oven for 40–45 minutes or until set.

Chocolate Chip Pecan Pie

1 cup sugar
4 tablespoons cornstarch
2 eggs, slightly beaten
½ cup butter or margarine, melted and cooled
1 teaspoon vanilla
1 6–ounce package semi–sweet chocolate chips
1 cup finely chopped pecans
1 9–inch unbaked deep–dish pie crust
Vanilla ice cream, optional

- Combine sugar and cornstarch and beat in eggs.
- Mix in butter, vanilla, chocolate chips and pecans.
- Pour into pie crust and bake in a preheated 350° oven for 40 minutes or until puffy and lightly browned.
- Serve with vanilla ice cream, if desired.
  Variation: May add 3–4 tablespoons bourbon.

Chocolate Angel Pie

Meringue Crust:

2 egg whites
⅛ teaspoon cream of tartar
⅛ teaspoon salt
½ cup sugar
½ teaspoon vanilla
½ cup chopped pecans

- Beat egg whites until frothy. Add cream of tartar and salt and continue beating until whites stand in small peaks.
- Add sugar gradually, beating until very stiff.
- Fold in vanilla and chopped pecans.
- Turn into a greased 9–inch pie plate and shape like a pie crust in the dish.
- Bake in a preheated 275° oven for 45 minutes. Turn off oven and leave for an additional 15 minutes.
- Cool meringue thoroughly before adding filling.

Filling:

1 cake of Baker's German sweet chocolate
3 tablespoons hot water
1 teaspoon vanilla
1 cup heavy cream, whipped

- Melt chocolate in top of double boiler, add hot water. Blend and cool.
- Add vanilla and fold in whipped cream. Pour into meringue crust and refrigerate.
  Best made the day before serving.

Mud Pie

Pie:
- 2 cups crumbled chocolate sandwich cookies
- ½ cup butter or margarine, melted
- 1 quart coffee ice cream, softened

- Combine cookie crumbs and melted butter until all crumbs are moist.
- Press into a 9–inch pie plate.
- Fill pie crust with softened ice cream, top with Fudge Sauce and freeze.
- When ready to serve, slice and serve with additional warm Fudge Sauce, if desired.

Fudge Sauce:
- 5 1–ounce squares semi–sweet chocolate
- 1¾ cups sugar
- ½ cup butter or margarine
- ¼ teaspoon salt
- 1 13–ounce can evaporated milk
- 1 teaspoon vanilla

- Melt chocolate over low heat.
- Add sugar, butter and salt and bring to a boil.
- Add milk. Bring back to a boil and remove from heat.
- Cool; add vanilla and blend. Serve hot.
  Variation: Substitute chocolate graham cracker crumbs. You can also use chocolate ice cream softened and mixed with 1 table-spoon instant coffee granules dissolved in 3 ounces of Kahlúa.

Presidential Peanut Butter Pie

- 6 ounces cream cheese, softened
- 1 cup peanut butter
- 1 cup powdered sugar
- ½ cup milk
- 1 8–ounce carton non–dairy frozen whipped topping, thawed
- 1 9–inch graham cracker pie crust

- Beat cream cheese until fluffy.
- Add peanut butter and sugar, then gradually add milk.
- Stir in whipped topping.
- Pour into crust and freeze.
- Remove pie from freezer 30 minutes before serving.
- Garnish with chocolate syrup, if desired.
  Variation: Use a chocolate pie crust.

Apples and Cream Crumb Pie

Pie:

- 1½ cups sour cream
- 1 egg
- 1 cup sugar
- ¼ cup all–purpose flour
- 2 teaspoons vanilla
- ½ teaspoon salt
- 3 pounds Golden Delicious or Granny Smith apples, peeled, cored and cut into chunks
- 1 9- or 10–inch unbaked pie crust

- Mix all ingredients together, except apples, with a wire whisk.
- Stir in apples and pour into pie crust.
- Bake in a preheated 450° oven for 10 minutes. Reduce heat to 350° and bake for 35–40 minutes or until set.

Topping:

- ½ cup all–purpose flour
- 1 tablespoon cinnamon
- ¼ teaspoon salt
- ⅓ cup sugar
- ⅓ cup brown sugar
- ½ cup cold butter or margarine
- 1 cup coarsely chopped walnuts

- Combine flour, cinnamon, salt and sugars.
- Cut cold butter into dry mixture. Do not cream.
- Add walnuts.
- Spoon this mixture onto baked pie and return to oven for 15 minutes.

Great served with vanilla ice cream!

Southern Pecan Pie

- 3 eggs, beaten
- ½ cup sugar
- ⅓ cup butter or margarine, melted
- 1 cup white corn syrup
- 1 teaspoon vanilla
- 1 cup chopped pecans
- 1 9–inch unbaked pie crust

- Combine eggs and sugar.
- Stir in melted butter.
- Add remaining ingredients and pour into pie crust.
- Bake in a preheated 325° oven for 55 minutes.
- Pie will cut better if left to cool overnight.

Sour Cream Pecan Pie

1	9–inch pie crust
2	teaspoons all–purpose flour
½	teaspoon cinnamon
1	cup sour cream
2	eggs
1¼	cups sugar
1	teaspoon vanilla
1¼	cups chopped or halved pecans

- Bake pie crust at 350° for 7 minutes; set aside.
- Combine flour, cinnamon and sour cream and mix at medium speed.
- Beat in eggs, sugar and vanilla until well–blended. Stir in pecans.
- Pour into pie crust and bake in a preheated 350° oven for 40–45 minutes or until set.
- Serve at room temperature or slightly warm.

Strawberry Pie

1	quart fresh strawberries
3	tablespoons cornstarch
1	cup cold water
1	cup sugar
4	tablespoons strawberry gelatin
1	9–inch pie crust, baked
	Whipped cream or non–dairy frozen whipped topping

- Wash and stem berries, reserving 1 cup of prettiest berries for garnish.
- Slice other berries once or twice, depending on size.
- Mix cornstarch with a small amount of the cold water until smooth.
- Mix remaining water and sugar and add to the cornstarch.
- Cook on stove stirring constantly until almost clear, about 15–20 minutes.
- Add gelatin and cool.
- Arrange sliced berries in the baked crust.
- Pour cooled mixture over berries and refrigerate until it congeals.
- Top with whipped cream and garnish with the reserved whole berries.

Key Lime Pie

Irresistibly refreshing!

2   14–ounce cans sweetened condensed milk
4   egg yolks, beaten
¾   cup lime juice
1   tablespoon grated lime peel
1   9–inch graham cracker crust
2   cups heavy cream, whipped
8   lime slices
    Mint leaves

- Mix condensed milk with egg yolks, lime juice and peel.
- Pour into pie crust and bake in a preheated 300° oven for 5 minutes.
- Refrigerate for 1 hour.
- Cover with whipped cream and garnish with lime slices and mint.

Fresh Peach Pie

½   cup sugar
½   cup all–purpose flour
⅛   teaspoon salt
6   fresh peaches, peeled and sliced
2   9–inch unbaked pie crusts, room temperature
    Juice of 1 lemon
    Freshly grated nutmeg
    Milk
    Sugar

- Mix sugar, flour and salt and stir into sliced peaches.
- Pour peaches into one of the unbaked pie crusts and squeeze lemon juice over top. Dust with grated nutmeg.
- Dampen edges of pie crust with water and invert second pie crust over to make top crust.
- Mash the edges of the crusts with a fork. Pierce the top crust, brush it with milk, then sprinkle with a little sugar.
- Place pie on baking sheet and bake in a preheated 425° oven for 10 minutes. Reduce heat to 350° and bake 45–50 minutes longer.

Egg Custard Pie

2   cups milk
3   eggs, beaten
1   cup sugar
1   teaspoon vanilla
⅛   teaspoon nutmeg
1   9–inch unbaked pie crust

- Scald the milk, being sure to stir constantly so it won't stick.
- Mix scalded milk with remaining ingredients.
- Pour into pie crust.
- Bake in a preheated 325° oven for 50 minutes or until set.

236

Lemon Meringue Pie

Always a Favorite!

5 eggs
¾ cup sugar
5 tablespoons water
6–8 tablespoons fresh lemon juice
 Grated rind of 1 lemon
¼ cup butter or margarine
1 9–inch pie crust, baked
¼ teaspoon cream of tartar
6 tablespoons sugar

- Separate 3 eggs, saving 3 whites for meringue.
- Beat 2 eggs and 3 yolks until light; add sugar gradually, beating constantly.
- Add water, lemon juice and rind, then put in double boiler over hot water.
- Add butter and cook until thickened. Pour mixture into baked pie crust.
- Beat egg whites until frothy.
- Add cream of tartar and continue beating until stiff enough to hold a point.
- Gradually beat in sugar and continue beating until mixture is stiff and glossy. Spread on pie filling.
- Bake in a preheated 300° oven for 15–20 minutes.

Filling can also be used in a lemon cheese cake.

Yield: Serves 6–8

Banana Cream Pie

1 9–inch deep dish pie crust
2–3 bananas
2 tablespoons butter or margarine
¾ cup sugar
⅛ teaspoon salt
⅓ cup all–purpose flour
2 eggs, well beaten
2 cups milk, scalded
½ teaspoon vanilla
 Whipped cream

- Bake pie crust according to directions and cool.
- Slice bananas and put in pie crust.
- In a double boiler, combine butter, sugar, salt, flour and eggs.
- Slowly add scalded milk, stirring constantly.
- Cook over hot water until thick and smooth.
- Add vanilla and stir well. Set aside to cool.
- Pour cooled custard into pie crust and top with whipped cream.

Variation: Use fresh sliced peaches instead of bananas.

Lemon Cheese Pie

Graham Cracker Crust:
- 1½ cups graham cracker crumbs, finely crushed
- 2 tablespoons sugar
- ¼ cup unsalted butter or margarine, melted

• Mix ingredients and press into a 8–inch pie plate.

Filling:
- 2 eggs
- ⅔ cup sugar
- 12 ounces cream cheese, softened
- Grated rind of ½ lemon
- 1½ tablespoons fresh lemon juice

• Beat eggs and slowly mix in sugar, cream cheese, lemon rind and lemon juice.
• Pour into pie crust.
• Bake in a preheated 325° oven for 20 minutes.
• Allow pie to cool.

Topping:
- 1 cup sour cream
- 3 tablespoons sugar
- 1½ tablespoons fresh lemon juice

• Mix sour cream, sugar and lemon juice.
• Spread over cooled pie.
• Bake at 325° for 5 minutes.

Summertime Pie

- ½ cup chopped pecans
- 1 9–inch unbaked pie crust
- 1 cup whipping cream
- 1 8–ounce package cream cheese, softened
- 1 cup sugar
- 1 teaspoon vanilla

• Press pecans into the bottom of the pie crust.
• Bake pie crust in a preheated 375° oven for 12 minutes or until done. Set aside to cool.
• Whip cream and set aside.
• Beat cream cheese, sugar and vanilla.
• Fold in whipped cream.
• Pour in completely cooled pie crust and refrigerate until set.
• Garnish with sweetened fruit, such as strawberries, peaches or cherries.
Variation: Use low–fat cream cheese.

Chess Pie

3 eggs
1⅓ cups sugar
¼ teaspoon vanilla
1 tablespoon corn meal
1 tablespoon vinegar
6 tablespoons butter or margarine, melted
1 9–inch unbaked pie crust

- Mix all ingredients well and pour into un-baked pie crust.
- Bake in a preheated 350° oven for 50–60 minutes.

The Absolute Very Best Buttermilk Pie

2 cups sugar
½ cup butter or margarine, room temperature
4 tablespoons all–purpose flour
3 eggs, slightly beaten
1 cup buttermilk
1 teaspoon vanilla
1 9–inch unbaked deep–dish pie crust

- Cream together sugar, butter and flour.
- Add eggs, buttermilk and vanilla.
- Pour into unbaked pie crust and bake in a preheated 325° oven for 1 hour or until set.
- Cool before serving.

Cream Cheese Pumpkin Pie

1 3–ounce package cream cheese, softened
1 tablespoon milk or half–and–half
1 tablespoon sugar
1½ cups non–dairy frozen whipped topping, thawed
1 graham cracker crust
1 cup milk or half–and–half
2 3–ounce packages instant vanilla pudding mix
1 16–ounce can pumpkin
1 teaspoon cinnamon
½ teaspoon ground ginger
¼ teaspoon ground cloves
Whipped cream

- Mix cream cheese, 1 tablespoon milk and sugar until smooth.
- Stir in whipped topping and pour over crust.
- Mix 1 cup milk and pudding mixes until well blended and thickened.
- Add pumpkin and spices blending well.
- Spoon over cream cheese layer and chill at least 2 hours before serving.
- Serve topped with fresh whipped cream.

Southern Pecan Tarts

½ cup butter or margarine, softened
1 3–ounce package cream cheese, softened
1 cup all–purpose flour
1 egg
¾ cup brown sugar
½ teaspoon vanilla
⅓ cup finely chopped pecans

- Mix butter, cream cheese and flour.
- Shape into small balls and press into greased mini–muffin tins to form shells.
- Mix egg, brown sugar, vanilla and pecans together.
- Spoon filling into shells about ⅔ full.
- Bake in a preheated 350° oven for 15–20 minutes.
  Yield: 36 tarts

Candy Bar Brownies

4 eggs, lightly beaten
2 cups sugar
¾ cup butter or margarine, melted
2 teaspoons vanilla
1½ cups all–purpose flour
½ teaspoon baking powder
¼ teaspoon salt
⅓ cup cocoa
4 2.07–ounce Snickers candy bars, coarsely chopped
3 1.55–ounce Hershey chocolate bars, finely chopped

- Combine eggs, sugar, butter and vanilla in a large bowl.
- Stir in flour, baking powder, salt and cocoa.
- Fold in chopped Snickers bars.
- Spoon into a greased and floured 13x9x2–inch pan.
- Sprinkle with chopped Hershey bars.
- Bake in a preheated 350° oven for 30–35 minutes.
- Cool and cut into squares.
  Yield: 30 squares

Caramel Chocolate Layer Brownies
A chocolate lover's dream

Brownie layer:
- 1   18.25–ounce package German chocolate cake mix
- ⅓   cup evaporated milk
- 1   cup chopped pecans
- ¾   cup butter or margarine, melted

Caramel layer:
- 1   14–ounce package caramels
- ½   cup evaporated milk
- 1   cup milk chocolate chips

- Mix together cake mix, evaporated milk, pecans and melted butter.
- Pat half the brownie mixture into a non–greased 13x9x2–inch pan.
- Bake in a preheated 350° oven for 6 minutes.

- Mix caramels and evaporated milk over a double boiler or in the microwave.
- Sprinkle crust with chocolate chips.
- Pour heated caramel mixture over chocolate chips.

Assembly:
- Pat remaining brownie mixture over caramel mixture.
- Bake in a preheated 350° oven for 18 minutes. Cool for ½ hour.
- Refrigerate at least one hour before cutting into bars.

Freezes well.
Yield: 2 dozen

Double Chocolate Cream Cheese Brownies

Brownie layer:

  1 cup butter or margarine
  4 ounces unsweetened chocolate
  2 cups sugar
1½ cups all–purpose flour
  4 eggs, slightly beaten
  1 teaspoon salt
  1 teaspoon baking powder
  2 teaspoons vanilla
  1 cup semi–sweet chocolate chips

Filling:

  ¼ cup sugar
  2 tablespoons butter or margarine, softened
  1 egg
  1 3–ounce package cream cheese, softened
  1 tablespoon all–purpose flour
  ½ teaspoon vanilla

- Combine butter and unsweetened chocolate in a 2–quart saucepan.
- Cook over medium heat until melted, stirring occasionally.
- Stir in remaining brownie ingredients except chocolate chips.
- Remove from heat and fold in chocolate chips. Set aside.

- Combine all filling ingredients and mix until smooth.

Assembly:

- Spread HALF of brownie mixture into a greased 13x9x2–inch baking pan.
- Spread filling over brownie mixture.
- Spread remainder of brownie mixture over filling. Mixture will not entirely cover the cream cheese layer.
- Bake in preheated 350° oven for 30–35 minutes or until brownies begin to pull away from the side of the pan.

Yield: 3 dozen

Chocolate Carmelita Bars

Cookie layer:
1¾ cups quick or long–cooking oats
1½ cups all–purpose flour
¾ cup firmly packed brown sugar
¾ cup butter–flavored shortening, melted
1 tablespoon water
½ teaspoon baking soda
¼ teaspoon salt

- Combine all ingredients and mix well.
- Set one cup of mixture aside.
- Press remaining mixture into bottom of greased 13x9x2–inch pan.
- Bake in preheated 350° oven for 10–12 minutes or until light brown. Cool 10 minutes.

Caramel Filling:
1 12.5–ounce jar caramel ice cream topping
¼ cup all–purpose flour

- Mix caramel topping and flour until smooth. Set aside.

Assembly:
1 cup chopped pecans
1 cup semi–sweet chocolate chips

- Sprinkle pecans and chocolate chips onto cooled cookie layer.
- Drizzle caramel filling over pecans and chocolate chips to within ¼ inch of pan edge.
- Sprinkle with reserved cookie batter.
- Bake in a preheated 350° oven for 18–22 minutes until golden brown.
- Cool completely before cutting into bars.
Yield: 32 bars

Chocolate Pecan Bars

Cookie Layer:
1 cup all-purpose flour
1 cup graham cracker crumbs
⅔ cup sugar
½ teaspoon salt
¾ cup butter or margarine, softened
1 egg, beaten

- In a large bowl, stir together flour, graham cracker crumbs, sugar and salt.
- Add butter and cut in until mixture resembles coarse meal.
- Stir in 1 beaten egg.
- Press evenly into bottom of a non-greased 13x9x2-inch baking pan.
- Bake in preheated 350° oven for 25 minutes or until golden brown.

Chocolate Filling:
1 egg
1 14-ounce can sweetened condensed milk
½ cup cocoa
1½ teaspoons vanilla

- In large bowl beat the egg, sweetened condensed milk, cocoa and vanilla.
- Pour over cookie layer.

Topping:
½ cup flaked coconut
1 cup chopped pecans

- Sprinkle coconut and pecans over top and press into mixture with back of a spoon.
- Bake at 350° for 25 minutes or until set.
- Cool completely before cutting into bars.
  Freezes well.
  Yield: 2 dozen

Butter Pecan Turtle Bars

Cookie layer:
- ½ cup butter or margarine, softened
- 1 cup firmly packed brown sugar
- 2 cups all-purpose flour
- 1 cup chopped pecans

- Cream butter and brown sugar beating at medium speed.
- Gradually add flour, mixing well.
- Press mixture into non-greased 13x9x2-inch pan.
- Sprinkle with pecans and set aside.

Caramel Sauce:
- ⅔ cup butter or margarine, melted
- ½ cup firmly packed brown sugar

- Combine butter and brown sugar in a saucepan.
- Over medium heat, bring to a boil for 30 seconds, stirring constantly.
- Remove from heat and pour hot mixture over cookie layer.
- Bake in a preheated 350° oven for 18 minutes or until bubbly. Remove from oven.

Topping:
- 1 cup milk chocolate chips

- Sprinkle hot turtle bars with chocolate chips and allow chips to soften.
- After chips have softened, cut through chocolate with a knife to create a marbled effect.
- Cool and cut into squares.

Freezes well.
Yield: 3 dozen bars

Cinnamon Crisps

- 1 cup butter or margarine, softened
- 1 cup sugar
- 1 egg yolk
- 1 teaspoon vanilla
- 1 teaspoon cinnamon
- 2 cups all-purpose flour
- 1 egg white
- ¾ cup finely chopped pecans

- Mix first 6 ingredients well and spread into lightly greased jelly roll pan.
- Beat egg white with mixer in a small bowl.
- Spread over dough and sprinkle with pecans.
- Bake in a preheated 300° oven for 30-40 minutes.
- Cut immediately.

Almond Roca Bars

1 cup butter or margarine
½ cup brown sugar
½ cup sugar
1 egg
2 cups all–purpose flour
1 teaspoon vanilla
2 cups semi–sweet chocolate chips
¾ cup chopped nuts (almonds, pecans or walnuts)

- Combine butter and sugars, blending well.
- Add egg, flour and vanilla, mixing until dough is blended well.
- Press into an 11x18–inch pan.
- Bake in a preheated 350° oven for 15–17 minutes or until light brown.
- While hot, sprinkle with chocolate chips. When chips have melted, spread the chocolate over the cookie layer.
- Sprinkle with chopped nuts, pressing them down.
- Cut bars when cool.
  Variation: Substitute almond extract for vanilla.

Chewy Brown Sugar Brownies

½ cup butter or margarine
1 1–pound box brown sugar
3 eggs
2 cups self–rising flour
1 teaspoon vanilla
1 cup chopped pecans

- Melt butter; pour into large mixing bowl.
- Add sugar and stir.
- Add eggs one at a time, beating well after each addition.
- Add flour and vanilla, then beat well.
- Stir in pecans and pour into a greased 13x9x2–inch baking dish.
- Bake in a preheated 325° oven for 40 minutes.
- Cool, then cut into squares.
  Freezes well.
  Yield: 2–3 dozen

Walnut Shortbread

2 cups butter or margarine
1 cup sugar
1 cup chopped walnuts
1 teaspoon vanilla
¼ teaspoon salt
4 cups sifted all–purpose flour

- Cream butter and sugar until light and fluffy.
- Beat walnuts, vanilla and salt into the butter and sugar. Add flour and mix well.
- Spoon dough into a lightly greased 15½x 10½–inch pan. Smooth dough evenly to fill out pan.
- Bake in a preheated 350° oven for 40–50 minutes until lightly browned.
- Cool in pan and cut into bars.
  Yield: 6 dozen

Lemon Love Notes

An all–time favorite at showers and teas

Crust:
½ cup butter or margarine, softened
1 cup sifted all–purpose flour
¼ cup powdered sugar

- Cream butter, flour and powdered sugar.
- Pat into an 8–inch square glass dish.
- Bake in a preheated 350° oven until light brown, about 15 minutes. Cool.

Filling:
2 eggs
1 cup sugar
2 tablespoons all–purpose flour
½ teaspoon baking powder
3 tablespoons fresh lemon juice
  Grated rind of 1 lemon
  Powdered sugar

- Beat eggs; add next 5 ingredients and pour onto cooled crust.
- Bake in a preheated 350° oven until set, about 25 minutes.
- Cool at least 2 hours, then cut into squares.
- Dust with powdered sugar.
  Variation: Can easily be doubled and baked in a 13x9x2–inch pan.
  Yield: 16 2–inch squares

Black and White Cheesecake Bites
Wonderfully different

Crust:
- 1 12–ounce package semi–sweet chocolate chips
- ½ cup butter or margarine
- 2 cups graham cracker crumbs

Cream cheese layer:
- 1 8–ounce package cream cheese, softened
- 1 14–ounce can sweetened condensed milk
- 1 egg
- 1 teaspoon vanilla

- In a medium pan over low heat, melt chocolate chips and butter, stirring until smooth.
- Stir in graham cracker crumbs.
- Remove ¼ cup crumb mixture for later use.
- Press remaining mixture evenly into a 13x9x2–inch baking pan.

- In a large bowl with an electric mixer, beat cream cheese until smooth.
- Gradually beat in condensed milk, then egg and vanilla.
- Pour over prepared crust.
- Sprinkle with reserved ¼ cup crumb mixture.
- Bake in a preheated 325° oven for 25–30 minutes until set.
- Cool on counter top.
- Refrigerate at least two hours before cutting.
Yield: 2 dozen

Lemon-Raspberry Cheesecake Squares

Crust:

¾	cup butter–flavored shortening
⅓	cup firmly packed brown sugar
1¼	cups all–purpose flour
1	cup quick or long–cooking oatmeal
¼	teaspoon salt

- Beat shortening and brown sugar until fluffy.
- Add flour, oatmeal and salt, mixing well.
- Press into bottom of a greased 13x9x2–inch pan.
- Bake in a preheated 350° oven for 20 minutes or until light brown.

Filling:

½	cup seedless raspberry jam
2	8–ounce packages cream cheese, softened
¾	cup sugar
2	tablespoons all–purpose flour
2	eggs
3	tablespoons lemon juice
2	teaspoons grated lemon peel

- Spread jam over hot crust.
- Beat cream cheese, sugar and flour at medium speed until fluffy.
- Add eggs, one at a time, beating well after each.
- Add lemon juice and peel, mixing until smooth.
- Pour over jam and bake in a 350° oven 25 minutes or until set.
- Cool completely and chill.
- Store covered in refrigerator.
  Yield: 2 dozen

 ## Melting Moments

1	cup butter or margarine, softened
¾	cup sugar
½	teaspoon baking powder
½	teaspoon vinegar
1½	cups all–purpose flour
	Sliced almonds

- Cream butter and sugar. Add other ingredients except almonds and beat well.
- Drop by teaspoonful on a lightly greased cookie sheet. Top each with an almond slice.
- Bake in a preheated 300° oven for 18–20 minutes.
- Cool for 2 minutes before removing from pan.
  Yield: 5 dozen

Butter Cream Sandwich Cookies

Cookies:

2 cups butter or margarine, softened
1½ cups sugar
1 egg
4½ cups all–purpose flour
Food coloring, optional

- Beat butter and sugar well by hand.
- Add egg and beat again.
- Gradually add flour.
- Stir in food coloring if desired.
- Chill dough until firm, but not hard. Shape into small balls and place on lightly greased cookie sheet. Flatten with a fork.
- Bake in a preheated 325° oven for 9–12 minutes or until edges are light brown.

Cream Filling:

4 tablespoons butter or margarine, melted
2½ cups sifted powdered sugar
¾ teaspoon almond extract
2–3 tablespoons milk or cream
Food coloring, optional

- Mix all ingredients until smooth.
- Place small amount of cream filling between 2 cookies to make a sandwich.
  Variation: Make a festive Christmas cookie by using red and green food coloring.
  Yield: 2½ dozen

Crisp Sugar Cookies

1 cup powdered sugar
1 teaspoon cream of tartar
1 teaspoon baking soda
4¼ cups all–purpose flour
1 cup sugar
1 cup butter or margarine
2 eggs, well beaten
1 cup cooking oil
2 teaspoons vanilla
Sugar or decorative candy sprinkles

- Sift together powdered sugar, cream of tartar, baking soda and flour. Set aside.
- Cream together sugar, butter and eggs. Stir in oil and vanilla.
- Add dry ingredients and blend well.
- Chill dough. Form into ½–inch balls and place on a cookie sheet. Press with a fork and sprinkle with sugar or decorative candy sprinkles.
- Bake in a preheated 350° oven for approximately 15–20 minutes or until lightly brown.
  Yield: 6 dozen

Danish Cookies

3 cups all-purpose flour
2 cups butter or margarine, softened
2 cups sugar
1 teaspoon baking powder
1 egg white, beaten
8 ounces almonds, ground

- Combine, flour, butter, sugar and baking powder.
- Roll dough into a log and cover with waxed paper. Chill log in refrigerator overnight.
- Place log on a floured surface and cut dough into slices.
- Brush slices with egg white and sprinkle with almonds.
- Bake in a preheated 325°–350° oven for 10–12 minutes until lightly browned. Be careful not to overbake.
  Yield: 8 dozen

Iced Pecan Sandies

Cookies:
1½ cups butter or margarine, softened
½ cup powdered sugar
4 teaspoons vanilla
2 tablespoons water
4 cups sifted cake flour
2 cups ground pecans

- Cream butter, sugar and vanilla.
- Stir in water and flour.
- Fold in ground pecans. Dough will be stiff. Chill dough for one hour.
- Form dough into walnut-size balls and place on a non-greased cookie sheet. Flatten with back of spoon so that a slight depression is in the center of the cookie.
- Bake in a preheated 300° oven for 20–25 minutes or until lightly browned.
- Top cookie with icing.

Icing:
1 box powdered sugar
6 tablespoons butter or margarine, softened
1 teaspoon vanilla
Small amount of milk (about 2 tablespoons)
Food coloring

- Cream butter and sugar.
- Add vanilla and enough milk to give icing a nice spreading consistency.
- Add food coloring if desired.
  Yield: 7 dozen

Pecan Sticks

½ cup butter or margarine, softened
3 tablespoons sugar
3 teaspoons almond flavoring
1 cup all–purpose flour
1 cup chopped pecans
  Powdered sugar

- Cream butter, sugar and almond flavoring.
- Work in flour and pecans to form dough.
- Roll into fingers or sticks and bake in a pre-heated 300° oven for 20–25 minutes until light brown.
- Roll in powdered sugar.

Yield: 2 dozen

Special K Cookies

1 cup butter or margarine
1 cup sugar
1½ cups all–purpose flour
½ teaspoon salt
1 teaspoon baking soda
1 teaspoon vanilla
2 cups Special K cereal

- Cream butter and sugar about 15–20 minutes or until fluffy. This is very important.
- Combine next 3 ingredients and add to the butter and sugar mixture. Add vanilla and mix thoroughly.
- Stir in Special K and drop by teaspoonful onto non–greased cookie sheet.
- Bake in a preheated 350° oven: 10–12 minutes on an insulated cookie sheet, 8–9 minutes on a regular cookie sheet.

Yield: 75 cookies

Snickerdoodles

1 cup margarine or shortening
1½ cups sugar
2 eggs
2¾ cups all–purpose flour
2 teaspoons cream of tartar
1 teaspoon baking soda
½ teaspoon salt
2 tablespoons sugar
2 tablespoons cinnamon

- Mix margarine, sugar and eggs.
- Sift together flour, cream of tartar, baking soda and salt. Add to margarine mixture.
- Chill dough, then roll into balls.
- Combine sugar and cinnamon; roll balls in this mixture.
- Place on cookie sheet and bake in a pre-heated 350° oven for 10 minutes.

Yield: 6 dozen

Oatmeal Crispies

1 cup shortening
1 cup brown sugar
1 cup sugar
2 eggs, beaten
1 teaspoon vanilla
1 teaspoon salt
1 teaspoon baking soda
1½ cups all–purpose flour
3 cups quick oats
½ cup chopped walnuts

- Cream shortening and sugars. Add eggs and vanilla, beating well.
- Sift together salt, baking soda and flour and add to sugar mixture.
- Add oatmeal and walnuts, mixing well.
- Shape into rolls and wrap in waxed paper, chill, then freeze.
- While dough is frozen, slice cookies to ¼–inch thickness.
- Bake in a preheated 350° oven for 10–13 minutes.
Yield: 5 dozen

Chocolate Peanut Butter Cookies

4 cups sugar
3 squares unsweetened chocolate
½ cup butter or margarine
1 cup milk
1 cup crunchy peanut butter
4 cups quick cooking oats
2 teaspoons vanilla

- Mix sugar, chocolate squares, butter and milk in a saucepan.
- Bring to a boil and boil for 2 minutes.
- Add peanut butter, oats and vanilla, mixing well.
- Drop by spoonful onto waxed paper and allow to cool.
Yield: 4 dozen

Chocolate Chip Oatmeal Cookies

1 cup butter or margarine, softened
¾ cup sugar
¾ cup brown sugar
2 eggs
1½ cups all-purpose flour
1 teaspoon salt
1 teaspoon baking soda
1 teaspoon vanilla
1 teaspoon hot water
2 cups quick cooking oatmeal
1 cup semi-sweet chocolate chips

- Mix butter, sugar, brown sugar and eggs and beat until creamy.
- Add flour, salt, baking soda and vanilla, mixing well.
- Add hot water, oatmeal and chocolate chips. Mix well.
- Drop by the spoonful onto non-greased cookie sheets.
- Bake in a preheated 350° oven for 10–12 minutes.
  Variation: Add raisins and/or pecans.
  Yield: 5 dozen

Chocolate Chocolate Chip Cookies

Definitely for chocolate lovers!

⅔ cup butter or margarine, softened
⅔ cup sugar
⅓ cup brown sugar
1 egg
1 teaspoon vanilla
2 squares unsweetened chocolate, melted
1½ cups all-purpose flour
1 cup semisweet chocolate chips

- Cream butter and sugars. Add egg, mixing well.
- Add vanilla and melted chocolate, then flour.
- Stir in chocolate chips and drop by tablespoon on non-greased cookie sheets.
- Bake in a preheated 325° oven for 15–17 minutes.
  Yield: 5 dozen

Oatmeal Lace Cookies
Very light and crisp

½ cup all–purpose flour
¼ teaspoon baking powder
½ cup sugar
½ cup quick–cooking oats
2 tablespoons heavy cream
2 tablespoons light corn syrup
⅓ cup butter or margarine, melted
1 tablespoon vanilla

- Sift flour, baking powder and sugar together in a bowl. Add all remaining ingredients and mix together until well blended.
- Spray an aluminum foil–lined baking sheet with non–stick vegetable spray.
- Using a ¼ teaspoon measuring spoon, drop dough 4 inches apart onto baking sheet.
- Bake in a preheated 375° oven for 6–8 minutes or until lightly browned.
- Let stand a minute, then remove from pan.

Yield: 6 dozen 2–inch cookies

Gingersnaps

¾ cup shortening
1 cup sugar
¼ cup dark molasses
1 egg, beaten
3 cups all–purpose flour
¼ teaspoon salt
2 teaspoons baking soda
1 teaspoon cinnamon
1 teaspoon ground cloves
2¼ teaspoons ginger
Sugar

- Cream shortening and sugar. Add molasses and the egg.
- Combine dry ingredients in separate bowl. Add to shortening mixture, blending well.
- Roll into small balls and dip in sugar.
- Place on greased cookie sheet and bake in a preheated 350° oven for 10–12 minutes.

Yield: 5 dozen

Brown-Eyed Susans

Cookies:

1 cup butter or margarine, softened
¼ cup 4x powdered sugar
1 teaspoon almond extract
2 cups all–purpose flour
½ teaspoon salt

Frosting:

1 cup sifted 4x powdered sugar
2 tablespoons cocoa
2 tablespoons hot water
½ teaspoon vanilla

- Mix all ingredients and chill.
- Roll dough by tablespoon into balls.
- Place on a greased cookie sheet and flatten.
- Bake in a preheated 350° oven for 10–15 minutes.
- Top each cookie with ½ teaspoon of frosting.

- Mix all ingredients until well blended.
  Yield: 4 dozen

Peanut Butter Kiss Cookies

Children love these cookies!

1¾ cups all–purpose flour
1 teaspoon baking soda
½ teaspoon salt
½ cup sugar
2 tablespoons milk
½ cup firmly packed brown sugar
½ cup shortening
½ cup peanut butter
1 egg
1 teaspoon vanilla
Sugar, optional
48 milk chocolate kiss candies

- Combine in a large mixing bowl all ingredients except extra sugar and kisses. Mix on lowest speed until dough forms.
- Shape dough into balls, using a rounded teaspoonful for each ball. Roll balls in sugar, if desired.
- Bake in a preheated 375° oven for 8–10 minutes.
- Remove from oven and immediately top each cookie with a chocolate kiss. Press down firmly until cookie cracks around edges.

Fruit Cake Cups

A terrific holiday treat!

1   pound candied red cherries, chopped
½   pound candied pineapple, chopped
4   cups chopped pecans
½   pound chopped dates
1   3½–ounce can coconut
1   cup self–rising flour
1   14–ounce can sweetened condensed milk
¾   cup butter or margarine, softened

- Mix all ingredients well and spoon into greased mini–muffin tins.
- Bake in a preheated 350° oven for 15–20 minutes.
  Yield: 100 muffins

Chocolate Snacks

4   ounces saltine crackers
1   cup butter or margarine
1   cup brown sugar
1   12–ounce package chocolate chips
1   cup chopped pecans

- Spray jelly roll pan with vegetable oil spray and line pan with cracker squares.
- Boil butter and brown sugar for 3 minutes. Pour over crackers.
- Bake in a preheated 350° oven for 10-12 minutes (watch carefully or sugar mixture will burn).
- Remove from oven and sprinkle with chocolate chips and then pecans.
- Put back in oven long enough to melt chocolate chips.
- Put into refrigerator and break into pieces when cool.

Chocolate Fudge

1   6–ounce package semi–sweet chocolate chips
4   ounces German sweet chocolate, broken into pieces
3   cups marshmallow cream
1   cup chopped pecans
2½ cups sugar
1   5–ounce can evaporated milk
    Pinch of salt
1   tablespoon butter or margarine
1   teaspoon vanilla

- Mix first 4 ingredients in a large bowl. Set aside.
- Combine next 4 ingredients in a saucepan and boil exactly 6 minutes.
- Pour boiling syrup over the chocolate mixture.
- Add vanilla and beat until the chocolate is melted.
- Pour into a well–greased pan and let stand several hours in a cool place before cutting into squares.

Peanut Brittle

1½ cups sugar
½   cup white corn syrup
¼   cup hot water
1   ½–inch thick slice of a 2½–inch square of paraffin
2   cups raw peanuts
1½ heaping teaspoons baking soda

- Cut a ½–inch slice of paraffin from a 2½–inch square of paraffin.
- Place sugar, corn syrup, water and paraffin in a boiler and cook until it spins a long thread.
- Stir in 2 cups of raw peanuts.
- Cook until syrup is a light caramel color.
- Stir frequently, then add the baking soda. Remove from stove at once and stir very fast.
- Quickly pour onto greased marble or large greased cookie sheet. Do not try to spread, it won't.
- Run spatula under the candy while it is still warm.
- Break into small pieces and store in tightly covered container.

 *Sheri's Chocolate Delight*

Crust:
- 1 cup all–purpose flour
- 2 tablespoons powdered sugar
- ½ cup butter, melted
- ½ cup pecans, chopped

- Mix flour and powdered sugar. Add melted butter and pecans.
- Using a fork, press mixture into a 13x9x2–inch glass dish.
- Bake in a preheated 350° oven for 20 minutes. Let cool.

Cream Cheese Layer:
- 1 8–ounce package cream cheese, softened
- 1 cup powdered sugar
- 1 cup non–dairy frozen whipped topping, thawed

- Mix all ingredients and spread over crust.

Chocolate Pudding Layer:
- 2½ cups cold milk
- 1 large box instant chocolate pudding mix

- With electric mixer, blend milk and instant pudding.
- Spread over cream cheese layer.

Topping:
- 2 cups non–dairy frozen whipped topping, softened
- ¼ cup chopped pecans
  Shaved chocolate, optional

- Spread whipped topping over pudding layer to completely cover.
- Sprinkle with chopped pecans and shaved chocolate.
  Variation: Substitute 1 container of lemon or blueberry pie filling for chocolate pudding and milk.

  Can be made a day ahead.

Charlotte Russe
A century–old favorite

2 dozen lady fingers
2 cups whipping cream
5 eggs, separated
⅛ teaspoon salt
⅔ cup sugar
2 packages unflavored gelatin
¼ cup cold milk
½ cup milk, heated
2 ounces sherry
1 teaspoon vanilla

- Split lady fingers and line sides and bottom of a large springform pan or bowl.
- In first bowl, beat cream until stiff.
- In second bowl, beat the egg yolks, then add the salt and sugar. Blend well.
- In third bowl, beat egg whites until stiff and set aside.
- In measuring cup, dissolve gelatin in ¼ cup cold milk.
- In small saucepan, heat ½ cup milk and add dissolved gelatin. Allow to cool.
- Pour cooled gelatin into yolks and beat. Continue to beat as you slowly add the sherry and vanilla.
- Fold in cream, then stiffly beaten egg whites.
- Spoon mixture over ladyfingers and place split ladyfingers across the top.
- Allow to chill for several hours before serving and serve within 48 hours.

Oreo Sundae

½ gallon vanilla ice cream, softened
1 16–ounce package Oreo cookies, crushed
¾ cup cocktail peanuts
1 12–ounce carton non–dairy frozen whipped topping, thawed
4 ounces German chocolate, melted

- Layer these ingredients in the following order in a 13x9x2–inch glass baking dish: ⅓ ice cream, ¾ cookie crumbs, remaining ice cream, peanuts, remaining cookie crumbs and whipped topping.
- Drizzle melted chocolate over top and freeze until firm.
- Remove from freezer 10 minutes before serving.
Variation: Low–fat frozen yogurt can be substituted for the ice cream.
Yield: 15 servings

Easter Bird's Nests

Children will want to help make these!

12 ounces semi–sweet chocolate chips
¾ cup peanut butter
6 large shredded wheat cereal rectangles
Small jelly beans or peanut M & M candies

- Melt chocolate chips and peanut butter in a double boiler or microwave.
- Crumble shredded wheat and add to chocolate mixture.
- Place a spoonful of mixture on waxed paper and shape into a nest. Repeat.
- When nests have hardened, fill with jelly beans or peanut M & M candies.

Yield: 18 nests

Egg Custard

4 eggs
½ cup buttermilk biscuit baking mix
⅔ cup sugar
3 tablespoons butter
1 teaspoon vanilla
2 cups milk

- Put all ingredients in a blender and mix.
- Spray 6 custard cups with non–stick vegetable spray.
- Pour into cups and bake in a preheated 400° oven for 30 minutes.

Variations: For Egg Custard Pie, pour mixture into a pie crust and bake for 45 minutes. For a lower fat version, use low–fat buttermilk biscuit baking mix and egg substitute.

Yield: 6 servings

Crème Caramel

½ cup sugar
4 eggs
⅓ cup sugar
2 cups milk
1 teaspoon vanilla
¼ teaspoon salt
Nutmeg
Lemon peel

- Grease six 6–ounce custard cups.
- Place ½ cup of sugar in a small saucepan and heat until melted and a light caramel color. Stir constantly.
- Immediately pour melted sugar into custard cups.
- Place eggs and ⅓ cup sugar in a large bowl and beat with a wire whisk until well blended.
- Add milk, vanilla and salt mixing until well blended.
- Pour into custard cups.
- Place custard cups in a 13x9x2–inch baking pan and fill pan with hot water to come half way up the sides of the custard cups.
- Bake in a preheated 325° oven for 50 minutes or until a knife inserted in the center comes out clean.
- Remove from oven and remove cups from water.
- Cover and refrigerate 1½ hours.
- Remove from mold by running a knife around the edge.
- Serve on chilled dessert plates.
- Sprinkle with nutmeg and garnish with a lemon peel twist.
Yield: 6 servings

Fresh Fruit Tart

Crust:

½ cup butter or margarine, softened
¼ cup brown sugar
1 cup all–purpose flour
¼ cup quick cooking oats
¼ cup finely chopped walnuts

- Lightly grease a pizza pan or baking sheet.
- Beat butter and brown sugar until fluffy.
- Add the remaining ingredients.
- Press mixture onto prepared pan, forming a rim around the edge. Prick with a fork.
- Bake in a preheated 375° oven for 10–12 minutes, until lightly browned. Cool.

Cream Filling:

1 8–ounce package cream cheese, softened
⅔ cup sugar
1 teaspoon vanilla

- Mix ingredients until creamy and chill.
- Spoon chilled filling onto crust.

Fruit Topping:

Fresh fruit, such as sliced strawberries, grapes, bananas, kiwis or mandarin oranges

- Arrange fruit on top of filling.
- Keep refrigerated until ready to serve.
  Variation: For a speedier crust, use 1 roll of refrigerator sugar cookies. Slice cookie dough into circles and slightly overlap in concentric pattern in prepared pan.
  Yield: 8–10 servings

Easy Apple Crisp

4 or 5 medium Granny Smith apples
½ teaspoon cinnamon
1 cup self–rising flour
1 cup sugar
½ cup butter
¼ teaspoon salt
½ teaspoon cinnamon

- Peel, core and slice apples.
- Place in a greased 1½–quart baking dish.
- Sprinkle ½ teaspoon cinnamon over apples.
- Mix flour, sugar, butter, salt and ½ teaspoon cinnamon together with a pastry blender until crumbly.
- Sprinkle mixture over apples.
- Bake for 1 hour in a preheated 350° oven.
  Yield: 6 servings

 *Peach Cobbler*

2   cups peaches, peeled and sliced
2   cups sugar, divided
½   cup butter
¾   cup all–purpose flour
2   teaspoons baking powder
    Pinch of salt
¾   cup milk
    Whipped cream or ice cream, optional

- Mix peeled and sliced peaches with 1 cup sugar.
- Melt butter in 2–quart casserole dish in oven.
- In a medium bowl, mix 1 cup sugar, flour, baking powder, salt and milk. Pour over melted butter. DO NOT STIR.
- Place the sugared peaches on top of batter. DO NOT STIR.
- Bake in a preheated 350° oven for 1 hour. Batter will rise to top and will be brown and crisp when cobbler is done.
- Serve warm with whipped cream or ice cream.

Cherry Dessert

1   cup butter or margarine, softened
1½   cups sugar
4   eggs
1   teaspoon almond extract
2   cups all–purpose flour
2   teaspoons baking powder
1   21–ounce can cherry pie filling
       Whipped cream

- Cream together butter and sugar in a large mixing bowl.
- Add eggs and beat until fluffy.
- Stir in almond extract, flour and baking powder, then mix until smooth.
- Pour batter into a greased 13x9x2–inch baking dish.
- Using large spoonfuls, place the pie filling over the batter.
- Bake in a preheated 350° oven for 45–50 minutes.
- Serve topped with whipped cream.
  Yield: 12 servings

Chocolate Éclair Dessert

Cake:
- 2 3.4–ounce boxes instant vanilla pudding mix
- 3 cups milk
- 1 8–ounces non–dairy frozen whipped topping, thawed
- 1 box graham crackers

Icing:
- 2½ squares unsweetened chocolate
- 3 tablespoons butter or margarine
- 2 teaspoons white corn syrup
- 1½ cups powdered sugar
- 3 tablespoons milk
- 2 teaspoons vanilla

- Mix pudding with milk. Fold in whipped topping.
- Place a layer of graham crackers in bottom of a 13x9x2–inch pan.
- Spoon ⅓ of pudding mixture on top.
- Layer crackers and pudding two more times, ending with a layer of crackers.

- Melt chocolate and butter in the microwave on low.
- Add remaining ingredients, mixing well.
- Pour icing over top layer of crackers.
- Refrigerate overnight.
- To serve, cut into squares.

Yield: 8–10 servings

Brownie Pudding Cake

- 1 cup self–rising flour
- ½ cup sugar
- 2 tablespoons cocoa
- ½ cup milk
- 2 tablespoons cooking oil
- 1 teaspoon vanilla
- ½ cup chopped pecans
- ¾ cup sugar
- ¼ cup cocoa
- 1½ cups water, boiling

- Sift together flour, ½ cup sugar and 2 tablespoons cocoa.
- Add milk, oil and vanilla, stirring until smooth. Stir in pecans.
- Pour into a non–greased 8x8–inch pan.
- Combine ¾ cup sugar and ¼ cup cocoa. Gradually stir in boiling water.
- Pour evenly over batter in pan. DO NOT STIR.
- Bake in a preheated 350° oven for 30 minutes or until cake tests done.
- Serve immediately or brownie cake will absorb sauce.

Delicious served with vanilla ice cream.
Yield: 8 servings

Double Chocolate Torte

Like eating a big, wonderful candy bar!

Torte:
1¾ cups all–purpose flour
1¾ cups sugar
1¼ teaspoons baking soda
1 teaspoon salt
¼ teaspoon baking powder
⅔ cup butter or margarine, softened
4 ounces unsweetened chocolate, melted and cooled
1¼ cups water
1 teaspoon vanilla
3 eggs

Chocolate Filling:
6 ounces semi–sweet chocolate
¾ cups butter or margarine
½ cup chopped pecans

Cream Filling:
2 cups whipping cream
1 tablespoon sugar
1 teaspoon vanilla

Assembly:
Chocolate curls or shavings, optional

- Prepare four 9–inch round cake pans by spraying them with non–stick vegetable spray.
- In a large mixing bowl, blend well the flour, sugar, baking soda, salt and baking powder.
- Add the butter, melted chocolate, water and vanilla and blend at low speed. Mix for 2 minutes at medium speed, scraping sides and bottom of bowl frequently.
- Add eggs and beat an additional 2 minutes.
- Spoon approximately 1¼ cups of batter into each of the 4 prepared pans. Layers will be very thin.
- Bake in a preheated 350° oven for 15–18 minutes or until a wooden pick comes out clean. Two layers can be baked at a time.
- Cool slightly, then remove from pans. The layers may be frozen at this point.
- Melt chocolate and cool. Mix in butter and add pecans. Chill if filling is too thin to spread.

- Whip cream with sugar and vanilla until soft peaks form. Do not overbeat.

- Place bottom layer of cake on serving plate and spread with half the chocolate filling.
- Add another cake layer and spread with half the cream filling.
- Repeat layers, ending with cream filling on top. Do not frost sides of torte.
- Refrigerate until firm, then cover. Remove from refrigerator shortly before serving.
- Garnish with chocolate curls or shavings, if desired.

Yield: 12–16 servings

Old Fashioned Gingerbread

Makes your house smell like Grandma has been cooking!

Gingerbread:

½ cup butter or margarine, softened
1 cup sugar
1 egg
1 cup molasses
2½ cups all-purpose flour
1½ teaspoons baking soda
1 teaspoon ground cinnamon
½ teaspoon salt
1 teaspoon ground ginger
1 cup hot water

Lemon Sauce:

½ cup butter or margarine
1 cup sugar
¼ cup water
Juice and rind of one lemon
1 egg, beaten
Lemon rind strips for garnish, optional
Whipped cream, optional

- Beat butter at medium speed with an electric mixer. Gradually add sugar, beating well.
- Add egg and molasses, mix well.
- Combine flour, soda, cinnamon, salt and ginger. Add to creamed mixture alternately with water, beginning and ending with flour mixture. Mix after each addition.
- Pour batter into a greased 13x9x2-inch pan and bake in a preheated 350° oven for 35–40 minutes, or until a toothpick inserted into the center comes out clean.

- Melt butter in a saucepan.
- Add remaining ingredients. Cook over medium heat, stirring constantly, until mixture reaches 160°.
- Cut gingerbread squares and spoon lemon sauce over top.
- Garnish with lemon rind, if desired, or serve with whipped cream.

Pâte Brisée

Pastry:
- ½ cup butter or margarine
- ¼ teaspoon salt
- 1¾ cups all–purpose flour
- 3 tablespoons sugar
- ½ cup cold water

- Cut the butter and salt into the flour until the mixture resembles coarse meal.
- Add sugar and then water to mixture and mix until it is a soft dough. The amount of water needed may vary.
- Form into a ball and allow to rest for about 30 minutes.
- Grease and flour a tart pan with a removable bottom.
- After dough has rested, roll out and press smoothly into tart pan.

Filling:
- Sugar
- Fresh fruit (apples, peaches, kiwi, strawberries, etc.)

- Sprinkle pastry with sugar until evenly coated.
- Arrange peeled slices of fresh fruit in a circular manner in pastry.
- Bake in a preheated 350° oven for approximately 30 minutes.

This is a very versatile pastry and can be used for quiches or pizza, but omit sugar.

 # Blueberry Cobbler

Berries:
- ¾ cup sugar
- ¾ cup water
- 1 teaspoon lemon juice
- 1 quart blueberries

- Dissolve sugar in water.
- Add lemon juice and berries.
- Place mixture in a 13x9x2–inch baking dish.

Topping:
- ½ cup butter or margarine
- 1½ cups self–rising flour
- 1 cup sugar

- Mix butter, flour and sugar with a pastry blender until it is the consistency of meal.
- Spoon over blueberry mixture.
- Bake in a preheated 350° oven for 25–30 minutes.
- Serve with whipped cream or ice cream.

Mrs. Storey's Boiled Custard

1 quart milk
¾ cup sugar
3–4 large eggs
1 teaspoon vanilla

- Heat milk and sugar in heavy saucepan or double boiler until it reaches room temperature.
- Beat eggs until frothy.
- Pour milk mixture into eggs and pour all back into saucepan.
- Cook over medium heat stirring constantly, until mixture will coat a spoon.
- Cool, then add vanilla.
- Strain.

Sweet Mouthful

4 egg whites
Pinch of salt
¼ teaspoon cream of tartar
1 cup sugar
6 ounces semi–sweet chocolate pieces
3 tablespoons water
3 cups whipping cream
⅓ cup sugar
1 pint fresh strawberries, sliced
Whole strawberries, for garnish

- Beat egg whites with a pinch of salt and cream of tartar until stiff.
- Gradually beat in 1 cup sugar and beat until meringue is stiff and glossy.
- Line a baking sheet with waxed paper and trace on the paper 3 8–inch circles.
- Divide meringue in 3 parts and spread evenly on the 3 circles.
- Bake in a preheated 250° oven for 20–25 minutes.
- Melt the chocolate in a double boiler with the water.
- Whip cream until stiff and gradually add ⅓ cup sugar.
- Spread a thin coating of chocolate on 1 of the meringue rounds, then cover chocolate with a ¾–inch layer of whipped cream. Place half the sliced strawberries on top.
- Repeat once.
- Place last meringue on top.
- Frost sides and top with remaining whipped cream.
- Decorate top with whole strawberries.

Poached Pears in Red Wine with Vanilla Custard Sauce

Pears:

8   underripe Bartlett pears, stems attached
2   cups red table wine
1   cup water
½   cup sugar
1   tablespoon ground cinnamon (or 2 cinnamon sticks)
½   teaspoon nutmeg, freshly ground
6   whole cloves
3   tablespoons fresh lemon juice
     Peel of 1 lemon, removed in strips with potato peeler

- Peel the pears with a potato peeler, being careful to leave the stems on.
- At the base of the pear, insert the potato peeler vertically and remove the core. It will come out easily if the peeler is rotated.
- Trim the base flat with a knife so the pear will stand upright.
- Put the remaining ingredients into a 1½–quart saucepan and bring to a boil. Lower the heat and slip the pears into the liquid with a spoon.
- Simmer gently for 45 minutes. Turn the pears with a spoon occasionally if the liquid doesn't completely cover them.
- Remove the pears from the liquid with a slotted spoon and let them drain on paper towels.
- Place the warm pears in individual serving dishes and spoon warm Custard Sauce around them or keep sauce warm in a thermos until ready to serve.

Vanilla Custard Sauce:

2   eggs, slightly beaten
⅛   teaspoon salt
¼   cup sugar
2   cups milk, scalded
1   teaspoon vanilla

- Combine eggs, salt and sugar.
- Add the scalded milk slowly, while whisking, and cook in the top of a double boiler until the mixture coats a spoon.
- Add vanilla and stir thoroughly.

How to make ahead: Both the pears and sauce may be made several days ahead. Store the pears in the poaching liquid in the refrigerator and the custard sauce in a jar. On serving day, remove the pears several

Continued on next page

**Poached Pears in Red Wine with
 Vanilla Custard Sauce (continued)**

hours ahead of time and bring to room temperature. Reheat the sauce in a double boiler over very low heat. The water is just hot, not boiling. If the sauce begins to curdle, remove from heat, drop an ice cube into it, and stir rapidly, or quickly pour into a blender or food processor and run machine for 10–15 seconds or until the lumps are gone.
Yield: 8 servings

Oranges in Red Wine

An elegant ending

½ cup sugar
1 cup water
¾–1 cup dry red wine
2 cloves
2 slices lemon
1 stick cinnamon
6 oranges, peeled and sectioned

- Dissolve sugar in water in saucepan.
- Add rest of ingredients, except orange sections and boil until slightly syrupy, about 20 minutes.
- Strain into serving bowl and cool slightly.
- Add oranges and refrigerate until very cold.

Lemon Ice Dessert

6 large lemons
1 cup sugar
1 pint half–and–half

- Grate rind from 2 lemons.
- Slice in half and juice them.
- Combine rind, juice and sugar and stir until sugar is dissolved.
- Add half–and–half slowly and mix until well blended.
- Pour in ice tray or bowl and freeze.
- Take 4 remaining lemons, halve and remove pulp and rind.
- Fill with frozen lemon mixture and garnish with mint leaves.

Great for luncheons or following a heavy dinner.
Yield: 8 servings

Lemon Soufflé

1	envelope unflavored gelatin
2	tablespoons water
	Grated rind of 4 lemons
½	cup lemon juice, strained or juice of 8 lemons
1	cup super fine granulated sugar
7–8	egg whites
1	cup heavy cream
	Lemon slices, cut paper thin

- Dissolve gelatin in water.
- Add grated lemon rind, strained juice and sugar.
- Stir over low heat until completely dissolved, then chill until gelatin thickens and begins to set.
- Beat egg whites and heavy cream separately until stiff. Fold into gelatin mixture.
- Scotch tape a 2–inch collar of waxed paper around the rim of a 1–quart soufflé dish.
- Pour in the lemon soufflé and chill.
- Remove waxed paper collar before serving.
- Decorate with paper–thin lemon slices.
  Yield: 6 servings

Peach Champagne Sorbet

1	teaspoon unflavored gelatin
¼	cup water
6	large fresh peaches, peeled and quartered
1	cup sugar
2	tablespoons fresh lemon juice
2	cups champagne

- Soften gelatin in water in a small saucepan; stir over low heat until gelatin is dissolved.
- Combine peaches, sugar and lemon juice in a large bowl and mix well to combine.
- Place half the mixture into a blender or food processor and blend until smooth. Repeat with remaining mixture.
- Combine gelatin mixture, peach purée and champagne in a metal bowl or pan.
- Freeze until slushy.
- Remove from freezer and beat until smooth.
- Re–freeze until firm.
  This keeps well in the freezer for a month.
  Yield: 2 quarts

Lemon Ice Cream

6–8 lemons
3 cups sugar
2 quarts half–and–half

- Slice 2 of the lemons in thin slices.
- Combine slices with the juice of the remaining lemons and pour over sugar.
- Let stand several hours.
- Put half–and–half in ice cream churn and freeze until semi–stiff.
- Remove cover and add lemon and sugar mixture and finish freezing.

Butter Pecan Ice Cream

Such Southern appeal

1 cup light brown sugar, loosely packed
½ cup water
   Dash of salt
2 eggs, beaten
2 tablespoons butter
1 cup whole milk
1 teaspoon vanilla
1 cup heavy cream
½ cup finely chopped toasted pecans

- Combine sugar, water and salt in top of double boiler.
- Cook until sugar is dissolved.
- Pour a small amount over beaten eggs and return eggs to sugar mixture.
- Stir and cook over boiling water until thickened, just a few minutes.
- Add butter and cool.
- Add milk, vanilla and cream (not whipped).
- Stir in pecans.
- Freeze in ice cream freezer until firm.

Peppermint Ice Cream

6 cups milk
3 heaping teaspoons all–purpose flour
3 cups crushed peppermint sticks (about 22 ounces)
3 cups whipping cream

- Warm milk in a pan on the stove or the microwave.
- Remove from heat and add flour.
- Grind peppermint in blender or food processor. Add to milk.
- Add whipping cream to milk mixture.
- Pour into an ice cream freezer and freeze according to manufacturer's instructions.

Peach Ice Cream

1 quart peaches, peeled and mashed
2 cups sugar, divided
1 quart half–and–half
3 drops almond extract

- Mix peaches with 1 cup sugar and chill.
- Add remaining cup of sugar to half–and–half and chill.
- Place cream mixture in ice cream freezer, add almond extract and freeze until semi–stiff.
- Add peaches and finish freezing.
  Variation: You may add 4 teaspoons Amaretto before freezing.

Orange Pineapple Sherbet

2 14–ounce cans sweetened condensed milk
48–56 ounces orange soda
1 8–ounce can crushed pineapple, drained

- Pour all ingredients into an electric ice cream freezer and freeze according to manufacturer's directions.
  Yield: 15 servings

Chocolate Cinnamon Ice Cream

3 eggs
1 cup sugar
2 quarts half–and–half
1 16–ounce can chocolate syrup
½ teaspoon ground cinnamon
1 tablespoon vanilla
¼ teaspoon almond extract

- Beat eggs at medium speed until frothy.
- Gradually add sugar, beating until thick.
- Heat half–and–half in a 3–quart saucepan over low heat until hot.
- Gradually stir about ¼ of the hot mixture into the eggs.
- Add remaining hot mixture, stirring constantly.
- Cook over low heat until mixture is slightly thickened and reaches 165°, stirring constantly.
- Remove from heat, and stir in chocolate syrup and remaining ingredients.
- Cool in refrigerator.
- Pour into a 1–gallon ice cream freezer and freeze according to manufacturer's instructions.
- Let ripen at least 1 hour before serving.
  Yield: About 1 gallon

Special Thanks

The members of the Junior League of Columbus express their appreciation to those who have contributed to **A Southern Collection Then and Now** by providing valuable assistance and professional expertise.

Basset & Becker Advertising
Mary Bradley
Callaway Gardens
Christenson Studios
Ruth Flowers

Mike Fowler
Georgia Crown Distributing
    Company
Eleanor Hardegree
Sally Hatcher

Chris Henson
Nell Hudson
Charleton Kennon
Memory Martin
Virginia Norman

Barbara Page
Margie Richardson
Sally Spencer
Connie Van Blarcum
Kathryn Vaught

 The recipes in **A Southern Collection Then and Now** which are marked with a pineapple are favorites from previous cookbooks published by The Junior League of Columbus, Georgia, Inc. The following individuals are the original contributors of those particular recipes:

Mrs. Robert Addison
Mr. Oscar Betts
Mrs. Reynolds Bickerstaff
Mrs. James J.W. Biggers, Jr.
Mrs. Jane K. Blackmar
Mrs. Donald L. Bloebaum
Mrs. J.R. Bocell
Mrs. Charlotte Golden Boyd
Mrs. Richard Y. Bradley
Mrs. Thomas R. Bryan
Mrs. Carl Bryant
Mrs. John Bussey
Mrs. Cason J. Callaway
Mrs. Cason J. Callaway, Jr.
Mrs. Harrison W. Clark
Mrs. Jack Collins
Mrs. C.W. Curry
Mrs. William E. Dillard, Jr.

Mrs. J.W. Feighner
Mrs. Charles M. Flowers
Mrs. Jack A. Gantt, Jr.
Mrs. George J. Golden
Mrs. Theo Golden
Mr. P.C. Graffagnino
Mrs. Freddie Hall
Mrs. B.H. Hardaway, III
Mrs. William B. Hardegree
Mrs. J. Madden Hatcher
Mrs. J. Madden Hatcher, Jr.
Mrs. Michael Henry
Mrs. Patrick Holder
Mrs. W. Lloyd Hudson, Jr.
Mrs. A. Illges, Jr.
Mrs. John P. Illges, III
Mrs. G. Gunby Jordon
Mrs. James W. Key

Mrs. E. Buford King, Jr.
Mrs. James B. Knight
Mrs. Jack Lawler
Mrs. David G. Lewis
Mrs. Frank K. Martin
Mrs. William H. Martin
Mrs. Leighton W. McPherson
Mrs. David Mills
Mrs. W. Watt Neal
Mrs. Brown Nicholson, Jr.
Mrs. A. Henry Nordhausen
Mrs. Francis Norman, Jr.
Mrs. B.H. Petersen, Jr.
Mr. Clarke Prather
Mrs. Henry Reeves
Mrs. J. Ralph Richards
Mrs. Harry S. Roberts, Jr.
Mrs. Jac H. Rothschild

Miss Fannie Schnell
Miss Mamie Schnell
Mrs. J. Kyle Spencer
Mr. James Stanley
Mrs. W.B. Stotesbury
Mrs. Carter S. Terrell
Mrs. John B. Thompson
Mrs. L.Z. Thrasher, Jr.
Mrs. Tom Tuggle
Mrs. Constance Van Blarcum
Mrs. J. Barrington Vaught
Mrs. Charlton H. Williams
Mrs. Joseph A. Willman
Mrs. John H. Winn, Jr.
Mrs. Joseph P. Zollo

The Junior League of Columbus, Georgia, Inc. thanks its members, families and friends who have contributed recipes for **A Southern Collection Then and Now**. It is our sincere hope that no one has been inadvertently omitted.

Terrell Tuggle Adams
Julie Smith Alexander
Margaret Neal Amos
Jean Rea Anderson
Jennifer Magoni Andrews
Patti Paine Andrews
Lisa Mercier Arnold
Jennifer Wood Badcock
Kyle Avery Bair
Becky Nye Bickerstaff
Catherine Zimmerman Bickerstaff
Sara Bussey Bickerstaff
Betsy King Binns
Dorris Pappas Bishop
Kimberly Hagler Bishop
Courtney Calhoun Blackmar

Frances Dixon Blackmar
Jane Kendrick Blackmar
Amelie Burrus Blackmon
Jana Rittenhouse Blanchard
Angela Carey Blankenship
Gayle Fremaux Boland
Dodie Bowen
Mary Sprouse Boyd
Mary Bickerstaff Bradley
Minnie Rowe Bradley
Nell Hunt Bradley
William C. Bradley
Frances Watkins Branch
Lu Ann Binns Brandon
Sherrell Beach Braxton
Kimberly Flournoy Brennan

Virginia Young Browder
Karan Cargill Brown
Linda Lee Brown
Mary Singer Bruce
Leslie McClendon Bryan
Erie Sue Bloodworth Buck
Louann Clements Buck
Carden Flournoy Burdette
Ann Bishop Byars
Mary Tippins Cain
Winifred Battle Cain
Dell Turner Caldwell
Betsy Wellman Calhoun
Helen Langley Calhoun
Susan Martin Calhoun
Marla Burr Caligaris

Nancy Hodges Callaway
Lisa Butts Callaway-Wood
Linda Henry Callier
Julie Woodruff Camp
Valerie Whitney Camp
Joan Cargill
Jane Barders Chancellor
Mary Mullino Clason
Louisa Cargill Clinkscales
Rhonda Pritchett Clippinger
Cindy Carns Collins
Cynthia Woodsmall Collins
Mary Larabee Condron
T.J. Temple Connaughty
Faye Cook
Sandra Tally Coolik

Janet Mims Corbin
Betsy Whitaker Covington
Shirley Monacelli Craddock
Jean Beresford Crim
Dean Russ Crowe
Joanna Harris Culbreth
Joan Edrington Culpepper
Susan Sledge Culpepper
Virginia Pekor Culpepper
Jane Hester Cummings
Mary Daniels
Bettyesue Caproni Dedwylder
Kay Holliday Denes
Claire Patraude Derr
Roxann Gray Dismuke
Susie Bankston Dismuke
Alice Gentry Douglas
Lea Lewis Dowd
Twyla Pifer Dudley
Sherry Sexton Duncan
Louise Spencer Dupra
Brooks Cunningham Dykes
Eugene T. Dykes, Jr.
Sheryl Walsh Edgar
Martha Joan Humes Edrington
Jane Etheridge
Catherine Suntell Evans
Sherry Hinson Evans
Kimetha Inman Eysel
Nicole Long Farley
Courtney Lane Farmer
Carol Rabbit Faulkner
Nancy Ogie Fay
Carol Turner Flournoy
Lucile Redmond Flournoy
Martha Martin Flournoy
Billie Powell Flowers
Jean Rogers Flowers
Loretta Sparrow Flowers
Melanie Wood Flowers
Ruth Combs Flowers
Dana Williams French
Cynthia Cox Garrard
Vickie Portwood Gilbert
Mauren Callahan Gottfried
Jane Drury Graffagnino
Elizabeth Dudley Graham
Laura Mims Grantham
Peggy Beck Gray
Christine Fort Griffin
Ethel Kilgore Griffin
Kay Enloe Gudger
Nancy Riley Hallman
Isla Hunter Hamburger
Susi Pickenpaugh Hamlett
Donna Sears Hand
Christian Lorraine Harcourt

Dorothy Stevenson Harcourt
Mary Browder Harcourt
Sarah McDuffie Hardaway
Eleanor Glenn Hardegree
Sarah Harding
Patricia Hoffman Hargarten
Elinor Martin Harper
Barbara Benoit Harrell
Lee Chambers Harrell
Amy Harris
Elizabeth Burgin Harris
Melissa Jurgensen Harris
Angie Scott Hart
J. Madden Hatcher, Jr.
Martha Gilliam Hatcher
Sara Bickerstaff Hatcher
Aleta Cochrane Henderson
Karon Henderson
Kathleen Griffin Hendrix
Sue Boykin Henson
Betsey Henard Hewitt
Susan Cooper Hickey
Jane Wallich Hoffman
Beth Joiner Hofstetter
Carla Wickizer Hollek
Virginia Daniel Holman
Jennifer Terrell Horne
Brenda Bragg Hubbard
Joanne Alexander Hudson
Maude Martin Huff
Mary Phil Hamilton Illges
Linda Lewis Jackson
Elizabeth Roberts James
Laura Newman Jefferson
Celia Crawford Jenkins
Kim Giles Jinks
Karen McLendon Johnson
Pamela Pitts Johnson
Amy Pate Johnston
Carol Woolfolk Johnston
Jane McLeod Jones
Barbara Bauman Kamensky
Ann Greene Key
Pegi Hewitt Kimbrell
Nancy Driver King
Rebecca Hardaway King
Lucy Fay Knight
Jill Matthews LaForce
Deborah Ridings Lane
Devon Eastman Levy
Penny Browder Lewallyn
Jeanne Anderson Lewis
Jane Logan
Peggy Askew Love
LuWanda G. Lugo
Sandra Barton Majure
Nancy Snider Martin

Charlene Roberts Marx
Marsha Eaton Mason
Gail Green McClure
Tracy Lyn McCormick
Adelaide Hutto McGurk
Susan Blanchard Metcalf
Louise Key Miller
Carolyn Hewitt Mitchell
Julie Crowder Mitchell
Susan Hickey Mitchell
Bonnie Browder Mize
"J" Passailaigue Mize
Genie Graetz Mize
Chris Reaves Moore
Marie Turner Moshell
Suzanne Isom Mullin
Helen Harlin Neal
Alice Tartt Bailey Nicholson
Elizabeth Vail Nigh
Ann Ogletree Noble
Sean Dodd Norman
Marilu Hickey Novy
Barbara Brown Page
Michelle Knox Parker
Dorothy Mitchell Patterson
Lloyd Jackson Pease
Kathy Miller Peebles
Marjorie Cargill Petri
Mary Louise Duffee Philips
Jeannie Duncan Pierson
Marjorie Maxine Pifer
Susan Cashwell Pitts
Charlene Podger-Gay
Kelly Simpson Pollard
Anne Bogart Porter
Laura Passailaigue Porter
Helen Watkins Posey
Kathryn Rogers Postma
Brinkley Burks Pound
Carroll Kenimer Pound
Nancy Toney Prescott
Kelly Flournoy Pridgen
Elizabeth Strickland Redden
Mary Reed
Deborah Rykard Rhodes
Marjorie Thrasher Richardson
Jean Guy Rittenhouse
Grace Champion Robbins
Emily Sharp Robinson
Ann Schwan Robison
Becky Whisnant Roddenbery
Sam Roney
Samuel C. Ruffner
Rebecca Welsh Rumer
Sharon Enfinger Sanders
Ellen Petty Sargent
Kay Wike Saunders

Charles Stephens Scarborough, Jr.
Susan Harrell Scarborough
Molly Morgan Scarbrough
Elizabeth Robinson Scarbrough
Margaret Horsey Schley
Marilee Nuckolls Schomburg
Glenda Langston Sexton
Pamela Schladensky Shuler
Elizabeth Schwan Simmons
Leslie Hall Slaughter
Louise Tennent Smith
Nancy Saunders Smith
Rebecca Perkins Smith
Stephanie Sears Snavely
Cynthia Black Sparks
Rita Fillion Sparrow
Kathelen Van Blarcum Spencer
Sally Davis Spencer
Mary Stafford
Judi Freedman Steinberg
Julie Blattner Straus
Barbara Hamby Swift
Jeanne Robert Swift
Kathryn Wright Tanner
Catherine Freeman Tanzine
Sally Tarsitano
Barbara Little Tavenner
Eugenia Smithwick Taylor
Pamela Sutton Thompson
Marjorie Graves Thrasher
Lisa McLendon Torbert
Jenny Davis Trawick
June Peterson Turner
Starla Culbreth Turner
Alice Allen Upchurch
DeAun Watson Upchurch
Elizabeth Finlay Vingi
Donna Eskew Voynich
Laura Duncan Wagner
Kathy Combs Warner
Mary Munn Watkins
Sherrie Williams Watkins
Viola Hubbard Watson
Amy Dougherty White
Lisa Lane White
Laura Smith Wickham
Katherine Ward Wike
Ann Hubbard Williams
Rebecca Calvert Williams
Sandra McKenzie Williams
Kimberly Adcock Willis
Richard H. Wilson
Lane Roberts Woolfolk
Jane Hoffman Worthington
Gayle Johnson Yarbrough
Beth Lane Young
Dorothy McNeel Young

Index

A

Absolute Very Best Buttermilk Pie, The, 239
Alfred Lunt Pot Roast, 117
Almond Roca Bars, 246
APPETIZERS
  Almond Pinecones, 10
  Artichoke and Crab Dip, 13
  Avocado Dip, 13
  Baked Pecan Brie, 9
  Black Bean Torte, 30
  Boursin Cheese Spread, 10
  Broiled Crab Melt-A-Ways, 22
  Caviar Mousse, 20
  Cheese and Mushroom Toast, 23
  Cheese in Pastry, 8
  Cheese Straws, 26
  Cherry Tomatoes Stuffed with Avocado, 31
  Chutney Bacon Cheese Hors D'Oeuvres, 28
  Creamy Dip for Apples, 12
  Curry Dip for Raw Vegetables, 11
  Deviled Pecans, 26
  Easy Shrimp Dip, 16
  Easy Sweet and Sour Sauce, 32
  Fresh Fruit Dressing, 14
  Green Chile Tortillas, 24
  Ham Delights, 24
  Herbed Dip for Vegetables, 11
  Homemade Salsa, 18
  Hot Seafood Spread, 13
  Hot Tuna Dip, 15
  Layered Shrimp Spread, 16
  Low Fat Cheese Spread, 9
  Marinated Broccoli, 16
  Mary Mobley's Shrimp Mold, 27
  Mexican Cheese Dip, 19
  Mushroom Pâté, 21
  Mushroom Turnovers, 29
  Olive and Pecan Canapés, 22
  Olive Surprises, 22
  Pickled Shrimp, 20
  Pineapple Cheese Ball, 9
  Pizza Dip, 17
  Rich Cinnamon Bits, 27
  Salmon Bacon Ball, 8
  Salmon Mousse with Sour Cream Dill Sauce, 17
  Sausage Bacon Delights, 25
  Sesame Asparagus Roll-ups, 23
  Shrimp Curry Mold, 28
  Shrimp Rémoulade, 31
  Snappy Cheese Wafers, 25
  Southern Salsa, 19
  Spinach Cheese Squares, 19
  Spinach Vegetable Dip, 12
  Steak Dip, 15
  Sugared Pecans, 26
  Sun-Dried Tomato Cheese Spread, 11
  Surprise Dip, 14
  Tenderloin with Béarnaise, 32
  Tex Mex, 18
  Vidalia Onion Dip, 12
  Water Chestnut Dip, 14
  Whole Wheat Cheese Straws, 24
  Zesty Broccoli Dip, 15
  Zucchini Squares, 21
Apple Blossom Punch, 37
Apple Cider Salmon, 180
APPLES
  Apple Pecan Bread, 79
  Apple Pecan Cake, 226
  Apples and Cream Crumb Pie, 234
  Baked Oranges, 200
  Creamy Dip for Apples, 12
  Easy Apple Crisp, 263
Applesauce Mini-Muffins, 82
APRICOTS
  Apricot Chicken, 139
  Hot Curried Fruit, 201
ARTICHOKES
  Artichoke and Crab Dip, 13
  Artichoke and Spinach Casserole, 209
  Chicken Shrimp Artichoke Casserole, 169
  Chicken–Artichoke Pasta Salad, 97
  Curried Saffron Rice, 59
  Marinated Green Beans and Artichokes, 202
  Tangy Romaine Toss, 65
  Tarragon Chicken, 135
  Tomato Well Stuffed, A, 63
ASPARAGUS
  Asparagus and Pea Casserole, 192
  Asparagus Caesar, 192
  Asparagus Vinaigrette, 66
  Chicken Asparagus Casserole, 136
  Cold Potato Soup with Asparagus, 42
  Creamy Lemon–Chive Pasta with Asparagus, 104
  Marinated Asparagus, 192
  Sesame Asparagus Roll-ups, 23
AVOCADOS
  Avocado Dip, 13
  Caribbean Salad, 59
  Cherry Tomatoes Stuffed with Avocado, 31
  Tex Mex, 18

B

Baked Chicken Breasts with Scallions and Lime, 148
Baked Chicken Parmesan, 139
Baked Grits, 214
Baked Ham, 128
Baked Oranges, 200
Baked Pecan Brie, 9
Baked Red Snapper, 163
Baked Squash Casserole, 209
Balsamic Chicken and Peppers, 149
BANANAS
  Banana Cream Pie, 237
  Banana Nut Cake, 224
  Ponte Vedra Innlet Banana Bread, 78
Barbecue Sauce, 190
Barbecue Shrimp, 172
Barbequed Ribs, 188
Basil Chicken, 185
Bay Point Bloody Mary, 36
Bay Point Milk Punch, 35
BEANS
  Bean and Ham Soup, 52
  Black Bean Soup, 53
  Black Bean Torte, 30
  Drunken Beans, 202
  Marinated Green Beans and Artichokes, 202
  Picnic Black Beans, 64
  Sausage with Red Beans and Rice, 127
  Sautéed Green Beans, 203
  Soul Satisfying Chili, 125
  Tex Mex, 18
  Three Bean Bake, 193
  Venison Chili, 158
  White Chili, 153
BEEF
  Alfred Lunt Pot Roast, 117
  Barbecue Sauce, 190
  Beef Shish Kabobs, 179
  Beef Stir–Fry, 118
  Beef Stroganoff, 120
  Beef Tenderloin, 111
  Beef Tips, 118
  Bourbon Steaks, 176
  Cabernet Sirloin with Garlic, 111
  Carnonnades Flamandes (Beef Stew), 119

Easy Swiss Steak, 121
Elegant Beef Tenderloin, 117
Fabulous Flank Steak, 177
Fantastic Flank Steak, 116
Green Peppercorn Sauce, 126
Individual Beef Wellington, 115
Kentucky Bar–B–Q, 125
Marinated Beef Tenderloin, 178
Mexican Cheese Dip, 19
Mexican Cornbread Casserole, 122
Mexican Supreme, 121
Midnight Marinade, 126
Old Fashioned Meat Loaf, 120
Olde English Prime Rib, 112
Oriental Beef, 176
Peppered Beefsteaks with Jack Daniel's
    Sauce, 113
Pot Roast, 116
Pot Roast with Vegetables, 115
Quick Barbecue Sauce, 189
Reuben Casserole, 122
Soul Satisfying Chili, 125
Spaghetti Pie, 123
Steak au Poivre, 114
Steak Dip, 15
Sweet Soy Marinade, 126
Tenderloin with Béarnaise, 32
Vegetable Soup, 50
Zesty Barbecue Sauce, 189
Zesty Marinated Flank Steak, 177
Berries Berries Berries, 58
Berry Mallow Yambake, 210
BEVERAGES
Apple Blossom Punch, 37
Bay Point Bloody Mary, 36
Bay Point Milk Punch, 35
Crock Pot Cider, 33
Fiesta Slush, 33
Frosted Orange, 36
Frozen Pink Vodka, 35
Georgia Mint Iced Tea, 34
Georgia Watermelon-Wine Punch, 37
Homemade Kahlúa, 35
Instant Cocoa Mix, 33
Mexican Mocha Coffee, 37
Mr. John's Eggnog, 36
Party Punch, 35
Raspberry Apéritif, 37
Rum Slushes, 34
Strawberry Margarita, 34
Tea Punch, 33
Yellow Bird, 34
Yogurt Smoothie, 38
BISCUITS
Breakaway Vegetable Bread, 92
Cheddar Drop Biscuits, 86

Monkey Bread, 92
Black and White Cheesecake Bites, 248
Black Bean Soup, 53
Black Bean Torte, 30
BLACK-EYED PEAS
Southern Salsa, 19
Spicy Black-eyed Peas, 193
Blue Cheese Dressing, 72
Blue Cheese Tomato Dressing, 73
BLUEBERRIES
Blueberry Cobbler, 268
Blueberry Soup, 40
Williamsburg Blueberry Muffins, 84
Boo's Potato Salad, 61
Bourbon Steaks, 176
Boursin Cheese Spread, 10
BREADS
Apple Pecan Bread, 79
Applesauce Mini-Muffins, 82
Bran Muffins, 83
Breakaway Vegetable Bread, 92
Carrot Pineapple Bread, 80
Cheddar Drop Biscuits, 86
Cricket Tea Room Cornbread, 86
Dilly Cheese Bread, 80
Flavorful French Toast, 93
Honey of a Spread!, 94
Marshmallow Cinnamon Puffs, 91
Melt Away Muffins, 85
Mexican Cornbread, 85
Millionaire Muffins, 83
Miracle Rolls, 91
Molasses Squash Muffins, 84
Monkey Bread, 92
Mother's Refrigerator Rolls, 87
Parmesan Herb Loaves, 81
Peachy Almond Muffins, 82
Pecan Muffins, 85
Ponte Vedra Innlet Banana Bread, 78
Sour Cream Coffee Cake, 93
Sour Cream Cornbread, 86
Sour Dough Bread, 88
Sweet Cinnamon Quick Bread, 94
Sweet Potato Nut Bread, 78
Toasted Thyme Sticks, 81
Versatile Seasoned Butter, 94
Williamsburg Blueberry Muffins, 84
Worth-the-Wait Rolls, 90
Zucchini Bread, 79
BROCCOLI
Broccoli Lorraine, 195
Broccoli Soufflé, 195
Broccoli Soup, 45
Cheesy Broccoli and Rice, 196
Chicken Divan, 152
Cream of Broccoli Soup, 46

Fresh Broccoli Salad, 61
Marinated Broccoli, 16
Zesty Broccoli Dip, 15
Broiled Crab Melt-A-Ways, 22
Brown Rice and Almond Salad, 60
Brown Sugar and Cinnamon Pound Cake,
    217
Brown–Eyed Susans, 256
Brownie Pie, 231
Brownie Pudding Cake, 265
Brunswick Stew, 51
Butter Cream Sandwich Cookies, 250
Butter Pecan Ice Cream, 273
Butter Pecan Turtle Bars, 245
Butterflied Lamb, 175
Butternut Squash Puff, 209

C

CABBAGE
Cole Slaw, 68
Red Cabbage, 213
Sour Cream Cole Slaw, 68
Cabernet Sirloin with Garlic, 111
Caesar Salad Dressing, 75
CAKES
Apple Pecan Cake, 226
Banana Nut Cake, 224
Brown Sugar and Cinnamon Pound
    Cake, 217
Brownie Pudding Cake, 265
Cake in a Pan, 227
Carrot Cake, 224
Chocolate Cake, 222
Chocolate Chip Pound Cake, 216
Chocolate Dish Cake, 218
Chocolate Pound Loaf Cakes, 216
Chocolate Praline Cake, 219
Cream Cheese Pound Cake, 218
Easy Chocolate Frosting, 229
Favorite Jam Cake, 225
Fruit Cake Cups, 257
Gran's Lemon Cheese Cake, 229
Hershey Chocolate Cake, 223
Lemon Cake, 228
Mary's Caramel Icing, 230
Never Fail White Icing, 230
Orange Blooms, 228
Oreo Cheesecake, 220
Peanut Butter Chocolate Chip
    Cheesecake, 221
Plum Cake, 225
Poppy Seed Cake, 227
Sour Cream Cheese Cake, 222
Sour Cream Cinnamon–Nut Pound
    Cake, 217

Sour Cream Coffee Cake, 93

CANDIES
Chocolate Fudge, 258
Chocolate Snacks, 257
Easter Bird's Nests, 261
Peanut Brittle, 258
Candy Bar Brownies, 240
Caramel Chocolate Layer Brownies, 241
Caribbean Salad, 59
Carnonnades Flamandes (Beef Stew), 119

CARROTS
Apple Pecan Bread, 79
Carrot Cake, 224
Carrot Pineapple Bread, 80
Company Carrots, 197
Cool Dill Carrots, 196
Glazed Carrots, 197
Grilled Vegetables, 174
My Favorite Carrot Soup, 47
Casserole Arroz, 207

CAULIFLOWER
Cauliflower, 194
Cauliflower Bloom, 194
Caviar Mousse, 20
Charlotte Russe, 260

CHEESE
Almond Pinecones, 10
Artichoke and Crab Dip, 13
Baked Pecan Brie, 9
Baked Squash Casserole, 209
Blue Cheese Dressing, 72
Blue Cheese Tomato Dressing, 73
Boursin Cheese Spread, 10
Broccoli Soufflé, 195
Broiled Crab Melt-A-Ways, 22
Casserole Arroz, 207
Cheddar Drop Biscuits, 86
Cheese and Mushroom Toast, 23
Cheese in Pastry, 8
Cheese Soup, 54
Cheese Straws, 26
Cheesy Broccoli and Rice, 196
Cheesy Broiled Flounder, 165
Chicken Divan, 152
Chicken Parmigiana, 140
Chicken Tetrazzini, 145
Chutney Bacon Cheese Hors
   D'Oeuvres, 28
Crab Au Gratin, 161
Creamy Dip for Apples, 12
Crunchy Chicken Cheese Bake, 143
Delightful Zucchini, 212
Dilly Cheese Bread, 80
Easy Spinach Lasagna, 103
Eggplant Patrice, 200
Fresh Fruit Tart, 263

Green Chile Tortillas, 24
Ham Delights, 24
Holland Rusk Salad, 63
Hot Chicken Salad Casserole, 135
Hot Seafood Spread, 13
Hot Tuna Dip, 15
Italian Boneless Chicken, 138
Italian Tomato Pie, 211
Lasagna, 124
Layered Shrimp Spread, 16
Louisiana Grits, 214
Low Fat Cheese Spread, 9
Mary Mobley's Shrimp Mold, 27
Mexican Cheese Dip, 19
Mexican Supreme, 121
Mushroom Pâté, 21
Mushroom Turnovers, 29
Olive and Pecan Canapés, 22
Olive Surprises, 22
Parmesan Herb Loaves, 81
Parmesan Vidalias, 205
Pesto, 106
Pineapple Cheese Ball, 9
Pizza Dip, 17
Rich Cinnamon Bits, 27
Salmon Bacon Ball, 8
Salmon Mousse with Sour Cream Dill
   Sauce, 17
Sea Island Salad, 70
Seafood Medley, 169
Sesame Asparagus Roll-ups, 23
Sheri's Chocolate Delight, 259
Shrimp Aspic, 70
Shrimp Curry Mold, 28
Snappy Cheese Wafers, 25
Southern Pecan Tarts, 240
Spaghetti Pie, 123
Spinach Cheese Squares, 19
Sun-Dried Tomato Cheese Spread, 11
Swiss Cheese Grits, 213
Tex Mex, 18
Tomato Bacon Cheese Onions, 204
Tomato Cheese Mold, 58
Veal Parmesan, 110
Versatile Seasoned Butter, 94
Vidalia Onion Dip, 12
White Chili, 153
Whole Wheat Cheese Straws, 24
Zesty Broccoli Dip, 15
Zucchini Squares, 21

CHEESECAKES
Black and White Cheesecake Bites,
   248
Cream Cheese Pumpkin Pie, 239
Gran's Lemon Cheese Cake, 229
Lemon Cheese Pie, 238

Lemon–Raspberry Cheesecake Squares,
   249
Oreo Cheesecake, 220
Peanut Butter Chocolate Chip
   Cheesecake, 221
Sour Cream Cheese Cake, 222
Summertime Pie, 238

CHERRIES
Cherry Dessert, 264
Fruit Aspic, 71
Hot Curried Fruit, 201
Sweet and Sour Chicken, 142
Cherry Tomatoes Stuffed with Avocado, 31
Chess Pie, 239
Chewy Brown Sugar Brownies, 246

CHICKEN
Apricot Chicken, 139
Baked Chicken Breasts with Scallions
   and Lime, 148
Baked Chicken Parmesan, 139
Balsamic Chicken and Peppers, 149
Barbecue Sauce, 190
Basil Chicken, 185
Brunswick Stew, 51
Chicken and Wild Rice Soup, 47
Chicken Asparagus Casserole, 136
Chicken Breast Lombardy, 150
Chicken Diablo, 142
Chicken Divan, 152
Chicken Fajitas, 182
Chicken in Dill Sauce, 140
Chicken Marengo, 100
Chicken Marinade, 190
Chicken Parmigiana, 140
Chicken Pie, 150
Chicken Salad Vinaigrette, 67
Chicken Shrimp Artichoke Casserole,
   169
Chicken Soufflé with Mushroom Sauce,
   137
Chicken Tetrazzini, 145
Chicken with Muscadine Sauce and
   Almond Pasta, 101
Chicken–Artichoke Pasta Salad, 97
Country Captain, 146
Cranberry Chicken, 142
Crunchy Chicken Cheese Bake, 143
Curried Chicken Salad With Chutney,
   66
Devilish Chicken, 149
French Chicken, 144
Garlic Chicken, 134
Gourmet Champagne Lentil Soup, 54
Hawaiian Chicken, 183
Herbed Chicken and Pasta Salad, 96
Honey Mustard Chicken, 182

Hot Chicken Salad Casserole, 135
Hunter's Chicken, 147
Individual Chicken Pockets, 152
Italian Boneless Chicken, 138
Lemon Mushroom Chicken with Parsley, 137
Lime Chicken with Honey Butter, 184
Mulligatawny Soup, 49
Mustard Sauce, 159
Oven Barbecued Chicken, 143
Pecan Chicken, 141
Pineapple Chicken, 144
Poppy Seed Chicken, 136
Poultry Marinade, 159
Quick Barbecue Sauce, 189
Ranch Style Chicken, 183
Roasted Chicken Feast, 134
Rotisserie Chicken, 184
Royal Chicken Crêpes, 151
Sesame Chicken, 141
Sesame Ginger Chicken, 181
Sliced Chicken with Lime and Basil, 67
Southwest Chicken, 154
Stir-Fry Chicken and Vegetables, 153
Sweet and Sour Chicken, 142
Tarragon Chicken, 135
White Chili, 153
Zesty Barbecue Sauce, 189
Chili Sauce Dressing, 72
Chinese Pork Tenderloin, 130
Chocolate Angel Pie, 232
Chocolate Carmelita Bars, 243
Chocolate Chip Oatmeal Cookies, 254
Chocolate Chip Pecan Pie, 232
Chocolate Chip Pound Cake, 216
Chocolate Chocolate Chip Cookies, 254
Chocolate Cinnamon Ice Cream, 274
Chocolate Dish Cake, 218
Chocolate Fudge, 258
Chocolate Peanut Butter Cookies, 253
Chocolate Pecan Bars, 244
Chocolate Pound Loaf Cakes, 216
Chocolate Praline Cake, 219
Chocolate Snacks, 257
Chutney Bacon Cheese Hors D'Oeuvres, 28

CLAMS
Clam Chowder, 49
Quick Clam Chowder, 43

COFFEE CAKE
Sour Cream Coffee Cake, 93
Cold Cucumber Soup, 40
Cold Potato Soup with Asparagus, 42
Cold Squash Soup, 41
Cole Slaw, 68
Company Carrots, 197

Congealed Citrus Salad, 71
Congealed Cranberry Salad, 72
COOKIES AND BARS
Almond Roca Bars, 246
Black and White Cheesecake Bites, 248
Brown–Eyed Susans, 256
Butter Cream Sandwich Cookies, 250
Butter Pecan Turtle Bars, 245
Candy Bar Brownies, 240
Caramel Chocolate Layer Brownies, 241
Chewy Brown Sugar Brownies, 246
Chocolate Carmelita Bars, 243
Chocolate Chip Oatmeal Cookies, 254
Chocolate Chocolate Chip Cookies, 254
Chocolate Peanut Butter Cookies, 253
Chocolate Pecan Bars, 244
Cinnamon Crisps, 245
Crisp Sugar Cookies, 250
Danish Cookies, 251
Double Chocolate Cream Cheese Brownies, 242
Gingersnaps, 255
Iced Pecan Sandies, 251
Lemon Love Notes, 247
Lemon–Raspberry Cheesecake Squares, 249
Melting Moments, 249
Oatmeal Crispies, 253
Oatmeal Lace Cookies, 255
Old Fashioned Gingerbread, 267
Peanut Butter Kiss Cookies, 256
Pecan Sticks, 252
Snickerdoodles, 252
Special K Cookies, 252
Walnut Shortbread, 247
Cool Dill Carrots, 196
CORN
Corn Pudding, 197
Corn Tomato Zucchini Casserole, 198
Low Country Boil, 167
CORNBREAD
Cricket Tea Room Cornbread, 86
Divine Dressing, 90
Mexican Cornbread, 85
Mexican Cornbread Casserole, 122
Sour Cream Cornbread, 86
CORNISH HENS
Orange Glazed Cornish Hens, 155
Texas Style Game Hens, 185
Country Captain, 146
CRABMEAT
Artichoke and Crab Dip, 13
Broiled Crab Melt-A-Ways, 22

Crab Au Gratin, 161
Crab Cakes, 162
Crab Fettuccine, 98
Easy Seafood Bisque, 46
Hot Seafood Spread, 13
Julia's Crabmeat, 162
Pappy Prather's Seafood Gumbo, 56
Seafood and Leek Bisque, 48
Seafood Medley, 169
CRANBERRIES
Berry Mallow Yambake, 210
Congealed Cranberry Salad, 72
Cranberry Chicken, 142
Cranberry Relish, 201
CRAWFISH
Crawfish Fettuccine, 100
Cream Cheese Pound Cake, 218
Cream Cheese Pumpkin Pie, 239
Cream of Broccoli Soup, 46
Creamy Dip for Apples, 12
Creamy Lemon–Chive Pasta with Asparagus, 104
Crème Caramel, 262
Creole Shrimp, 168
Cricket Tea Room Cornbread, 86
Crisp Sugar Cookies, 250
Crock Pot Cider, 33
Crunchy Chicken Cheese Bake, 143
CUCUMBERS
Cold Cucumber Soup, 40
Curried Chicken Salad With Chutney, 66
Curried Rice Salad, 60
Curried Saffron Rice, 59
Curried Scallops and Shrimp, 171
Curry Dip for Raw Vegetables, 11

D

Danish Cookies, 251
Delightful Zucchini, 212
DESSERTS
Blueberry Cobbler, 268
Brownie Pudding Cake, 265
Butter Pecan Ice Cream, 273
Charlotte Russe, 260
Cherry Dessert, 264
Chocolate Cinnamon Ice Cream, 274
Chocolate Éclair Dessert, 265
Crème Caramel, 262
Double Chocolate Torte, 266
Easter Bird's Nests, 261
Easy Apple Crisp, 263
Egg Custard, 261
Fresh Fruit Tart, 263
Lemon Ice Cream, 273
Lemon Ice Dessert, 271

Lemon Soufflé, 272
Mrs. Storey's Boiled Custard, 269
Old Fashioned Gingerbread, 267
Orange Pineapple Sherbet, 274
Oranges in Red Wine, 271
Oreo Sundae, 260
Pâte Brisée, 268
Peach Champagne Sorbet, 272
Peach Cobbler, 264
Peach Ice Cream, 274
Peppermint Ice Cream, 273
Poached Pears in Red Wine with
	Vanilla Custard Sauce, 270
Sheri's Chocolate Delight, 259
Sweet Mouthful, 269
Deviled Pecans, 26
Devilish Chicken, 149
Dill Shrimp, 170
Dilly Cheese Bread, 80
DIPS AND SPREADS
Almond Pinecones, 10
Artichoke and Crab Dip, 13
Avocado Dip, 13
Baked Pecan Brie, 9
Black Bean Torte, 30
Boursin Cheese Spread, 10
Caviar Mousse, 20
Cheese in Pastry, 8
Creamy Dip for Apples, 12
Curry Dip for Raw Vegetables, 11
Easy Shrimp Dip, 16
Herbed Dip for Vegetables, 11
Homemade Salsa, 18
Honey of a Spread!, 94
Hot Seafood Spread, 13
Hot Tuna Dip, 15
Layered Shrimp Spread, 16
Low Fat Cheese Spread, 9
Mary Mobley's Shrimp Mold, 27
Mexican Cheese Dip, 19
Mushroom Pâté, 21
Olive and Pecan Canapés, 22
Pineapple Cheese Ball, 9
Pizza Dip, 17
Salmon Bacon Ball, 8
Salmon Mousse with Sour Cream Dill
	Sauce, 17
Shrimp Curry Mold, 28
Southern Salsa, 19
Spinach Vegetable Dip, 12
Steak Dip, 15
Sun-Dried Tomato Cheese Spread, 11
Surprise Dip, 14
Tex Mex, 18
Versatile Seasoned Butter, 94
Vidalia Onion Dip, 12

Water Chestnut Dip, 14
Zesty Broccoli Dip, 15
Divine Dressing, 90
Double Chocolate Cream Cheese
	Brownies, 242
Double Chocolate Torte, 266
DOVE
Grilled Dove Breasts, 187
Mamie's Quail or Dove, 157
Sauce for Venison, Dove or Duck, A,
	158
DRESSING
Divine Dressing, 90
Drunken Beans, 202
DUCK
Sauce for Venison, Dove or Duck, A,
	158

E

Easter Bird's Nests, 261
Easy Apple Crisp, 263
Easy Brown Rice, 208
Easy Chocolate Frosting, 229
Easy Congealed Peach Salad, 71
Easy Seafood Bisque, 46
Easy Shrimp Dip, 16
Easy Spinach Lasagna, 103
Easy Sweet and Sour Sauce, 32
Easy Swiss Steak, 121
Ed's Frozen Turkey Breast, 155
Egg Custard, 261
Egg Custard Pie, 236
EGGPLANT
Eggplant Patrice, 200
Oven Fried Eggplant, 199
Tomato and Eggplant Casserole, 199
Elegant Beef Tenderloin, 117

F

Fabulous Flank Steak, 177
Fantastic Flank Steak, 116
Favorite Jam Cake, 225
Fettuccine Carbonara, 102
Fiesta Slush, 33
FISH
Baked Red Snapper, 163
Cheesy Broiled Flounder, 165
Fish with Crumbs, 164
Greta Sauce, 172
Grilled Catfish Fillets, 179
Grouper Greco, 164
Marinated Orange Roughy, 179
Mustard Sauce, 159

Orange Roughy with Cucumber and
	Dill, 165
Pan Fried Snapper, 163
French Chicken, 144
French Onion Soup, 55
FRENCH TOAST
Flavorful French Toast, 93
Fresh Broccoli Salad, 61
Fresh Fruit Dressing, 14
Fresh Peach Pie, 236
Fried Green Tomatoes, 198
Frosted Orange, 36
FROSTINGS
Easy Chocolate Frosting, 229
Mary's Caramel Icing, 230
Never Fail White Icing, 230
Frozen Pink Vodka, 35
Fruit Aspic, 71
Fruit Cake Cups, 257

G

GAME
Grilled Dove Breasts, 187
Ground Venison Casserole, 158
Mamie's Quail or Dove, 157
Sauce for Venison, Dove or Duck, A,
	158
Southern Quail, 157
Venison, 159
Venison Chili, 158
Garlic Chicken, 134
Georgia Mint Iced Tea, 34
Georgia Watermelon-Wine Punch, 37
German Potato Salad, 62
Gingersnaps, 255
Glazed Carrots, 197
Glazed Ham Steaks, 127
Glorified Italian Dressing, 75
Gourmet Champagne Lentil Soup, 54
Gourmet Potatoes, 205
Gran's Lemon Cheese Cake, 229
GRAPEFRUIT
Congealed Citrus Salad, 71
Fruit Aspic, 71
GRAPES
Minted Grapes in Melon Boats, 59
GREEN CHILES
Casserole Arroz, 207
Green Chile Tortillas, 24
Green Goddess Salad Dressing, 74
Green Peppercorn Sauce, 126
Greta Sauce, 172
GRILLING
Apple Cider Salmon, 180
Barbecue Sauce, 190

Barbequed Ribs, 188
Basil Chicken, 185
Beef Shish Kabobs, 179
Bourbon Steaks, 176
Butterflied Lamb, 175
Chicken Fajitas, 182
Chicken Marinade, 190
Fabulous Flank Steak, 177
Grilled Catfish Fillets, 179
Grilled Dove Breasts, 187
Grilled Lamb Chops, 175
Grilled Lamb Roast, 176
Grilled Salmon Steaks, 180
Grilled Shrimp, 181
Grilled Vegetables, 174
Hawaiian Chicken, 183
Honey Mustard Chicken, 182
Lime Chicken with Honey Butter, 184
Marinated Beef Tenderloin, 178
Marinated Orange Roughy, 179
Oriental Beef, 176
Quick Barbecue Sauce, 189
Ranch Style Chicken, 183
Rosemary Marinated Pork Tenderloin, 186
Rotisserie Chicken, 184
Savory Grilled Potatoes, 174
Sesame Ginger Chicken, 181
Sesame Pork Tenderloin, 186
Smoked Turkey, 187
Teriyaki Pork Chops, 188
Texas Style Game Hens, 185
Zesty Barbecue Sauce, 189
Zesty Marinated Flank Steak, 177

GRITS
Baked Grits, 214
Louisiana Grits, 214
Swiss Cheese Grits, 213
Ground Venison Casserole, 158
Grouper Greco, 164

H

Ham Delights, 24
Hawaiian Chicken, 183
Hearts of Palm Salad, 64
Herbed Chicken and Pasta Salad, 96
Herbed Dip for Vegetables, 11
Herbed Pork Tenderloin, 131
Hershey Chocolate Cake, 223
Highland Gourmet's Marinated Rice, 207
Holiday Turkey with No Basting, 156
Holland Rusk Salad, 63
Homemade Kahlúa, 35
Homemade Salsa, 18
Honey Mustard Chicken, 182

Honey of a Spread!, 94
Hot and Sour Egg Drop Soup, 44
Hot Chicken Salad Casserole, 135
Hot Curried Fruit, 201
Hot Pineapple Casserole, 201
Hot Seafood Spread, 13
Hot Tuna Dip, 15
Hunter's Chicken, 147

I

ICE CREAM
Butter Pecan Ice Cream, 273
Chocolate Cinnamon Ice Cream, 274
Lemon Ice Cream, 273
Orange Pineapple Sherbet, 274
Peach Ice Cream, 274
Peppermint Ice Cream, 273
Iced Pecan Sandies, 251
Individual Beef Wellington, 115
Individual Chicken Pockets, 152
Instant Cocoa Mix, 33
Italian Boneless Chicken, 138
Italian Tomato Pie, 211

J

Joyce Christie's Fudge Pie, 231
Julia's Crabmeat, 162
Just Peachy Pork Chops, 129

K

Kentucky Bar–B–Q, 125
Key Lime Pie, 236

L

LAMB
Butterflied Lamb, 175
Grilled Lamb Chops, 175
Grilled Lamb Roast, 176
Lamb Curry in a Hurry, 109
Leg of Lamb, 109
Seasoned Leg of Lamb, 108
Lasagna, 124
Layered Shrimp Spread, 16
LEEKS
Seafood and Leek Bisque, 48
LEMON
Lemon Cake, 228
Lemon Cheese Pie, 238
Lemon Ice Cream, 273
Lemon Ice Dessert, 271
Lemon Love Notes, 247
Lemon Meringue Pie, 237

Lemon Mushroom Chicken with Parsley, 137
Lemon Soufflé, 272
Lemon–Raspberry Cheesecake Squares, 249
LENTILS
Gourmet Champagne Lentil Soup, 54
Lime Chicken with Honey Butter, 184
Louis Dressing, 74
Louisiana Grits, 214
Low Country Boil, 167
Low Fat Cheese Spread, 9

M

Mamie's Quail or Dove, 157
Marinated Asparagus, 192
Marinated Beef Tenderloin, 178
Marinated Broccoli, 16
Marinated Green Beans and Artichokes, 202
Marinated Orange Roughy, 179
Marshmallow Cinnamon Puffs, 91
Mary Mobley's Shrimp Mold, 27
Mary's Caramel Icing, 230
Mayo in a Blender, 76
Melting Moments, 249
Mexican Cheese Dip, 19
Mexican Cornbread, 85
Mexican Cornbread Casserole, 122
Mexican Mocha Coffee, 37
Mexican Supreme, 121
Microwave New Potatoes, 207
Midnight Marinade, 126
Minestrone Soup, 45
Minted Grapes in Melon Boats, 59
Miracle Rolls, 91
Mom's Chocolate Pie, 231
Monkey Bread, 92
Mother's Refrigerator Rolls, 87
Mr. John's Eggnog, 36
Mrs. Storey's Boiled Custard, 269
Mud Pie, 233
MUFFINS
Applesauce Mini-Muffins, 82
Bran Muffins, 83
Fruit Cake Cups, 257
Melt Away Muffins, 85
Millionaire Muffins, 83
Molasses Squash Muffins, 84
Peachy Almond Muffins, 82
Pecan Muffins, 85
Williamsburg Blueberry Muffins, 84
Mulligatawny Soup, 49
MUSHROOMS
Cheese and Mushroom Toast, 23

Lemon Mushroom Chicken with Parsley, 137
Mushroom Pâté, 21
Mushroom Soup, 52
Mushroom Turnovers, 29
Royal Chicken Crêpes, 151
Mustard Sauce, 159
My Favorite Carrot Soup, 47

N

Never Fail White Icing, 230
New Potatoes with Basil Cream Sauce, 206
New Potatoes With Dill, 62
New World Shrimp, 170
Noodles Supreme, 104
NUTS
Deviled Pecans, 26
Peanut Brittle, 258
Pecan Sticks, 252
Sour Cream Pecan Pie, 235
Southern Pecan Pie, 234
Sugared Pecans, 26

O

Oatmeal Crispies, 253
Oatmeal Lace Cookies, 255
OKRA
Okra and Tomatoes, 198
Old Fashioned Gingerbread, 267
Old Fashioned Meat Loaf, 120
Olde English Prime Rib, 112
OLIVES
Olive and Pecan Canapés, 22
Olive Surprises, 22
ONIONS
French Onion Soup, 55
Parmesan Vidalias, 205
Stuffed Vidalias, 203
Tomato Bacon Cheese Onions, 204
Vidalia Onion Dip, 12
Vidalia Onion Pie, 204
Orange Glazed Cornish Hens, 155
Orange Rice, 208
Orange Roughy with Cucumber and Dill, 165
ORANGES
Baked Oranges, 200
Caribbean Salad, 59
Congealed Citrus Salad, 71
Cranberry Relish, 201
Fruit Aspic, 71
Orange Blooms, 228
Orange Pineapple Sherbet, 274

Oranges in Red Wine, 271
Spinach Mandarin Orange Salad, 65
Oreo Cheesecake, 220
Oreo Sundae, 260
Oriental Beef, 176
Oven Barbecued Chicken, 143
Oven Fried Eggplant, 199
OYSTERS
Out of This World Oysters, 160
Oyster and Spinach Soup, 48
Pappy Prather's Seafood Gumbo, 56
Scalloped Oysters, 161

P

Pan Fried Snapper, 163
Pappy Prather's Seafood Gumbo, 56
Parmesan Herb Loaves, 81
Parmesan Vidalias, 205
Party Punch, 35
PASTA
Alfred Lunt Pot Roast, 117
Beef Stroganoff, 120
Beef Tips, 118
Chicken in Dill Sauce, 140
Chicken Marengo, 100
Chicken Tetrazzini, 145
Chicken with Muscadine Sauce and Almond Pasta, 101
Chicken–Artichoke Pasta Salad, 97
Crab Fettuccine, 98
Crawfish Fettuccine, 100
Creamy Lemon–Chive Pasta with Asparagus, 104
Devilish Chicken, 149
Easy Spinach Lasagna, 103
Easy Swiss Steak, 121
Fettuccine Carbonara, 102
French Chicken, 144
Herbed Chicken and Pasta Salad, 96
Lasagna, 124
Noodles Supreme, 104
Pasta Leon, 102
Penne Pasta with Fresh Tomato, Basil and Ricotta Sauce, 105
Pesto, 106
Picante Pasta, 103
Rigatoni with Ham and Mozzarella, 102
Sea Island Salad, 70
Shrimp and Angel Hair Pasta, 99
Shrimp with Feta Sauce, 99
Shrimp with Spinach Pasta, 98
Spaghetti Pie, 123
Spaghetti Sauce with Italian Sausage, 133

Spicy Sesame Pasta, 105
Veal Marsala, 110
Vermicelli Salad, 96
Pâte Brisée, 268
Patti Howard's Zucchini and Tomatoes, 212
Pea Soup, 50
PEACHES
Easy Congealed Peach Salad, 71
Fresh Peach Pie, 236
Hot Curried Fruit, 201
Just Peachy Pork Chops, 129
Peach Champagne Sorbet, 272
Peach Cobbler, 264
Peach Ice Cream, 274
Peach Soup, 42
Peachy Almond Muffins, 82
Peanut Brittle, 258
Peanut Butter Chocolate Chip Cheesecake, 221
Peanut Butter Kiss Cookies, 256
PEARS
Hot Curried Fruit, 201
Poached Pears in Red Wine with Vanilla Custard Sauce, 270
PEAS
Asparagus and Pea Casserole, 192
Pea Soup, 50
Surprise Dip, 14
Pecan Chicken, 141
Pecan Muffins, 85
Pecan Sticks, 252
Penne Pasta with Fresh Tomato, Basil and Ricotta Sauce, 105
Peppered Beefsteaks with Jack Daniel's Sauce, 113
Peppermint Ice Cream, 273
Pesto, 106
Picante Pasta, 103
Pickled Shrimp, 20
Picnic Black Beans, 64
PIES
Absolute Very Best Buttermilk Pie, The, 239
Apples and Cream Crumb Pie, 234
Banana Cream Pie, 237
Brownie Pie, 231
Chess Pie, 239
Chocolate Angel Pie, 232
Chocolate Chip Pecan Pie, 232
Cream Cheese Pumpkin Pie, 239
Egg Custard Pie, 236
Fresh Fruit Tart, 263
Fresh Peach Pie, 236
Joyce Christie's Fudge Pie, 231
Key Lime Pie, 236

Lemon Cheese Pie, 238
Lemon Meringue Pie, 237
Mom's Chocolate Pie, 231
Mud Pie, 233
Presidential Peanut Butter Pie, 233
Sour Cream Pecan Pie, 235
Southern Pecan Pie, 234
Southern Pecan Tarts, 240
Strawberry Pie, 235
Summertime Pie, 238
PINEAPPLE
Baked Oranges, 200
Cake in a Pan, 227
Carrot Pineapple Bread, 80
Congealed Citrus Salad, 71
Curried Chicken Salad With Chutney, 66
Easy Congealed Peach Salad, 71
Fruit Aspic, 71
Hawaiian Chicken, 183
Hot Curried Fruit, 201
Hot Pineapple Casserole, 201
Orange Pineapple Sherbet, 274
Pineapple Cheese Ball, 9
Pineapple Chicken, 144
Pizza Dip, 17
Plantation Rice, 208
Plum Cake, 225
Poached Pears in Red Wine with Vanilla Custard Sauce, 270
Ponte Vedra Innlet Banana Bread, 78
POPPY SEED
Poppy Seed Cake, 227
Poppy Seed Chicken, 136
Poppy Seed Dressing, 75
PORK
Baked Ham, 128
Barbecue Sauce, 190
Barbequed Ribs, 188
Bean and Ham Soup, 52
Brunswick Stew, 51
Chinese Pork Tenderloin, 130
Fettuccine Carbonara, 102
Glazed Ham Steaks, 127
Ham Delights, 24
Herbed Pork Tenderloin, 131
Just Peachy Pork Chops, 129
Lasagna, 124
Low Country Boil, 167
Mexican Cheese Dip, 19
Pea Soup, 50
Pork Tenderloin with Sour Cream Sauce, 128
Pork with Chutney Glaze, 129
Pork with Red Plum Sauce, 132
Quick Barbecue Sauce, 189

Rigatoni with Ham and Mozzarella, 102
Rosemary Marinated Pork Tenderloin, 186
Sausage Bacon Delights, 25
Sausage with Red Beans and Rice, 127
Seasoned Bar-B-Que Ribs, 127
Sesame Pork Tenderloin, 186
Spaghetti Pie, 123
Spaghetti Sauce with Italian Sausage, 133
Teriyaki Pork Chops, 188
Tomato Bacon Cheese Onions, 204
Willie Mae's Pork Chops, 133
Zesty Barbecue Sauce, 189
Pot Roast, 116
Pot Roast with Vegetables, 115
POTATOES
Boo's Potato Salad, 61
Cold Potato Soup with Asparagus, 42
German Potato Salad, 62
Gourmet Potatoes, 205
Low Country Boil, 167
Microwave New Potatoes, 207
New Potatoes with Basil Cream Sauce, 206
New Potatoes With Dill, 62
Potato Soup, 44
Savory Grilled Potatoes, 174
Thyme Potatoes, 206
Vichyssoise, 43
Poultry Marinade, 159
POUND CAKES
Brown Sugar and Cinnamon Pound Cake, 217
Chocolate Chip Pound Cake, 216
Chocolate Pound Loaf Cakes, 216
Cream Cheese Pound Cake, 218
Sour Cream Cinnamon-Nut Pound Cake, 217
Presidential Peanut Butter Pie, 233
PUMPKIN
Cream Cheese Pumpkin Pie, 239

Q

QUAIL
Mamie's Quail or Dove, 157
Southern Quail, 157
Quick Barbecue Sauce, 189
Quick Clam Chowder, 43

R

Ranch Style Chicken, 183

RASPBERRIES
Lemon-Raspberry Cheesecake Squares, 249
Raspberry Apéritif, 37
Red Cabbage, 213
RELISHES
Cranberry Relish, 201
Reuben Casserole, 122
RICE
Alfred Lunt Pot Roast, 117
Balsamic Chicken and Peppers, 149
Beef Stir-Fry, 118
Beef Stroganoff, 120
Beef Tips, 118
Brown Rice and Almond Salad, 60
Carnonnades Flamandes (Beef Stew), 119
Casserole Arroz, 207
Cheesy Broccoli and Rice, 196
Chicken and Wild Rice Soup, 47
Chicken in Dill Sauce, 140
Chicken Salad Vinaigrette, 67
Country Captain, 146
Crunchy Chicken Cheese Bake, 143
Curried Rice Salad, 60
Curried Saffron Rice, 59
Easy Brown Rice, 208
Easy Swiss Steak, 121
Highland Gourmet's Marinated Rice, 207
Hot Chicken Salad Casserole, 135
Lemon Mushroom Chicken with Parsley, 137
Orange Glazed Cornish Hens, 155
Orange Rice, 208
Plantation Rice, 208
Sausage with Red Beans and Rice, 127
Shrimp and Wild Rice Casserole, 166
Shrimp Jambalaya, 166
Stir-Fry Chicken and Vegetables, 153
Wild Rice Salad, 61
Rich Cinnamon Bits, 27
Rigatoni with Ham and Mozzarella, 102
Roasted Chicken Feast, 134
ROLLS
Marshmallow Cinnamon Puffs, 91
Miracle Rolls, 91
Mother's Refrigerator Rolls, 87
Worth-the-Wait Rolls, 90
Rosemary Marinated Pork Tenderloin, 186
Rotisserie Chicken, 184
Royal Chicken Crêpes, 151
Rum Slushes, 34
Russian Dressing, 73

S

SALAD DRESSINGS
Blue Cheese Dressing, 72
Blue Cheese Tomato Dressing, 73
Caesar Salad Dressing, 75
Chili Sauce Dressing, 72
Fresh Fruit Dressing, 14
Glorified Italian Dressing, 75
Green Goddess Salad Dressing, 74
Greta Sauce, 172
Louis Dressing, 74
Mayo in a Blender, 76
Poppy Seed Dressing, 75
Russian Dressing, 73
Salad Dressing for Fruit or Vegetables, 76
Secret French Dressing, 73
Shrimp Rémoulade, 31
Tangy French Dressing, 74

SALADS
Asparagus Vinaigrette, 66
Berries Berries Berries, 58
Boo's Potato Salad, 61
Brown Rice and Almond Salad, 60
Caribbean Salad, 59
Chicken Salad Vinaigrette, 67
Chicken-Artichoke Pasta Salad, 97
Cole Slaw, 68
Congealed Citrus Salad, 71
Congealed Cranberry Salad, 72
Curried Chicken Salad With Chutney, 66
Curried Rice Salad, 60
Curried Saffron Rice, 59
Easy Congealed Peach Salad, 71
Fresh Broccoli Salad, 61
Fruit Aspic, 71
German Potato Salad, 62
Hearts of Palm Salad, 64
Herbed Chicken and Pasta Salad, 96
Holland Rusk Salad, 63
Minted Grapes in Melon Boats, 59
New Potatoes With Dill, 62
Picnic Black Beans, 64
Sea Island Salad, 70
Shrimp Aspic, 70
Shrimp Salad, 69
Shrimp Salad With Capers, 69
Sliced Chicken with Lime and Basil, 67
Sour Cream Cole Slaw, 68
Spinach Mandarin Orange Salad, 65
Summer Tomato and Basil Salad, 63
Tangy Romaine Toss, 65
Tomato Aspic, 58
Tomato Cheese Mold, 58
Tomato Well Stuffed, A, 63
Vermicelli Salad, 96
Wild Rice Salad, 61

SALMON
Apple Cider Salmon, 180
Grilled Salmon Steaks, 180
Salmon Bacon Ball, 8
Salmon Mousse with Sour Cream Dill Sauce, 17

SAUCES AND GRAVIES
Barbecue Sauce, 190
Chicken Marinade, 190
Easy Sweet and Sour Sauce, 32
Green Peppercorn Sauce, 126
Greta Sauce, 172
Midnight Marinade, 126
Mustard Sauce, 159
Pesto, 106
Poultry Marinade, 159
Quick Barbecue Sauce, 189
Sauce for Venison, Dove or Duck, A, 158
Spaghetti Sauce with Italian Sausage, 133
Sweet Soy Marinade, 126
Zesty Barbecue Sauce, 189
Sausage Bacon Delights, 25
Sausage with Red Beans and Rice, 127
Sautéed Green Beans, 203
Savory Grilled Potatoes, 174
Scalloped Oysters, 161

SCALLOPS
Curried Scallops and Shrimp, 171
Scallops, 160
Seafood Medley, 169
Sea Island Salad, 70
Seasoned Bar–B–Que Ribs, 127
Seasoned Leg of Lamb, 108
Secret French Dressing, 73
Sesame Asparagus Roll-ups, 23
Sesame Chicken, 141
Sesame Ginger Chicken, 181
Sesame Pork Tenderloin, 186
Sheri's Chocolate Delight, 259

SHRIMP
Barbecue Shrimp, 172
Chicken Shrimp Artichoke Casserole, 169
Creole Shrimp, 168
Curried Scallops and Shrimp, 171
Dill Shrimp, 170
Easy Seafood Bisque, 46
Easy Shrimp Dip, 16
Grilled Shrimp, 181
Hot Seafood Spread, 13
Layered Shrimp Spread, 16
Low Country Boil, 167
Mary Mobley's Shrimp Mold, 27
New World Shrimp, 170
Pickled Shrimp, 20
Sea Captain, 167
Seafood and Leek Bisque, 48
Seafood Medley, 169
Shrimp and Angel Hair Pasta, 99
Shrimp and Wild Rice Casserole, 166
Shrimp Aspic, 70
Shrimp Curry Mold, 28
Shrimp Jambalaya, 166
Shrimp Rémoulade, 31
Shrimp Salad, 69
Shrimp Salad With Capers, 69
Shrimp with Feta Sauce, 99
Shrimp with Spinach Pasta, 98
Sliced Chicken with Lime and Basil, 67
Smoked Turkey, 187
Snappy Cheese Wafers, 25
Snickerdoodles, 252

SOUPS
Bean and Ham Soup, 52
Black Bean Soup, 53
Blueberry Soup, 40
Broccoli Soup, 45
Brunswick Stew, 51
Cheese Soup, 54
Chicken and Wild Rice Soup, 47
Clam Chowder, 49
Cold Cucumber Soup, 40
Cold Potato Soup with Asparagus, 42
Cold Squash Soup, 41
Cream of Broccoli Soup, 46
Easy Seafood Bisque, 46
French Onion Soup, 55
Gourmet Champagne Lentil Soup, 54
Hot and Sour Egg Drop Soup, 44
Minestrone Soup, 45
Mulligatawny Soup, 49
Mushroom Soup, 52
My Favorite Carrot Soup, 47
Oyster and Spinach Soup, 48
Pappy Prather's Seafood Gumbo, 56
Pea Soup, 50
Peach Soup, 42
Potato Soup, 44
Quick Clam Chowder, 43
Seafood and Leek Bisque, 48
Soul Satisfying Chili, 125
Soup for the Hunt, 49
Summer Gazpacho, 41
Tomato Consommé, 55
Tomato Dill Soup, 53
Vegetable Soup, 50
Venison Chili, 158

Vichyssoise, 43
White Chili, 153
Sour Cream Cheese Cake, 222
Sour Cream Cinnamon–Nut Pound Cake, 217
Sour Cream Coffee Cake, 93
Sour Cream Cole Slaw, 68
Sour Cream Cornbread, 86
Sour Cream Pecan Pie, 235
Sour Dough Bread, 88
Southern Pecan Pie, 234
Southern Pecan Tarts, 240
Southern Quail, 157
Southern Salsa, 19
Southwest Chicken, 154
Spaghetti Pie, 123
Spaghetti Sauce with Italian Sausage, 133
Special K Cookies, 252
Spicy Black-eyed Peas, 193
Spicy Sesame Pasta, 105

SPINACH
Artichoke and Spinach Casserole, 209
Caribbean Salad, 59
Easy Spinach Lasagna, 103
Oyster and Spinach Soup, 48
Spinach Cheese Squares, 19
Spinach Mandarin Orange Salad, 65
Spinach Vegetable Dip, 12

SQUASH
Baked Squash Casserole, 209
Butternut Squash Puff, 209
Cold Squash Soup, 41
Grilled Vegetables, 174
Molasses Squash Muffins, 84
Steak au Poivre, 114
Steak Dip, 15
Stir-Fry Chicken and Vegetables, 153

STRAWBERRIES
Strawberry Margarita, 34
Strawberry Pie, 235
Sweet Mouthful, 269
Stuffed Vidalias, 203
Sugared Pecans, 26
Summer Gazpacho, 41
Summer Tomato and Basil Salad, 63
Summertime Pie, 238
Sun-Dried Tomato Cheese Spread, 11
Surprise Dip, 14
Sweet and Sour Chicken, 142
Sweet Cinnamon Quick Bread, 94
Sweet Mouthful, 269

SWEET POTATOES
Berry Mallow Yambake, 210
Cake in a Pan, 227
Sweet Potato Casserole, 210

Sweet Potato Nut Bread, 78
Sweet Soy Marinade, 126
Swiss Cheese Grits, 213

T

Tangy French Dressing, 74
Tangy Romaine Toss, 65
Tarragon Chicken, 135
Tea Punch, 33
Tenderloin with Béarnaise, 32
Teriyaki Pork Chops, 188
Tex Mex, 18
Texas Style Game Hens, 185
Three Bean Bake, 193
Thyme Potatoes, 206
Toasted Thyme Sticks, 81

TOMATOES
Blue Cheese Tomato Dressing, 73
Cherry Tomatoes Stuffed with Avocado, 31
Chicken Marengo, 100
Corn Tomato Zucchini Casserole, 198
Fried Green Tomatoes, 198
Homemade Salsa, 18
Italian Boneless Chicken, 138
Italian Tomato Pie, 211
Mexican Cheese Dip, 19
Okra and Tomatoes, 198
Patti Howard's Zucchini and Tomatoes, 212
Penne Pasta with Fresh Tomato, Basil and Ricotta Sauce, 105
Soup for the Hunt, 49
Southern Salsa, 19
Spaghetti Sauce with Italian Sausage, 133
Summer Gazpacho, 41
Summer Tomato and Basil Salad, 63
Tex Mex, 18
Tomato and Eggplant Casserole, 199
Tomato Aspic, 58
Tomato Bacon Cheese Onions, 204
Tomato Cheese Mold, 58
Tomato Consommé, 55
Tomato Dill Soup, 53
Tomato Well Stuffed, A, 63
Vegetable Soup, 50

TUNA
Hot Tuna Dip, 15
Sea Island Salad, 70

TURKEY
Chicken Tetrazzini, 145
Ed's Frozen Turkey Breast, 155
Holiday Turkey with No Basting, 156

Smoked Turkey, 187
Soul Satisfying Chili, 125

V

VEAL
Veal Marsala, 110
Veal Parmesan, 110
Vegetable Soup, 50

VENISON
Ground Venison Casserole, 158
Sauce for Venison, Dove or Duck, A, 158
Venison, 159
Venison Chili, 158
Vermicelli Salad, 96
Versatile Seasoned Butter, 94
Vichyssoise, 43
Vidalia Onion Dip, 12
Vidalia Onion Pie, 204

W

Walnut Shortbread, 247
Water Chestnut Dip, 14

WATERMELON
Georgia Watermelon-Wine Punch, 37
White Chili, 153
Whole Wheat Cheese Straws, 24
Wild Rice Salad, 61
Williamsburg Blueberry Muffins, 84
Willie Mae's Pork Chops, 133
Worth-the-Wait Rolls, 90

Y

Yellow Bird, 34
Yogurt Smoothie, 38

Z

Zesty Barbecue Sauce, 189
Zesty Broccoli Dip, 15
Zesty Marinated Flank Steak, 177

ZUCCHINI
Corn Tomato Zucchini Casserole, 198
Delightful Zucchini, 212
Grilled Vegetables, 174
Pasta Leon, 102
Patti Howard's Zucchini and Tomatoes, 212
Zucchini Bread, 79
Zucchini Casserole, 211
Zucchini in Garlic Butter, 212
Zucchini Squares, 21

Junior League of Columbus, Georgia, Inc.
1440 Second Avenue
Columbus, GA 31901

Please send _____ copies of *A Southern Collection — Then and Now*

@ $22.95 each $ _____

Postage and handling   @ $4.00 each $ _____
Georgia residents add 7% sales tax, each book   @ $1.61 each $ _____
                                                                                 TOTAL $ _____

Name _____

Address _____

City _____ State _____ Zip _____

Make checks payable to *Junior League of Columbus, Georgia, Inc.*

- -

Junior League of Columbus, Georgia, Inc.
1440 Second Avenue
Columbus, GA 31901

Please send _____ copies of *A Southern Collection — Then and Now*

@ $22.95 each $ _____

Postage and handling   @ $4.00 each $ _____
Georgia residents add 7% sales tax, each book   @ $1.61 each $ _____
                                                                                 TOTAL $ _____

Name _____

Address _____

City _____ State _____ Zip _____

Make checks payable to *Junior League of Columbus, Georgia, Inc.*